I Like What I Know

ILLUSTRATED WITH PHOTOGRAPHS

I Like What I Know

A VISUAL AUTOBIOGRAPHY

by VINCENT PRICE

DOUBLEDAY & COMPANY, INC.

GARDEN CITY, NEW YORK

1959

Library of Congress Catalog Card Number 59–12830
Copyright © 1959 by Vincent Price
All Rights Reserved
Design: Alma Reese Cardi
Printed in the United States of America/First Edition

To Mary and Barrett
without whom I might not like what I know
—as much.

Foreword

I have always heard that a drowning man experiences his whole life over again as he goes down for the third time. Not having met many drowned men, I can't substantiate this as a fact, but during the past year and a half I have had close contact with a man who was living his life over again and if not drowning in it, at least he was wallowing in it, right up to the eyes, and liking it.

I find I've built a little edifice of soapboxes with picture windows in every wall, and there are a couple of rooms that have been added on, as the family grew, that are hard to get into, and at least one that's almost impossible to get *out* of. But it's home! And it has a comfortable corner here and there where, at least for me, I can sit comfortably and look back and, if I stretch around the clutter far enough, look ahead.

When you've furnished your house and dusted the objects, cleaned the glass on the pictures, patted the pillows and put a few flowers around, and your friends or new acquaintances have the feeling of being as much at home as you are, then I think you can say you're a lucky man. You can't do more than try to make people at ease in a new experience, and a successful home should always be a new experience. A good cook should be mysterious, but a good host should be well known for his appreciation of his guests.

Right away I've talked myself into liking whoever reads this story of my illustrated life. I feel toward you as I do toward the oculist who told me that my vision was good but a pair of glasses would help me read the fine print. He restored something I thought I'd lost and gave me back part of my youth.

In liking you, I'm restoring myself because I'm sharing your reaction to me. I'm lending you my glasses. Even if they don't fit, perhaps they'll reassure you that what sometimes seems blurred is curable by a simple prescription of looking at the same object through someone else's eyes.

This is how I've seen it, and it's looked mighty good to me, so I hope you enjoy the view from my window.

I Like What I Know

QUITE OBVIOUSLY, THE FIRST VIEW FROM MY WINDOW would be out onto my own back yard. But being an obtuse kind of guy, I'd rather stand out in the back yard and let you look in.

As you look into the interior, you will see a large and happy family: father, mother, two sisters, a brother, and myself, all neatly dressed and smiling. There is pride written on each face, and a lot of gratitude, but as the "camera" of my memory dollies in, it will end up on a close-up of my mother. Certainly, we all lived in this house, and certainly a man's home is his castle, but in this case the expression on Mother's face will leave no doubt in your mind as to who pulled the ropes of the drawbridge.

There is nothing smug about her, and there is great love and warmth oozing out of every pore, but let's just say that there is a certain look of knowing satisfaction with her achievements, which include not only the house but all of us.

My family belonged to that stratum of American society best described as "well to do." I've come to understand that to mean not rich enough to evoke envy and just successful enough to demand respect. It is the ultimate plateau in American life and is only reached by hard work, just enough ambition, and the guidance of a good woman. Of course, a man on his own, or with a bad woman, can be successful, but then another term must be applied: "well off." It's a subtle distinction, but one to which my mother clung with all her might—and she was a mighty good woman.

Good women can be dull, but she wasn't. She was fun for her children and fortunate for her husband. She had enough stamina for an Atlantic crossing, under her own steam, and she never let us get away with anything. If she lacked knowledge on a certain subject, she would (perhaps unconsciously) use her lack to pique our curiosity. In my case, Mother knew nothing about art, and I'm sure she had moments when my nagging curiosity almost got the better of her—and the entire family.

Father was beatified by her the day she set eyes on him, and he became a full-fledged saint as the years rolled by. They were married for fifty-three years, until death did them part, and he sat back to wait out the few years until he could join her.

They were my friends, and I remember so much about them that it's difficult to recall and to separate their warmth from their eccentricities, which were the springboard for my curiosity.

To give a picture of my "place de la Revolution," come inside our home with me.

Our home—that is, the one they were finally able to build after all the children, except myself, were educated and "on their own"—was semi-pretentious. The furniture was antique American from every period of our history, and most of it carried some legend, in Mother's careless hand, carefully glued underneath, along with the name of its inheritor. She wanted to be sure, since she couldn't take it with her, that none but the designated persons would take it with them; for while she enjoyed enthusiastic health, she constantly threatened that she was ready at any moment to leave us for a less wearing life in the life beyond. It was a threat that worried us not at all because of her vast vitality, and the warning only succeeded in calming our exuberant spirits momentarily at the realization that we were the ones who were wearing her out.

As these things happen, at the time of actual dispersal little was done about the labels, and the four children, seven grandchildren, and in-laws took, by mutual agreement, what they could house or what they needed to complete their sparsely furnished homes. We had all been hard up at times and actually were somewhat afraid to buy too much even when we could have, since Mother had indoctrinated us for so many years that this or that from her enormous stock of household goods was to be "ours." The knowledge that a Gothic Victorian table was to hold a flowery Dresden lamp with a lace shade somehow did leave its mark and made it a little difficult to guess what period we should buy on our own that would look good with it, or even be tolerable.

For instance, part of my lot was a pair of Biedermeier vases that Mother had bought in New Orleans on her thirtieth wedding anniversary. They have been placed in every room of my several domiciles, wired and unwired as lamps, stored and unstored, or stuffed carelessly in closets until I suddenly remember Mother's value on them. Then with nostalgic conscience they are searched for and tenderly packed in shredded newspaper until, once again, they start their futile journey from room to room. They belonged to my mother—but not to me. However, I love them because she loved them, if not for the same reasons. She bought them on a trip, a trip being her number-one cause for loving anything. Secondly, she loved them because they were expensive at that time and were guaranteed to make her contemporaries gasp at her good fortune in owning them. And finally, she loved them because she had wanted them for many years to occupy a specific place on the mantel of her living room, and their ultimate discovery and purchase represented a triumph of housewifely acquisitions.

Here I would like to describe that house in detail. It'll make me deliciously homesick, and I hope it will bring back memories of other houses—other families in the same circumstances. Beyond that, it will, I think, reflect the general atmosphere of a past generation of Americans and give a picture of the vanishing treasures of yesteryear.

As our circumstances improved we moved farther out of town.

Indeed, we helped start the ghastly rush into suburbia, which is the all-over American pattern of today. Our final family home was on a lot carefully selected for its address, its view, and its trees—four pin oaks, sturdy, shaggy, and shady. A few blocks farther out were open fields and the leftover land of fine old farms and estates. Today modern housing developments occupy every square inch.

The lot Mother chose was across from the university—not because of any hope that the view would rub off on us and we would slip across the street to higher education, but because the administration building was a squat elongation of Windsor Castle, and my mother's stepfather had been a British army officer. To her that made sense, just as the incorporation of a dozen or so broad "A's" into her much-better-than-average good American enunciation made her—one, traveled; two, interestingly related; and three, slightly more cultured than some of her other friends.

A few years before I was born, we had had a great world's fair, and the chief result of it seemed to have been an inordinate desire on the part of St. Louisans to see the world. I never stop meeting them wherever I go, from Peru to Istanbul. Unlike today's fairs, where each nation tries to be more modern architecturally than the other, at the St. Louis fair they tried to be more typical. There were buildings of all national types, and the university, which was growing at that time, took it upon itself to emulate the British.

But the view of our pseudo-Windsor Castle was charming. The building was flood-lit at night, and a broad field led up to it, making an uninterrupted view, very desirable for conversation from Mother's point of view, and future real estate value from Father's. And when, two years after we moved in, the university saw fit to interrupt our view of Windsor Castle with an equally pseudo-Roman copy of a dubious Greek building for the Architecture School, Mother's pen emitted a six-month scream of protest to the president of the university, the architect, and finally to the mayor. After her reluctant reconciliation with the marble-veneered monster in our line of vision, she had a handsome leather-bound scrapbook of her correspondence and the placating, servile, but fruitless replies. Mother never really recovered from it, however, and to "her dying day," (which was her stubborn assertion on all points of bull-doggedness—her way of saying she disapproved of something or someone) to her dying day she was cool to the architect's wife and not a little overjoyed when the guilty president of the university took the final sabbatical and passed into Higher Spiritual Education.

The address was another thing. Our lot was in the center of the new and most desirable district of town. There was an air of culture lent by the university and the fact that the two or three really artistic families lived not far away. The new and much discussed "progressive school" was a short, firm walk—good for a growing boy—and it was there that I, being the youngest, was to get my first setback in formal education. The name of the street was quickly and permanently changed by my mother to "road." This appellation gave it an air of "country," and she made it legal for herself, if not for the post office, by having several thousand sheets of pearl-gray writing paper and envelopes third-dimensionally embossed in Yale blue with "Road." (My father went to Yale, my brother went to Yale, my sister married a Yale man, and I was going to Yale—they hoped.)

The view, the address, and the trees having decided the location, now the question of architectural style had to be settled, and I will always regret that I was considered too young to be allowed in on what must have been some mighty spirited arguments. Furthermore, they must have been titanically one-sided, as Father hated arguments as much as Mother loved them.

Father was a descendant, on his mother's side, of Peregrine White, the first child born on the *Mayflower* as it hove into Plymouth Bay—a bad day for Mrs. White, I always thought. His father was a wonderfully black-haired, black-mustached, "black" Welshman whose family came on a later boat. These forebears were taken into consideration by Mother, of course, but it was naturally her background that was to become the setting for our future family life. She was French, Dutch, and English, but American through and through. Together, she and

Father had eighteen generations behind them, and every generation was considered in the architecture of our house. Of Father's generations, however, we knew little except of the first two and the last three, but Mother knew all eight of hers intimately. There was one who intrigued her and was perhaps the greatest influence on her taste. Her great-grandmother. It seems that on the way to church one day, this lady saw the light. She was dressed in all her Sunday finery, and enviable finery it must have been. Her husband was a six foot eight inch captain of a China clipper. Proud of his beautiful wife, he lavished all the silks of the Orient on her, and she was equally proud to wear them. Though it was never thoroughly explained to us what caused her to see the aforementioned light, my guess is that her pride was hurt when the thought occurred to her that "Vanity, vanity, all is vanity" not only applied to her but to all other women. She wanted to be different. I may be doing her an injustice, but anyway, one Sunday she did see the light, and she vowed to prune herself of her fine feathers and wear black for the rest of her life. The light obviously did not preclude her being sensible, for from the gorgeous silks she made an endless series of patchwork quilts as penance. Mother cherished them all, as she cherished this legend, even though she would never have thought of emulating it, and the quilts were neatly folded at the foot of every Early American bed in the house. It was her pride in these quilts that I feel was the predominate factor in the final architectural style and décor of our home.

The house was to be American, no question about that. The architects, a pair of nice young American men, were very much in vogue, naturally, since my parents had waited all these years and were going to have the best. For Mother, there was always an excuse to have the best—and the best she always had.

These two young men, I'm sure, matured rapidly as men and as architects after their endless losing rounds with Mother. If there ever was a woman who knew what she wanted, it was my mother. And she got it.

Because she generously took into consideration my father's ten generations and our, so far, distinguished and unsullied Yale background, the façade was to be New England. Pure, authentic, classic New England. It is fine for New England but a bit of a dust catcher in the Midwest, as Mother learned, year after year, when the yards of white trim had to be repainted. And the ivy (a requisite for New England which, in St. Louis, took four stubborn years to start at all) had to be nailed onto the house after each tornado or high wind.

But the façade was really pure, and I must admit that during its short-lived, monopolistic reign as the only house in the tract it glistened in American defiance at Windsor Castle across the street.

The two maturing architects were happy in this exterior triumph, but, unluckily for them, they wanted to carry it on inside. Here they met and fell before the whole eight generations of my mother's French-Dutch-English and American forebears, led by that able and much-admired Christian lady, the Priestess of Patchwork, my great-great-grandmother, the sea captain's muted peacock wife.

The interior design would have to accommodate Mother's belongings, and after thirty years of married life she had acquired more than her share of this world's goods. There was not a relative, near or distant, from whom she did not have some memento. These ranged from silver made by our first French forebear, Pierre Desnoyer of Detroit, to hand-hammered smoking sets made by my brother in craft class; from a hideous Victorian lamp some cousin had willed her to a really beautiful tip-top table, brought in a covered wagon by Father's father from Canandaigua, New York, to Chicago.

The furniture was as representative a collection of Americana as could be found. Gate-leg to Gothic, wicker to Washington-slept-here-looking and -feeling beds. All of these treasures had to be placed in Mother's mind and in the rooms before the interior plans could be okayed.

Then there had to be enough baths. In the cause of the multi-bathroom house, Mother was a positive pioneer. Let them be adequate in number and modern in design. So, in today's jargon, back to the old drawing board went the once-young architects.

There had to be a sunroom and there must be a small-scale grand staircase in a hall. The hall would accommodate the most hideous grand piano; a very beautiful grandfather clock which may have run in his day but refused in our time to tell the season, the year, the day, or even the hour (all of which it was equipped to do); and a treasured rug in now muted reds and blues, invisibly mended in spots where my brother had lit some firecrackers years ago when it was a recently acquired and hard-gained antique Persian. Mother also wanted a balcony on the stairway, from which she could hurl books at me when I idly put off my piano practice and sat waiting for dinner.

The fireplace had to be big and in proportion to the living room, which had to be oversized because my youngest sister was getting married (*not* to a Yale man!) the minute the house was done.

The dining room should be paneled, and the radiator casings— hardly a New England accessory—had to match. We couldn't afford a new dining-room suite, so the triumphant No-Period, invented in Grand Rapids, would have to do. After all, it had served us well for many years, and one look at it dispelled all doubt but that it would last many more years. In fact, its one recommendation, if you could call it that, was its threat of immortality.

Then there was that Dresden lamp, covered with blue china forget-me-nots and a lace shade made from the petticoat of Oliver Cromwell's daughter's wedding dress. Whom she married or how it got into our house (and out from under her dress), no one ever asked, but the whole glorious mess *had* to be in the living room. This information was supposed to be of great interest to the two aging architects, and I remember overhearing them describe this lamp, when Mother was out of the room, as a memorial to Lillian Russell. I asked Father what that meant, and he drew an airy diagram of Miss Russell's figure which described the lamp perfectly. He added, mysteriously, that his father, who had been very rich and, I gathered, rather racy, had backed Miss Russell in a play. Years later I thought this story unlikely but fraught with possibilities of an added interest in my family tree. I always regretted that my father's father had not lived long enough for me to know him. The history of his wealth and his vocabulary had made him my favorite relative. I also resented his dying poor.

Before the house was done, apparently a truce was reached somewhere. The architects won by getting some simplicity of line in the décor. They lost to Mother's housewifely sense of what was easy to keep clean by having to put in terrazzo floors throughout. That hideous gray conglomerate always looked dirty, so it never needed to be too clean. They won in the living room by pretty good proportions, which incensed Mother forever after whenever she had a party, because it wasn't roomy enough. Guests were known to stray into the hall for air, or stay in the dining room, or disappear into the sunroom where the liquor was kept. Since Midwesterners of the well-to-do class can drink more than the rich or poor of any other class in any other part of the world, this ran the party budget way up and put a strain on Father's "connections" during Prohibition.

But whatever the outcome, it was, as Mother described it and her friends concurred, a "gracious house." And because it housed a big family's big collection of whatnots, it did achieve the clutter of a genuine New England home. Besides, it had enough bathrooms to take care of all of us and our many guests. And there were enough closets to store four hundred and sixty yards of assorted laces, the fur trim from every garment that was fur trimmed, the feathers, flowers, fruits, birds, and abstractions of the hats of three generations of Episcopal women (and Episcopal women love hats), the remains of any kind of linen for dust cloths, my mother's wedding dress, and the largest known collection of suitcases and valises, which were my father's private folly, along with all family records—and we were the custodians of eighteen generations of them—plus drawers full of unframed photos of all of us, and everyone we knew from birth to grave. There was a concrete cellar of bank proportions which treasured a store of moldy newspaper clippings and moldier Mason jars of goodies my mother had preserved against the day of our incipient fall to utter poverty. The contents, I always felt, would have ended our misery in short order.

I think the architects never came back after the dinner party

Mother gave for them. She wanted them to see their achievement after she had peopled the house with all of us and her décor. She had had the help of an aged but beloved interior decorator who just happened to have set up business in what had been Mother and Father's first house in town—the house where my sister and I were born. I doubt if that really had anything to do with her choice—although the decorator's stock looked as though it might have been there before we were born—but Mother was sentimental.

Together, Mother and her decorator had created a sunroom that did have sun, thanks to the architects, but now was closer to a set for *The Shanghai Gesture* than anything else. The walls were green, a subtle split-pea green, shot with gold. Real gold leaf tipped every bump of the plaster. The curtains were striped black and orange, reminding my father, not happily, of Princeton. The furniture was America's first attempt at Chinese Modern. It couldn't have been less Chinese or less modern. Grand Rapids is a long way from both, after all. It was wood made to look like bamboo and richly enameled black, with every bamboo-like rung again gold. Tied on this frame of nondescript shape were lethal cushions of the same striped material as the curtains.

Since house plants were the triumph of housewives in Missouri, Iowa, and, in fact, in all of America, the room was alive with greenery. Leaf green fights with only one other green, and that green Mother had achieved on the walls—shot with gold. A bamboo (real, this time) cage sported the two angriest lovebirds in captivity. A silken tassel, which shortly was incorporated into a false nest for the "love" birds, hung from the cage. The Chinese square-holed coin which adorned it was later added to my coin collection. Quaint paintings of Chinese ladies in very tailored dresses by the Chinese branch of Peck & Peck were on the walls in black Chinese frames. And there was a brass bracket in the curly design of a dragon who held from his mouth a chain, at the end of which was a glass ball with that classic house plant, philodendron. It started as a cutting from a friend and miraculously grew into a long string of pale green with intermittent and infinitesimal leaves that dropped off as they reached a stunning, if stunted, maturity.

The rug was again imitation Chinese. It looked like a misshapen tweed coat, stretched out to accommodate the size of the floor. Two rubber pads finally had to be put under it to keep it from accompanying the family and guests as they left the room—or shooting them high into the air, to be blacked out on the terrazzo floor below. My father was heavily insured, of course, but my parents cherished their children and friends.

This room frightened the architects almost to death, but the results of Mother's "treatment" of the rather beautiful upstairs hall sent them sliding down the banisters and home to rededicate themselves to whatever is the architect's equivalent of the Hippocratic oath.

As you clumped up the grand staircase and paused for breath on the landing to draw courage for the last short flight into the hall, you were greeted at the top by a series of photographic copies of portraits of "The Pirates." Mother called them "The Pirates" just as a come-on to get the chance to explain further, which she always hastened to do. They were the elegantly dressed, in lace and armor, ruddy-cheeked, enormous-nosed antecedents of my British stepgrandfather. The originals hung in, of all places, Blarney Castle in Ireland. Now—why English in Ireland? Well, they were that breed of Irish, the English-Irish. Anyway, the present owners of Blarney Castle are the distant cousins of my stepgrandfather and therefore our distant stepcousins, too. Very anti-climactic, I always thought, but true, and there they were—"The Pirates"—to prove it.

As a key to the décor of the hall they were perfect. They were brown photographs of brown pictures, matted in beige in brown wood frames. They hung above a series of 1910 brown bookcases, filled with brown books behind leaded glass doors. If anyone had been tempted to read these books, it was impossible to get at them. The catches on the doors were inventions of genius and yielded to no one. I always suspected that the movers had to bring them, books and all, from our other house. The only thing to do was to break the glass, but no title

21

was exciting enough to use this four-alarm technique of securing a book. They were, in fact, sets which had been foisted off over the years on a family whose main collection of literature had to be, perforce, schoolbooks.

This gloomy row of brown objects ran up to the sewing-room french doors which Mother had temporarily curtained with an unbelievable tropical cretonne, and which—however temporary—lasted until "her dying day." On the opposite wall was one of the masterpieces of art in our home: an etching of three of the saddest cows ever seen, grazing in abject postures in a sepia valley which, to me, was always associated with the Twenty-third Psalm—"Yea, though I walk through . . ." It was the gift of three maiden ladies we called "cousins" and whom we children hated because they hated children. They camouflaged their hostile feelings with hypocritical gifts of stale jelly beans which came from their pocketbooks and tasted just like they smelled—of lavender. Later I learned to like them because, in retrospect, I learned to understand them. Their maiden ladyhood must have been severely painful when they visited friends with large families— families they never had. But the ogresses of my childhood became wonderful friends in adulthood, and my love for them increased with my years, although I never really forgave them the three sad cows which, of course, we named for them.

Beneath the cows was one of Victoria's great contributions to furniture. I forget Mother's story of where it came from, but I vaguely recall something about another covered wagon from New York getting stuck in the mud in Chicago, and because that was a sign of some sort, these particular ancestors bought the adhesive spot, which, after they sold it, inevitably turned out to be The Loop—worth at least a million an acre.

My family has a startling history of such misadventures. For instance, my father tried, nay, pleaded with some friends to pool together and buy stock in Ford. Nothing. They didn't. He didn't. My grandmother was offered stock in every paying gold mine in the Western hemisphere and turned it all down to buy non-paying ones *anywhere*. My grandfather loved "gold bricks." The only member of the whole outfit who hit the jackpot was a delightfully debauched uncle who bought half the state of Oklahoma (the right half), made millions, and was rumored to have owned half of a famous opera singer (the right half). Unfortunately, no one ever spoke to him; and my family, being honest if not smart, only spoke *about* him after he made good! Proof of my family's financial misadventures came to light years later when we unearthed enough magnificently engraved but worthless stocks to paper a small room—which I did in a New York apartment. I hope none of them turn out to be good . . . I've moved.

Other pictures in the house were family projects. A pastel of my mother's real father, "taken from life," as opposed to a tinted photograph after he was dead (a compliment, I think), hung over the mantelpiece. It was charming, and since he had drowned before Mother was born, it brought no tears to her ever ready eyes. Besides, she was very fond of her British stepfather, who, apart from being the only father she ever really knew, bequeathed her the monochromatic "Pirates," her circuitous relationship to Blarney Castle, her anglophile's view of Windsor Castle's counterpart, and her sprinkling of broad "A's."

"A man's home is his castle." Well, as I've said, our home was Mother's castle. Father paid for it, but he was really the consort to the Queen. He did have his chair—a woman's idea of a man's chair. It was low, deeply cut for his long legs, but short-lived functionally for him, as the crippling years stole the spring necessary to emancipate himself. Even at the resilient age of twelve I had to struggle to extricate *derrière* from chair.

His sparse collection of golf trophies, gifts of appreciation from clubs, etc., were scattered around the house, but Father's prize possession was a heavy ceramic vase with a juggled, incised inscription that was a monument to his essential and earthy humor:

I
FYO
UCAN
TKEE
PITD
OWN
THR
OWI
TUP

"If you can't keep it down, throw it up."

That was good advice, but scarcely necessary in a house where the greatest achievement was superb cooking. Recipes gleaned from all over the world from friends and relatives made meals a joy. In her kitchen Mother was inviolate, and the greatest tribute to inviolateness was her help. They feared her in a loving kind of way. She was a perfectionist in her teaching, and once they were taught, not a soufflé fell, not a hollandaise curdled. Distorted as her sense of home decoration was, just as straightforward were her menus—brilliant for parties, healthy and toothsome for family fare. Since I was well on my way to a gigantic six foot four, the food side of my cultural background was most appreciated, and I have never regretted my knowledge of how to eat well.

And eat well I did. Mother saw to it that each molecule, fiber, tissue, and gland was nourished. But about this time a new, almost subconscious taste was budding for which she didn't have a recipe and which was accompanied by an indefinable hunger.

The hunger was for knowledge. All kinds. I was at that age when boys discard their toys and take to books, especially books with pictures. But our library was made up, for the most part, of historical sets, and these are notoriously low on any art level—except to show the unlikely likenesses of illustrious world shakers. They tell the facts, so they don't feel they have to show them.

There was, however, (left over from my elder sister's skimpy art education) a book called *Apollo*, an illustrated history of art from "before" to "after." The reproductions were so small they could be used for postage, but I dug in with my youthful twenty-twenty until no fold or feature was unfamiliar.

And there I found the world I knew I wanted to live in for the rest of my life—the world of man's creation—art.

Even progressive school could not undo the magic of *Apollo*, and my love of art was tried much further when I finally went to the local boys' prep school where, except for a tender and tuneless approach to music, based presumably on our parents' determination that well-to-do young men need ear education, we could have been blind—for all we were taught to see.

The competition between the arts was almost non-existent in our house. Music won, hands down. My older sister played beautifully on the family piano, and my brother, modernist that he was, was a whiz at good jazz. My younger sister, while really as untalented musically as I was, didn't admit it for many years, during which we formed a polite group to listen to her unsure soprano renditions of "A Bowl of Roses" and the "Kashmiri Song."

Mother played by ear, though by whose ear we were never quite sure, but she was a dauntless lady and would sail into anything if she'd heard it twice. It was all great fun, though it left Father with the idea that music, while admittedly the food of love, came close to giving him an ulcer.

As for the visual arts, the whole family was blind. They not only didn't know *how* to see, they didn't particularly want to. So my fight to learn to *see* was difficult, indeed. They were too nice to scoff at it, so their attitude was kind of "look and be damned."

At first I felt a little left out. I had a good baritone and could join in the music louder than everyone. But my musical instinct was more for caricature; so my triumph, Christmas times, was a scorching imitation of Madame Schumann-Heink singing "Silent Night, Holy Night." My motto was if you can't lick 'em, join 'em. And I might have been a good singer if I hadn't always felt that the orchestra or the accompanist was bound to win. As always in families, the one who feels left out—even if it isn't a fact—turns to his own devices, passionately. And passionately, I wanted to see. Art books were rare, especially around our house, where no one made even the cultural gesture of leaving one casually on a table, as is the vogue today.

Mother may not have invented the saying, "I don't know anything about art, but I know what I like," but she lived by it. Certainly, she knew nothing about art. Pictures to her were photographs—preferably of people, and even more preferably of relatives. If you could sneak a not-too-distinct, but distinguished, landmark in the background, she knew that this was what she liked. We just escaped the embarrassment of a gallery of our childish school drawings by an unspoken pledge, on all our parts, to tear them up seconds after Mother had praised them.

Her opinion of paintings and sculpture and architecture was highly spiced by her own personality. For instance, when I became aware of the magnificence of Michelangelo via a reproduction, I quizzed her on the Sistine Chapel, which she had seen on her honeymoon. To her, it was just an enormous testament of Catholicism, and she regarded the glories of the Vatican as the unwarranted personal property of that usurper of the Presidency of Christendom, the Pope. Michelangelo was forgotten in a long story about how she would never kiss the Pope's ring, shoe, or anything else that was his.

There was no way for me to turn her discourse to the "Last Judgment." In her hands the art of transubstantiation became a drama only Max Reinhardt would tackle. Of Rome, the food, the fountains, and the Forum alone remained for her.

Mother was totally unaware of the magnitude of art, but she was dedicatedly aware of her duties as a mother and a citizen. In a combined mother-citizen effort—under the auspices of the progressive school—she traipsed dozens of children, in wiggling batches, through the City Art Museum. She may not have been equipped to expose her charges to a dissertation on the arts, but she certainly saw to it that overly progressive little girls refrained from peeking under the fig leaves of Adonis, Apollo, and Pan. She came away with a definite opinion of inquisitive little girls (other people's, of course!)—and a shallow but lasting impression of painter Rosa Bonheur. Perhaps Mademoiselle Bonheur had the edge with Mother because she was a woman. Or perhaps it was because she painted animals, which Mother could understand.

As modern art slunk in, she piled clichés on it with ditchdigger zeal: "What is it? A child could do it . . . Picasso can't draw." However, she loved flowers; Fantin-Latour and the Flemish flower masters pleased her, although she often wanted to redo the arrangements.

There were two or three families up the street who were "artistic."

They had connections with poets, painters, writers, musicians; and though they were not shunned by the straight social set, they posed a problem for my mother and friends at dinner parties. It was her way of admitting that her other friends were a little "square" by wondering whom to seat next to the artistic ones. But at those trying times Mother could usually solve it brilliantly by asking the bishop, who was a "known" liberal and an extremely delightful conversationalist on any subject. Secretly, she approved of this fast-thinking set, for they were renegade Catholics. They had no little trouble with a brace of divorces, an institution Mother heartily disapproved of as an Episcopalian. But she could also tolerate (even if it was with the other eye) anything that brought about excommunication or separation from the Pope.

I loved these families, their way of life, and one of their daughters, whom I was engaged to off and on from the age of eight to thirty-eight. They were something out of another world. They used money as though it was meant to spend, not to sustain. They were frivolous. My little fiancée didn't dress like the other progressive children. She put a color or two into her middy-blouse wardrobe—a bow, a sash—to assure me, especially, that she was not only progressive but different. Her family allowed this difference, and when we went to play at their house, there were costumes to wear and strange paintings to see, and her father often read to us beautiful little abstract poems of four lines each, having to do with beauty, nature, and love.

One day I was presented to a muffin lady all in silk, plum-colored silk, with violet beads. Her name was "The Poetess." She looked like one, the first one I'd ever met, and like all others looked from that meeting on. She read us a poem about the fog. It wooed me into a cloudy nap, and when I told Mother she was delighted, if a little wary, that I had been "exposed" to such interesting people. However, it was a month before I was allowed to go back to be exposed again.

It was not so much the artistic qualities of these people that fascinated me, or that their lives were happier than ours—I seriously doubt that they were. It was more their aura of excitement. I felt that they were taking some kind of chance with life—a chance to be different—to see differently and to think differently.

We, for instance, were considered the best-mannered children of any of my family's group. But other kids resented this when we were used as examples by their parents. We had politeness drilled into us. Mother expected it of us, and we came to expect it of ourselves. But politeness can invade other patterns of your life besides manners, and as far as I was concerned, as a family we had come to have *polite* vision. Our home and its décor, odd as it seems to me now, was indeed very politely correct. Our pictures were politely dull and our music politely prosaic.

Right here I should apologize to those millions of Americans whose manners have been formed by Emily Price Post (no relative) and say that it was the slightly rude, irreverent attitude toward the norm that made the aforementioned artistic families so interesting. They were offbeat but never downbeat; they were progressive and not tied to conventions that were uncomfortable. Where we had family pictures and an engraving of three sad cows, they had oriental objects, fuzzy impressionistic paintings, and provocative Indian rugs and pottery. Their homes looked like they'd been away from them, once or twice, while ours looked like we not only hadn't been away but didn't want to go.

Mother and Father both disliked change. They worked hard to have their home the way she wanted it, and Father wanted it the way she made it. Home was their religion. If I poke fingers of doubt into the minor aspects of it that offended me, it's because I didn't want to get trapped in any one way of living—and especially of *seeing*. They went along with my inquisitiveness, inch by inch, but their encouragement of and interest in my different approach to everything only spoke volumes of wishes . . . that I would one day become a standard American man and meanwhile, during that young moment, that I'd stop looking at new art and start practicing on our old piano.

28

MOST ART BOOKS (AND THIS ISN'T ONE) TELL YOU about the artists whom time has handed down to us with crowns of fame. They discuss his date of birth, his background, his teacher, his influences, and endless, detailed descriptions of his work. I want more to go back into my own history and produce negatives which can be developed into positive identifications of what I have seen; where and why I've liked what I've seen—or not. I would like to create a sort of verbal kaleidoscope, through which I may reveal to you (and to myself) answers to many "why's." For example, *why* did I begin to look at pictures? . . . *Why*, at my ripe age, do I find myself increasingly undogmatic in my taste? . . . And *why* am I still learning?

The preceding pages of my background may seem irrelevant, but they were my first reflections and conditioned my eyes. I'm sure that if art had been stuffed down my throat, I would have choked on it, spit it out, and played the piano with a social grace I do not possess in art. Painting is still a vehement subject with me, and a discussion of modern art can be as hazardous as that of politics or religion. I've found that even many connoisseurs, or people tolerant of every phase of life, still lean with Mother on that limping crutch: "I don't know anything about art, but I know what I like."

Of all the art I saw in my youth, outside of the museum, none left me with any particular exaltation, and only one gave me any insight at all into what the vast world of art would be like. This was a dreamy copy of Andrea del Sarto's dreamy "Madonna dell' Arpie," owned by the minister who catechized me. I knew her in postage-stamp size from *Apollo*, but when I saw her standing, full size in half-light on her pedestal, between companion saints, the little harpies attendant on them all, I felt something happen that, if it wasn't exaltation, was at least a preview of what might be if I could ever crash the Renaissance in person.

She is beautiful and worldly, this virgin, sad though triumphant; experienced at making a man identify her as a woman. She is pedestaled for a purpose . . . to solicit adoration. At first sight I recognized in her all future adoration of all women as the source of man. She is the tender girl friend, the loving mother, the goddess, all in one.

Then and there I started my unsubtle campaign to get to Europe—to examine her, firsthand. I sold magazines; I sold junk and fitfully built up a bank account against the age when my parents would consider it suitable for me to go into the world alone. I arrived sooner than I hoped, aided by my staggering ability to grow: three and a half inches in one year. I felt that if I could make an inch or two more, I might just burst like a cecropia moth from its tough cocoon and fly to Europe on my own damp wings.

During the monetary and chronological wait, I employed another method at home to build up my chances for departure. With singleness of purpose I monotonously hammered away at a painful curiosity about art. This procedure was also monotonously painful to my parents, since it tested and strained their educational prowess, digging for answers to my endless questions.

My sisters had only the most polite finishing-school acquaintance with art. Girls in the twenties were exposed to rudimentary samples—just enough to make them *seem* cultured—equipped to "carry on" over some two or three proper pictures in assorted museums, but no more. It was as if they were taught to forget what they had learned—

to remember only vaguely that someone other than God created any-thing—and the appearance of their first baby canceled, in their minds, even God's creative ability, as there it was, the "sum and substance" of life's eternal purpose in their own hands.

And Mother and Father could only throw up their hands at my artistic curiosity, and throw me to whatever and what few artistic lions they knew, with a whispered warning to them that I was artistic, too. For all the love and security they had to offer, they had no knowledge of my chosen love, and from what they told me of Europe, I guess they had traveled through it locked in each other's embrace, seeing only what had to be seen for future conversations' sake and collecting more recipes for unique dishes than any museum could possibly house. As I said previously, our board groaned with lively concoctions from the corners of the earth, Mother being convinced that the way to a man's heart was through the usual tract.

I exhausted the three artistic families up the street. They knew a lot and had seen a lot, but at that time they were so concerned with their own poetic battle to make a different contribution to the same-ness of the lives around them, they were apt to negate other creative work, absorbing only enough from it to make theirs click.

The art dealers in my home town were limited, too. There was only one. His ample stock of Icart prints, portraying lascivious French ladies (holding even more lascivious French dogs and cats) gave one a sly peek into the sexual behavior of the human female. These publicly approved "filthy pictures" were considered, at that time, proper for wedding presents. My sister, for instance, received six, and I always wondered if my brother-in-law drew inspiration or disappointment from them.

Occasionally, the dealer would brave the storm and offer an exhi-bition of fine etchings and engravings: Rembrandt, Dürer, Van Ley-den, etc., and especially those of contemporary masters, popular at the time, like Anders Zorn, Joseph Pennell, and Whistler.

But the one who opened my eyes was Rembrandt. It was at one of these daring exhibitions that I fell financially in love with a work of art

31

for the first time, and, bless that dealer, he let me price everything from the "Hundred Guilder Print" to the one I finally bought for much less than the American equivalent of one guilder.

Like a young father-to-be, laying his financial status before the doctor who is to deliver his first child, I stuttered out my savings and my allowance to this trusting man. I confessed to hidden fortunes, tucked away in books; small Christmas gifts and one unholy sum I knew about but could not quite divulge—my lenten mite box, which I knew, right then and there, would never swell the funds for Christian ministry abroad.

He let me put five dollars down, with Boy Scout promises to pay off the $32.50 balance in the next six months. The next day I was there, the mite box burned so I could swindle Mother into believing I'd lost it, cash and all. Five dollars down. At twelve, that's all the world, and more. It's future sweets, future trespasses on cigarettes, dates with girls, and movies sneaked on Sunday afternoons. But it was worth it all, though it meant six long months of hoarding, work, and abstinences beyond the call of adolescent propriety.

"Two Nude Models, One Standing" by Rembrandt Harmensz van Rijn (1606–69)—price, $37.50. First state from the A. Artaria collection. My first privately owned work of art, and by Rembrandt . . . the Rembrandt! Oh, joy; oh, rapture unforeseen, but now seen with the most loving pair of eyes ever to look upon a picture, I think. The two rather emaciated men posed in true artist's model attitudes in the densely suggested studio. One arm of the standing figure rests languidly (but with a natural vitality) on a pedestal. The model looks at me, and while he looks at me, I know his gaze was set on Rembrandt, long ago— and I become Rembrandt as I return the look with no less love and possibly more appreciation of the model there, himself. I see the man that Rembrandt saw (and no man saw men as he saw them). Abstract, complete humanity in each, mankind in every man, civilization individualized. With adolescent awe, I saw his genius-interest in the human form, its grace—even in these imperfect specimens of man. The narrow shoulders, sunken chests, and spindle legs; the bony fingers and, close to the bone, the protecting flesh. Tough, wiry, and yet with all the startling grace—just as startling as is a gracefully gestured hand, held out from trucks at corners, and, following to the face, you see the rough uncouthness of its owner. The other model languishes on the floor behind. Another pose. An attitude to know and study and put down. Not in the classic group, my work of art; not even to be set beside the Tobit Angel series, the "Virgin's Death," "Three Trees," "Three Crosses," "Lazarus," or "Jan Six,"—just a page cut from the history of man, brought to life through the touch of Rembrandt . . . important as the sparrow . . . and as much of God.

This picture went with me from prep school to college, and throughout my life. It was a high standard to set, and one I could seldom live up to. And it doesn't follow, unfortunately, that a twelve-year-old boy, whose first art purchase was a Rembrandt etching, continues in this exalted vein. In the first place, it took me a whole year (instead of six months) to pay for that etching, and there was no more money for art works, good or bad. So I had to content myself with the wonders of the local museum.

The City Art Museum in St. Louis stands high on a hill in the great city park. It was one of the few permanent buildings which remained after the exposition of 1904. It is Roman, impressive, and for me, after *Apollo*, the open-sesame to art. Not that the collection housed there in my youth was great, or even adequate for study or inspiration, but it abounded in copies of great works, some masterpieces, and an atmosphere at once sacred and profane. My first visits were from the progressive school, with Mother leading the entourage and keeping a watchful eye on the little lascivious girls.

We walked through a lovely park on these trips up to the hill— Art Hill, we called it—up to the imposing entrance. On either side were limestone ladies, semi-nude, firm-bosomed, muses of the arts, but more like stately mothers who could make the kiddies feel at home. These statues are ever present in America, guarding Art and Justice, Architecture and Government, Music and, in many cases, nothing in particular. They are our bid for beauty and our diploma seal in emulation

33

of the Greek and Roman cultures which we all must study in school and, it would seem, only emulate but not go beyond. We love to copy, not invent.

The entrance hall of the museum was copied after the baths of Caracalla, or someone. Thank heaven the Romans were clean. Their public baths left an indelible mark on American public buildings. It made them roomy. We copied their baths rather than the temples, more impressed by their social graces than by their gods. And in the case of museums, they are cool and high, with light source distant as the sun itself as it approaches morning from the equally distant east. This hall was filled with casts, seamed mockeries of ancient glories, ancient gods and goddesses; of warriors and virgins; the later vestals, crowned with pagan or Christian symbols on the same old ancient drapes. From the central place of honor the confident majesty of Verrocchio's "Bartolomeo Colleoni" rode high, making a futile pass at the proportionately midget entrance door that could only have admitted the sacks of plaster lath and excelsior that comprised its bulk. And it alone stands out as comparable to the original when I finally saw it, being high, aloof, and tempered rotted-green, to simulate the natural patina of the past.

But Venus from the Isle of Melos, Demeter, and those preposterous, overly theatrical daughters of Niobe withheld their charm in plaster, being shy in anything but their original material. How luckless, lumpy, and unlifelike they all seemed. Venus, the perfect woman— waistless and taller than Miss Steuck, my Sunday-school teacher. This made our local Venus pretty damn tall, since Miss Steuck, in her haughty horsiness, even towered above the bishop—a big man. As a matter of fact, she and Venus had the same hairdo: parted in the middle, soft as marble, currycombed and careless, in the mode of aging spinster ladies of the middle twenties.

Like all museums, ours tried to give to the present visitor a quick impression of the past of all countries, from Stonehenge, kaleidoscopically almost, to our own not nearly so distant Salem sailor ancestors. There were "rooms." Classical, Gothic, Renaissance, New England,

and Victorian. The classical room made no attempt to copy Pompeii or any other geographic location. Fortunately, it was just a simple room with "classic" lines. There was a slight concession to authenticity in the "classic" ornaments—classic and classroom, straight out of the textbook—Ionian, Doric, or Corinthian. Since the early 1900 edifice in which it resided already included, indiscriminately, all forms of classic décor, this room seemed most "at home." In it were housed a sparse collection of fragments of antiquity, mostly the inevitable Roman copies of Greek art. The Romans must have been a little like us in their lack of originality. It has always seemed to me they did nothing but copy Greece, having completely destroyed it first, so no one would find them out in their chameleon propensities.

In one corner was a fragment of a Pompeiian fresco which filled me with delight and took me from suppressed giggles, on first viewing, to several surreptitious return engagements when the giggles gave way to adolescent yearnings. It was a satyr, chasing a pneumatic nude girl through a room with similar architectural ornamentation as the "classic room" itself. He was, of course, satyrically well equipped and became the private god of all the little boys and girls of the progressive school. He was having such an unashamedly good time, his purpose compass-clear. Even she, we felt, would stop her only half-harassment and give in when we weren't looking—that is, if she had any sense at all, for the look in her eyes as she gleamed over her shoulder at his glorious pursuit was rather one of wonder than of shock. I always visit this scene when I go home, in hopes she's given up and both have concluded what, for all these years, has been such a waste of time and energy.

At that time the other "rooms" didn't impress me too much. Certainly not the Early American one, which came too close to being what Mother was trying to achieve in the guest rooms at home. There she had collected, as the museum had, the most inquisitional group of Early American furniture ever assembled. In this motley mishmash was a bed, original to the last rung and spindle-turning. Only common decency had caused her to replace the rope "slats" with wooden ones,

35

which still came through the mattress to leave stripes instead of waffle welts on the unhappy guests. The chairs were designed for penance, and the desk—something called a "Jenny Lind"—had the only known surface which automatically folded the letter as you wrote it. There was a chair, upholstered in petit point, guaranteed to have been done by the Kaiser's second wife—and which, I shivered to think, was labeled to be left to me. The seat was as the cigarette ad said—round and firm and fully packed—as, indeed, were the mattresses, one of which actually hurled one of my nieces onto the floor in the middle of the night, breaking her small arm. How the early Americans achieved drawers which were hermetically sealed without locks will always be a mystery to me. Or mirrors in which the mirrored one took on the shape of the frame. Mother never would allow this genuine original distorter of the human form to be changed. Progress, for her, was something she was entirely willing to leave in the hands of her youngest child's educators.

The Early American room I *never* wished to visit in the museum, for it was a museum, a place of escape, and—it was for me! I preferred the Gothic Room, bleak and bare, or the wonderfully ornate, improbable and furnitureless Moorish interior from Spain, with its charming and inventively shaped little fountain, into which every school child in our city used to throw pennies, and which, I'm sure, went some short way to keep the museum running.

The picture collection was indecisive. It never made up its mind (or the viewer's) as to what was good, bad, or indifferent art. Good paintings by good painters were hung beside bad paintings by good painters or beside bad paintings by bad painters. These were the years before America and American collectors took it upon themselves to transport European art, *in toto*, to our shores, to assure us (or try to) of never having any incentive of our own to produce great art. It was that time before a famous publisher had seen and bought so much European art that he was moved to say there had been "no great art since the eighteenth century," a statement which I resented because it always left me with the feeling of living in a vacuum.

36

Most of the paintings and much of the furniture, rugs, and "objets d'art," a term which included sculpture at that time, were the gifts of wealthy citizens. The best that can be said about these donors is that they left a wealth of material to the museums of America. Those who gave to museums were either dead and wanted to be remembered (there were a great many "in-memory-of's"), or they were house cleaning. The great collectors whose collections were made under the influence of either great artists or dealers were only just beginning, and they kept their treasures close to home for many years—at least they did until it became the last "tax relief" in sight.

Then all at once our museums grew up and bulged with authentic opulence, as they do now. But these collections, whether they hung in a room named after the donor (and where their indecisive quality was most apparent) or whether they were seen all together, scattered in galleries which attempted to show the successive schools and trends in art, they were all we had. The almost without exception second-rate Renaissance paintings, for example, gave little indication of the splendor of that past period when art was the achievement, not the proof, of culture.

Yet there were some whose beauty, mystery, and deep-felt grace startled my wits. For example, there was a tiny portrait of a man in a gently shaped velvet hat to match his velvet robe, against a green background that poor-rich nature, except on willows at the point of spring, could not produce. His face was the face of any man his age, of any time, his gaze intent on being his own for all the years ahead—a tiny picture by the master of his time, Corneille de Lyons. I loved this image so much I never visit in the world of art that I don't try to see Corneille and all that perfect little world of likenesses he wandered in to set them down—impartial of their beauty, class, or strength of visage.

Another "Portrait of a Man" (strange how these sitters lose their identity in time, but not their individuality) was attributed to Sebastiano del Piombo. It was a wary, bearded man, one baleful eye blasé to portraiture, the other fixed to see that the painter did right by his wall-eyed superiority. His clothes are a dictionary of dress and manners as he sits before a fabric of design—again a fraction off the greens of nature.

About that museum phrase, "attributed to," who really cares if Sebastiano did it, or someone else? We benefit, and another attribution does not change the sitter, or his portrait, or its original plan at last to please the viewer.

And there were English portraits, too. There always are in American museums. The British being our most immediate identity with culture, American art patrons approved and collected them. These classy gentlefolk gave respectability to their drawing rooms, and proved we're still not here too long to lose what, in our local past, we fought to loose us from. The English portraitists painted themselves into their own backgrounds, but strangely enough it took a couple of visiting artists to see them best. Vandyke and Holbein. St. Louis had a Vandyke, and I could see that he gave the British glamour which they could not give themselves. Their own artists painted at home as their poets wrote away from it—nostalgically.

But for the children of our town, one frame alone contained the essence of our pictorial taste. It was enormous, this canvas by an unremembered French artist, bold and brave—at least as far as the subject went. It was a giant illustration of a gruesome scene, designed to make us shudder and have dreams. A tragic lady in the middle, put to test— facial and otherwise—must drink a glass of blood, the nice warm fresh blood of an executed Huguenot (French for Episcopalian, my mother told me, as she gave me a feeling recital of Catherine de' Medici's atrocities against our sect), or else her father's blood is let. The shaggy executioner holds out the glass of blood, which the wonderfully French painter couldn't resist making look like the best burgundy. The lady shudders. Grieving victims around her, by their expressions, sense her lot, but there's not one would disapprove her thirst.

And so we leave that blackest day of St. Bartholomew, assured that she drinks and that she and Papa live, if not forever, for a goodly time to tell this inflammatory story of how they threw bad Catherine out and rid the land of that accursed foreigner. The French wouldn't have given a damn if Catherine had killed every Huguenot in France—

even our bloodthirsty heroine—if Catherine had been French and not Italian.

That was our favorite picture, and when news came years later that the museum had sold it, I think a thousand kids, at least, then grown up, must have gone in mourning. The picture was passé. It had to go, I guess. But it had become part of the legend of our youth, and somehow, even though it was theatrical and not too well done, it captured us and made us admit that art could be interesting. It was a springboard for taste, for even as I began to know more about art and formed opinions of what I liked in the museum collection, I would always go back to see my old friend, the bloody lady. She and the "Madonna dell' Arpie," strange roommates as they were—and perhaps only because they were my first consciousness of the possibilities in art—will always be pictures in the back of my album of memories of how I learned to see.

Curiosity, which was to be the undoing of my home-town shackles, was never the undoing of my mother. She was only curious about what I'd grow up to be, since I was obviously not going to follow in my father's footsteps. Father had made a success in a business which I later learned he hated. But the pattern at home was "like father, like son," and while I was exactly like him, he wasn't about to admit it. Perhaps he'd forgotten what he was really like, or perhaps he wanted me to be different. He understood my need to fulfill my curiosity and made it possible for me to go to Europe. His generosity was so subtle that he made me feel I'd earned the right to go, as well as most of the money, by teaching me to save. He added little sums of trust and love to Christmas gifts and birthdays until, by my sixteenth year, I had almost the right amount.

For some unknown reason Mother, whose maternal instincts were highly developed, had not the slightest qualm about her baby boy going off alone to Europe. Before I left she gave me her usual warning about girls under bushes, and to beware of them. I took it straight-faced, as always, but wished I could have told her my reaction to the first time she told me this at fourteen—the age when boys were supposed to learn about sex for the first time. I went with the news to a worldly friend of fifteen and asked what the hell she meant about girls under bushes. He said she meant "fast" girls. Well, I swore from that day on never to leave a bush unturned, but I have yet to find one— under a bush, anyway.

My eyes may not have been filled with art at home, but my heart was full of love and gratitude to these two individuals who knew the art of parenthood so well, they could afford to be my friends. Mother's artistic mistakes, I've made a thousand times. For her lack of knowledge of the arts, I lack her warmth. My parents gave their blessing to my curiosity, and through that curiosity they knew I'd find my way, somehow, to be in love with life . . . a different love than theirs, perhaps, but I knew then, as they did, it would be full of sights they'd never see.

E UROPE AT SIXTEEN! HOW OR WHY MY PARENTS EVER GOT up the courage to let me go to Europe alone at sixteen, I'll never know. One reason might have been that the sight of another travel folder could well have snapped their minds. Secondly, I was six feet one and growing fast. A third possibility was that my four years of constant curiosity and questions about the rest of the world had run them out of answers.

But the most likely reason was my grandmother. As the youngest of her four grandchildren, I had become delightfully and enrichingly close to her. This frosted beauty lived with us more and more, as the limitations of age gradually prohibited her wandering to warmth in Florida and California—or just "taking off" for the then more economical countries across the sea, as she had always adored to do on her limited income. In addition to my basic love for her, we had a rapport regarding said countries across the sea; a little lopsided, to be sure, since it was comprised of endless queries from me and patiently understanding answers from her. That's why I say she was a likely reason for my departure. Her sympathetic attitude stemmed from her own fond memories of world travels. During her life with my English step-grandfather she had toured the world with him—toured as the British do, not for the usual reasons but just so they can be homesick and write lovely poems about being in England, now that spring is here . . . a wish of fantasy, to be sure, since nothing is slower to arrive or quicker to go than an English spring.

Her world wanderings during marriage and after her second widowhood had armed her with the answers to my interminable questions. I bent her ear for a description of every inch she'd covered, and she pictorially replied, in knowing prose. She told me tales of Mexico, of Spain, of Greece and Egypt—whetting my appetite all the more.

But I *had* to see for myself! With Grandmother pitching on my team, whatever objections Mother might have had to the idea of my long-anticipated journey were dissipated, for their relationship was one of deep devotion and mutual respect. Apart from this, Mother had always appreciated the fact that Grandmother didn't mope about in her youth after her first husband (Mother's father) had drowned. She was also grateful to her for marrying my English stepgrandfather, because, after all, how else would she have come by her affiliation with castles Windsor and Blarney—and that, to us, embarrassing habit of pushing food onto her fork with a knife? So, the dream gradually became a reality.

For reasons which escape me Father decided to sell our summer home, and from the sale, he put a modest sum aside for each of us to use as we would use it. He might as well have bought the boat passage for me, then and there, and saved a transfer of this generous gift.

Mine went, with their immediate permission, toward "Tour 22" . . . "Seven Capitals of Europe, Tour 22." I studied all the twenty-four in the folder, but it was 22 which covered most. Whoever wrote the propaganda for Tour 22 had written it just for me. The sights which would be covered were my dreams come true. Where other tours included famous battlefields and natural phenomena, like rocks which look like ladies fast asleep, Tour 22 was heavy on the churches and museums, with just enough enticing treats to mysteries like the Catacombs outside Rome and castles like Chillon.

I sailed in mid-June at midnight on an old Cunarder. My cabinmate, also on Tour 22, was a youngish man, with the air of a fugitive from the future. I later discovered this was true. Perhaps Pat Frank knew what life wherever he came from was to be, so he left it to see what he could of the world before the ax of incarcerating responsibility cut him down. I've often wondered if this trip turned him into the successful novelist he is today. It was great that night, sailing from New York, and while I knew Tour 22 had other members I would meet next day, that night I was Columbus, vice versa, Marco Polo, young Leonardo—going to see the wonders of the world. I stood on the upper deck like the seagoing hero in the last scene of a movie, with hair awind, watching the magic city disappear as the long gray valleys of the open ocean took us in. The world was not yet "too much with me, late and soon, getting or spending," to lay waste my powers of imagination. I was fully aware of the opportunities of this adventure—half equipped to meet them perhaps—but certain I would stand on this same deck ten weeks later, better than half equipped to meet the world and introduce myself to it, to live and love it. I slept that night like some enchanted creature, waiting to be awakened by a magic word.

The morning came, a morning made to celebrate the creation of the world, the thrill of a ship, the ecstasy of the sea, along with breakfast and the assemblage of Tour 22, a lovely group . . . ladies of all ages, accents, costumes, and, with all the world of ladies, one thing in common—that ugliest of headgear, the suffocating cloche; that hat which, in the twenties, turned females into warriors of old, cut the chance of conversation right in half, and leveled noble brows to idiocy. The men were standard, in plus fours, slacks, and caps, if not in age. They ranged from my sixteen to eighty-four. But, male and female, boy and girl, we had a purpose and a goal . . . Europe.

Our keepers were two divergent characters, a professional tourmaster and "Mademoiselle," a French schoolteacher with barracuda teeth and the most foreign accent, real or otherwise, I'd ever heard. We reviewed the tour, made friends, and settled down to enjoy the balmy crossing.

The romantic painter, Eugène Delacroix, on seeing the fastest sailing ship afloat in the middle of the nineteenth century, bemoaned its speed. He was quoted as saying that the quicker you get where you're going, the longer you have to be bored when you get there. That was the adage of an aging man, a Frenchman and an artist set in life, but not the motto for a middlewestern boy on his first trip to the moon. I couldn't wait. I loved the ocean, loved the ship, enjoyed the sense of being on my own. But the moment when my foot touched England's shore . . . that, I was positive, was the ultimate—the Moment of Truth! . . . I had arrived in Europe . . . and in life!

The English countryside is the side of that country most people rave about, and it is beautiful. But I've seen bluebells on the redbud hills at home, when dogwood flakes an April day—all white. I've seen a rug of violets and Mayflowers beneath their green umbrellas in the rain. I've seen Missouri flower, frost, and fry. So countrysides were countrysides, in England or at home. I'd seen enough. I waited for a city . . . London! And London *is* a city.

Approaching it from the country, we entered an opaque tunnel of rust and gray. The town surrounds you and, as its vast environs slip you down its open throat, you lose identity at last, like Jonah, in the belly of the station. The steel-ribbed, sooty-skinned interior, in constant fog of snorting trains, depresses one—as if on purpose—so that being belched forth into the rocking traffic of the city, one feels free—free and immediately a part of it, of London, of the life of England. It is impressive that this little land contains the world's greatest city, and it is equally impressive that its citizens have brought so much beauty into the welter of their poverty of space.

I took London on like the biggest hick ever to hit a big city. Several years before, I'd worn Father to a frazzle when he took me to New York for the first time, and now our good guide and Mademoiselle had to bear the brunt of my bursting curiosity. Much as I wanted to see everything on our schedule, I decided one day, with their permission, to forego another Christopher Wren church and head straight for my ultimate London goal on my own.

There is really only one mysterious museum in the world: the

44

British Museum. Nothing can touch it for clutter, for atmosphere, for gravity of purpose, that purpose being to collect civilization complete, under one roof. The past pops up around you as though it had sought refuge there from the present. Secretively, crouching in every corner, treasures await discovery. If the British didn't succeed in colonizing the world, they succeeded in preserving it here. And if it is true that they are the most civilized people on the face of the earth, their source of inspiration—the sun from which they take their shine and polish—orbits here. It is the home of discovery, the Rosetta Stone, that key to conversation; the doors, lintels, pylons, caryatids, architraves, tympana, all the supports of our ultimate necessity—the roof over our heads. Here they all are. If the ravages of British conquests, such as Benin, sometimes shock us, the spoils as gathered here can only delight us, for what they have gathered lives safer here, perhaps, than anywhere. Those sensitive souls who feel the Elgin Marbles would be better off in Athens should remember those centuries of neglect of the Parthenon, when it was a powderhouse and all the samplers of the past picked its anatomy apart so that heads, hands, and bodies are irretrievably separated.

For some inexplicable reason, I have always felt a pre-relationship with Greece. I was at home with anything Greek, and I felt I could make my bed right here. The glory that was Greece; perfection of the pose, living marble. Clichés rose and fell, only to seem utterly inadequate before this art. This marble was indeed alive! . . . Half in the fact that God made it marble but more in the knowledge that man made it live. The body underneath; the bosoms bursting through the tons of drapery; the grace and power.

I wrote a poem that night. I have it still, and if it fails to fill the bill we owe to Phidias, it shows my years, all sixteen of them, and best, the immediate identification of a lover with his beloved:

"Marbles of Greece! Made magically by man from that divine material begun by God. Divine gift, humanly accepted, worked to perfection from the perfect rock. For them, the end of learning, and for me, *necessity* to learn."

There is more, but that's enough. Not Wordsworth's, but a young man's recognition of the chance from here to learn, to gather curiosity (that word again) about how man could make these wonders and achieve this height, then slip away, destroy it, lose the lesson, learn it, and achieve again. One thing to learn, seeing great achievements of the past, is that the possibility is always there and that whenever man and his civilization strike the top—they strike it rich.

With Mademoiselle snapping at our heels to "get on with it," my hurried opinion of that other masterpiece in the British Museum, the Portland Vase, was that it looked like a reproduction by Wedgwood. And its importance escaped me to the point almost of condoning the maniac who, years before, had hurled a brick at it.

When you are doing seven capitals in seven weeks, you don't see very much of everything, and being with a group, you do as they do. So the British Museum was the only museum considered a "must" in our three days in London. The National Gallery, which I lived in later on (on another trip), I'd have to wait to see then. We had to eat, sleep, see the zoo, the Square, and Piccadilly. So all we could assume, jumping from one bus to another and walking endless miles of London streets, was that London was certainly the biggest city, that the British were intolerantly tolerant of American tourists, and that I, for one, wanted to come back.

So one capital down and six to go. For my money, the most exciting thing about Paris was the boat ride across the channel. I hated Paris then, though I've learned to love it. I'm sure it's not a city for the very young. At sixteen (even at six feet one) you're too young to night club and too hungry to enjoy the paradise of French cuisine. The charm of the brain, put under a glass bell and served with a delicious sauce which couldn't disguise the texture, will always escape me. Even my schooling at Mother's culinary breast could never teach me the charms of snails, octopuses, or brains.

At sixteen I resented the French for having torn down the Bastille; for burying Napoleon in a sarcophagus which gave you no idea of his size; for killing King Louis and Marie Antoinette; for having perfected champagne, which gave me my first hang-over; and for their language, which even the children could speak and which had me so confused that no matter what I ordered on any menu, it turned out *brains*. I thought the Arc de Triomphe was too far from the Louvre, and I felt the fountains of Versailles were a waste of water. This last resentment I inherited from my father, to whom a leaking tap was, along with an unextinguished light bulb, the primal cause of poverty.

I'll admit the Louvre was impressive, but I missed the clutter of the British Museum and I missed the kings. I would have foregone its treasures gladly, if those golden sovereigns still held sway. And after the Elgin Marbles, the "Winged Victory" looked much too fussy—as if she were in a hurry to get out to lunch—or like those chiffony leading ladies who always come on stage, no matter where they have just exited, by floating down the stairs. She reminded me of Ethel Barrymore, without her head (which was the best part of Ethel, because that's where her voice lived), making an entrance in the play, *The Constant Wife*.

I've had to eat my opinions, which always taste worse than words, but I hated Paris. The whole effect was a forced laugh, and I only learned to appreciate it years later when my own laugh was a little forced too, and hers seemed more familiar.

I'd visit the Louvre again, I knew, for I had been bright enough to see the sun behind the "Mona Lisa's" gloomy smile, and I knew that someday I'd be able to feel something, other than homesickness, looking at "Whistler's Mother," though why she made me homesick, I'll never know. (My mother, God knows, wouldn't have been caught dead in that cap, or slumped in a rocking chair. Rocking made her seasick.) I might even see the Venus de Milo as other than a symbol of homework, her unflattering likeness stamped on a pencil box. But I felt one thing, even then. When the time came for me to understand Mantegna, Zurbarán, Bellini, and Veronese, I would come back and sit beneath the warning finger of Leonardo's St. John, plumbing the rocks, the landscape, and the golden forestry of curls in that sentient masterpiece. But for now, I really didn't like Paris, and we were on our way to Rheims.

I loved the Rheims Cathedral, mainly because it had been bombed. Only the first dollars of the Rockefeller money had been spent to start to restore it, and it was still a shambles. But somehow you could see how it had been when those legions of artisans, so many centuries before, had worked on it to pile it there. There is always something really religious about a church being built. Of most churches, I feel that when people have finished working on them, they often have finished worshiping in them as well. They seem to sit and contemplate what has been done and thought before.

We were told how long and how much love it had taken to build it, originally, and I was pleased to see that loving going on again. I remember a stonecutter, copying a post card of a figure which had been destroyed, and inside, in the great nave, the sky came in. The sun was bright without that sieve of roses to strain through. It was a skeleton of faith, something essential and historical, but still new.

I loved Rheims, too, because it was the only French city I saw that wasn't half hysterical with hurry. The smiles seemed genuine . . . and I found a menu without brains.

We drove to Belgium in a bus. We saw the trenches and the rows of crosses in Flanders fields, so peaceful now. But I could sense the anguish in the people, still—and when two of our Tour 22 requested that we visit at the graveyard of their son—at least, they thought it was the graveyard—I was brought up short by the individuality of war. I had been too young to remember much of World War I, except the flags, food restrictions, saving tin foil, and the gaiety of the armistice. But these two people, standing at the gateway to the graves with heads bowed, their secret silent in themselves, I wouldn't forget. They never mentioned it again, nor did any of us, but Belgium had identity for all of us, from that time on.

In Brussels we were burdened with only one work of art: a famous statue of a little boy. Everyone knows the feeling, but why make a monument to it?

Holland was so damned quaint my feet began to hurt. The thought of wearing wooden shoes, even through fields of daffodils, gave

48

me such psychosomatic corns I could hardly walk. And walk we had to . . . through endless villages and towns . . . seeing the sights. I understand the sea is a constant threat to Holland, but there were moments, then, when I wished that boy had pulled his finger out of the dike.

Amsterdam, however, was another thing. A city of canals and homey houses, clean and lean, lined up like neat children to admire their reflection in the polished streams. And there was Rembrandt. He was the first artist I had ever known, personally—being the private owner of one of his etchings in its first state—so when we visited the Rijksmuseum, I lost myself from the rest of the tour to wander, stunned by these magnificently dramatic visions of mankind. There is in any collection of an artist's work the sense that the painter himself is there, giving you a personally conducted tour of his pictures. But with Rembrandt he is really there in those superb self-portraits. I think the truth of the greatest proverb: "to know yourself" must have appealed to Rembrandt more than to any other artist. The understanding of his personality, as seen by himself, is so intense there seems no secret of it left unrevealed. And it follows that, knowing himself so well, he could not prove false to any man. There is absolute truth in Rembrandt's approach to each of his sitters.

In *Apollo*, the "Night Watch" is the size of a special-delivery stamp; the "Anatomy Lesson" is an airmail, and the "Syndics" has more people in it than a commemoration stamp. So, when I came upon these masterpieces in actuality, it was the size which brought me to a halt—the fact that people were life-sized and lifelike, at the same time, was almost too much to take. In other big canvases I had seen (in the Louvre, for example), there was always a still-life quality, as if the action had been instantly and permanently suspended. But here, in the "Anatomy Lesson," for instance, the doctor, for all the ridiculous conceit of not bothering to remove his hat, lifts his attention to explain a point of surgical etiquette, but only for a second—that second the painter saw him. And there's resumption in his attitude. He will return and finish what he started the minute you look away. The Civic Guard *are* actually marching out, taking direction from what they leave behind, the life around them.

And here in the Rijksmuseum I entered for the first time the serenity of Dutch interiors, helped by the hands of Vermeer, de Hooch, and Terborch. I never did get to see a *real* Dutch interior, but I didn't need to. Through these masters I was let inside, in the sunlight, in the gleaming miracle of light they alone could achieve. I touched the surfaces and smelled the flowers in these monuments to realities. I shared a dewdrop with the thirsty flies Jan van Huysum populates his flower bouquets with. I was startled for a moment by a daring dead-blue Christ of Hugo van der Goes but overcome by Rembrandt and Vermeer. I had no room to taste these great Flemish masters of the early Renaissance, but I caught a glimpse of those red-eyed virgins, weeping at the spectacle of mankind crucified, that haunts me to this day.

Rubens remained an enigma. Those massive, livid mansions of crude flesh were too high a protein diet for my forming appetite. And even Hals, for all his virtuosity, his happy nature, and his presto style, escaped me then.

I took on a toothsome blonde, the only contemporary appetizer on Tour 22, and determined to explore, firsthand, what Rubens had reveled in: the flesh! This girl, with a lovely, semi-southern accent, was the only one of the ten assorted ladies on our tour anywhere near my age, yet there was a decent difference in her favor and, I felt, in mine, for I hoped she'd lead me to the garden of delights and crown my young years with conquest. I tried hard, God knows, and she almost complied, but it would have to be a night in Nice, some weeks later, before my quest was satisfied. After all, a love of art is a fine thing for a young boy, but art is long—and life can be pretty damned long too, without our just desserts!

Before we leave Holland and my pursuit of learning and the semi-southern blonde, I'd like to recall an evening when I stood alone on the shores of the North Sea, thinking of home. Mother had been reading a lot about "thought transference," and we'd agreed to try it while I wandered about Europe. It was a good idea, for the ache of homesickness dulled away as I remembered home, itself. I thought of happiness at home; my sisters and brother; Father and Mother; of how lucky I was to have them there, and yet how lucky I was to be here. It wouldn't have been half as much fun being here if they weren't there, and the thought of them concentrated my memories. I rehearsed recitals of my journey, thus far, that I would give to them when I got home. I realized that evening that what I thought was going to be my greatest experience in Europe, truly was. The firsthand contact with creative man. Even if I made my point with my charming blond target, that would simply be the first of many. But each contact with the creative act would have the difference of always seeming like the last. The mind's creation is a definite statement, while the adventure of the flesh is often better left unsaid. Throughout our lives we are apt to speak it many times, but at the end of life—as before the beginning— the statement exists and survives, for it is the truth, and the other often proves us false.

Three weeks of intense sight-seeing had passed, and the next two countries were considered sport: Germany and Switzerland. While this book is to be mostly a visual experience, I must honestly say that we ate more than we saw in these two countries. Cologne was impressive, and its cathedral made me realize how minutely we Americans had achieved Gothic opulence in our assimilation of that great architectural tradition. We've never been able to make such forests of stone, and the nave in Cologne seems as if it could contain the Woolworth Building. Those opening vaults, reaching the roof and branching away to a solid interlacing of foliage, expand the mind to think of their conception. The fact that this cathedral was in the process of being built for a thousand years (and was only completed in the last century) tempts us to accept its vastness almost as though it had a mind of its own and knew the world would increase in population, if not in faith, and could put its enormity to good use. It stands there, symbolic of the unaccepted open-armedness of faith.

In Germany sausage, boiled potatoes, sauerkraut, and beer are actually almost visual experiences. More honest than French cooking, where the object is obscured by sauces, these plates of succulence not only promise visually to satisfy, but do. If anyone can achieve a happier glow than having these inside you, boating down the Rhine, then I'd like to go where that glow glows.

We didn't go to Berlin. Very few Americans did then, because the Berliners apparently were having a rather vulgar recovery from the ravages of war.

But we did go to Nuremberg, thank God. If I had never seen this city, or could only see it later—pastures of rubble—I would have missed the realization of the German Renaissance and the fact that it's from that Renaissance that we inherit so many moments of our modern life. Dürer, above all . . . and Luther, Cranach, our love of etchings, the invention of the printed book . . . a hundred things. The city itself is pure romance—the walls, towers, lovely churches, houses that have changed nothing but the inhabitants—and Dürer's house where, as far as I'm concerned, he lives still.

For me, Dürer is one of the few supreme artists, not only because of his incomparable skill, but because of his aliveness. As Rembrandt was alive to men, Dürer was alive to nature. He is an exciting painter, though not the greatest. He is the master engraver, not the most profound. But when he looks at nature, when he draws from nature, no man extracts the essence more.

You can fall in love with Dürer and his art more readily and more completely than with most, but if the sheer beauty of "The Praying Hands" seems enough to most people, it is when you know what they are praying for that you really understand his genius. These hands are in supplication, that you may see him through to the complete communion he achieved with nature and natural life. See how he parts the grasses to explore the roots, and parts the roots to probe the sod, then discovers in the sod the roots of life itself.

I think I am as moved as the next man by the beauties of nature, though I sometimes agree with the American comedy writer who wrote that he "loved nature because it was so natural." I still can "Oh" and do "Oh" at sunsets, mists, mountains, trees, and mirroring lakes; and

I never have failed to "Ah" at the dawn. It frightens me properly each time I see it. I love being in at the birth of a new day, though sometimes it seems the world is overpopulated with days—just as it is with people. I worry properly about dusk. The sun, though still passionate, is spent, its limp light leaking around the corners of the earth, and I only feel reassured that I'm still alive and kicking when I see the Wishing Star. That single eye makes me feel protected. Then when they all appear, and the calculating night resets the mathematics of the spheres, I'm quite content to let it be and sleep it off, warm in the knowledge that it will solve itself . . . and let me enjoy another day.

And so I took Switzerland in like a deep breath. I didn't dare exhale until the threat of indigestion from visual overindulgence in grandeur was past. I remember nothing about that country except the views, and I compliment the Swiss on creating an architectural style that is nature, camouflaged . . . it doesn't get in the way of it. They have even placed their cities so that, by a short walk up from one, you can overlook it completely.

One incident happened to me in Switzerland that illustrates that point. In Interlaken my lady friend and I decided to picnic on an alp. Hours of climbing later, we arrived at the daring summit of a modest alp, only to discover, leading down the other side, a charming stairway.

The Swiss think of everything. The only mountain they have left unstaired or unfuniculared is the Matterhorn. I suppose they have to leave something for fools to climb.

The train trip from Switzerland to Austria is not much longer than a trip around the world. Nothing more arduous has been invented by man. This Trans-Siberian experience is enough to surfeit the soul forever with natural beauties. It is one breath-taking view after another, until you're completely breathless. Since this particular railroad takes particular pride in its unsurpassed scenic route, the schedule includes an unscheduled two-hour stop outside Vienna . . . so you can get your breath, I guess.

But we made Vienna, Capital Number Five, and all we were to see of it was Vienna herself. It is a combination city—old and not so old;

one about which someone always says something good, especially when referring to "former times." Personally, I thought it all right, right then. The food was good, the people nice, and the wine and dancing superb. I loved Vienna right away, and I encountered there a friend it took me years to cultivate: the art of the rococo and baroque. There's something fascinating about seeing something you don't like at first but directly know you will love—in time. People are that way, all through life. You come against a personality, and it questions yours. You shy away but know there are gratifying secrets there, and the half-open door is often more exciting than the wide.

The Karlskirche and the library were my first discoveries of this gold of the baroque. I threw my hat in the air at seeing it, then sat down to wonder if I wanted to be that rich. My conclusion was poverty. I found I couldn't handle the wealth of this discovery . . . not yet.

Schönbrunn I preferred to Versailles, but I still missed royalty. I think, if they'll admit it, all Americans do in a way. Those men we here call "honorable" because they have served us well are all "honorable" men, I'm sure. But they lack glamour. Being born to something is much more glamorous than acquiring it through hard work. Our only princesses are the contenders for the title of "the richest girl in the world." They may be just that, but no one I've ever heard of made the money for herself. That's why we pamper them with publicity. A castle, in the much more socially secure hands of a people-governed state, seems unprofitable compared to the glory of its former state. And when the royal family has moved out suddenly, leaving behind everything but their bath water, I always feel a little sad—like a trespasser—and I want to look the other way when signs point "this way" or "that."

Museums are different, if they are public buildings to begin with, and one of the great ones is the Kunsthistorisches in Vienna. It is great for its many masterpieces, but one especially, in my estimation, would justify even the train trip from Switzerland.

She's sitting there, a creature skinned in moonlight milk—like sea light, leaping in the night, she shimmers in one corner of the frame. Behind her, little pleasantries of life go on, and in the middle distance, two old men, comparing senile platitudes about a naked girl . . . listen and leer. This story of "Susanna and the Elders" has everything to delight the painter, for painters seem unusually naïve in their selected literature. They choose a story for its "picture possibilities" . . . and this one has them all: a landscape, the architectural distance, possibilities of portraiture both in Susanna herself (being in the nude) and in the dirty old men.

For whatever reason Tintoretto chose this subject, he succeeded, heaven knows, in creating a woman anyone would gape at. For me, this triumph (and his "Origin of the Milky Way" in London) sets him apart from other painters as a special dramatic entity, although almost everything he did has greatness.

The Kunsthistorisches also boasts the largest collection of Brueghels in the world. I was terribly impressed by this inventor of the candid panoramic point of view of religious, historical, and mythological stories. It is such a joy to wander in his villages and countrysides, in his contemporary vision, and discover Icarus, falling in the sea; or with a telescopic eye, come close to see the weeping virgin and His friends, alive in Brueghel's time through Brueghel's eyes. The museum had assembled almost every work of his to commemorate the anniversary of his (ancient) death. It wasn't big, this exhibition, for what he saw he saw completely, and his output was meticulously small. Yet, before the viewer, he displays his world entirely—a world that he created from the past and projected into his time. Brueghel succeeds where many fail—to make believable the fact that ancient voices can be understood, or heard, in modern tongue—that real-life actions in another age can happen now. A modern-dress Hamlet is a bit ridiculous, for the mood is helped by sets and costumes of a more passionate period than ours. But less complicated tragedies, more basic, more everyday—like "man's inhumanity to man"—exist forever, and Brueghel's success attests itself in his presenting of "The Way of the Cross," where Christ's Crucifixion is a holiday in Flanders, within which this most potent plot unfolds.

Here, too, I saw my first painting of the mythological loves of Jove: Correggio's "Io and Jupiter." The great gray cloud of love devours her and sets her fastidious flesh afire. What ecstasy for both of them—and only in this great artist's hands could cloud be flesh, as much as flesh is flesh. Correggio and Tintoretto, lovers in paint. They opened up to me the possibility of emotion in art. I could see the chances here for a complete visual life, and I was glad I'd seen these previews of the Renaissance away from Italy. They were appetizers before the great meal that Italy had been preparing for centuries. (Just for me?)

We left Vienna after a few hectic days and nights. The nights, it seemed, were spent in trying every wine and tasting every dish. *Schnitzel* and *Heurige* . . . the latter that juice of youth . . . of youthful grapes . . . a wine to die young . . . innocent and potent as a saint. The days were spent in an agony of repentance. However, when you are sixteen and in Vienna for the first time, it just might be the last time— and a hang-over was worth it.

And for dessert, the Viennese have exploded eggs to mountains of delight and fun. *Salzburger Knockerln*—a dream to be pictured by your tongue . . .

All through our lives we check off days to come, leading to something "big." Vacations, birthdays, a special anticipated event, and even if the days we scurry over toward our goal may be the finest we could ever live, that moment just ahead is precious and desired.

On our itinerary Tour 22 offered no diamond in its glamorous array to touch the hope of Italy. If you're in love with art, the honeymoon is there. All other art seems distant and a little strange without the eyes of Italy to see it through. You may have scattered affairs with other arts—deep passions, even—but the golden wedding partner is waiting for you at home in Italy.

The moment came. We took the train to Venice. Continents of natural beauties lay between: the Dolomites, the mountains, lakes, lovely towns. But dreams of Venice blinded me, and I'll never forget, for all this poetic dreaming, the force with which the squalor of Venice hit me. On a tour like ours—so cheap, so all-inclusive—the economy was hotels. In any language, we found ourselves at the Hôtel du

Gare . . . next door to the station. This was an easy way to keep us all together, and to get us off for the next place. For comfort, nothing could compare to them. They had none. The food was miserable, the beds were hard, and the baths so involved and tepid that you almost preferred to stay dirty. But I must say they were good places with which to compare the rest of the surroundings! Almost anything looked glorious, in comparison. All over Europe they were the same—especially in color. Soot brown.

Venice, from the station hotel, could be Hoboken with wet pavements. Arriving as we did in the dead of night, one had the suspicion that the advertised beauties of this gem of the Adriatic were elsewhere. Maybe another fourteen-hour train trip away? . . . Even the Venetian morning light lent little glamour to that scene around the station. You could only hope that such glamorous items as gondolas did exist, since only some shabby, high-prowed canoes were anchored in front.

Not speaking Italian, I tried my German on the breakfast waiter, which he feigned to understand. Having had the softest, scarcely coddled, boiled eggs in Vienna, I asked for *"Zwei Eieren, sechs Minuten gekocht"* . . . two six-minute eggs. Then, waiting a long multiple of *sechs Minuten*, I was delivered—*sechs* eggs, *zwei Minuten gekocht*— six two-minute eggs! You can't win with eggs in Europe, but it was fun throwing them in the canal.

Sure enough, Venice did exist. We cruised down the Grand Canal and there was the Rialto, the "business end" of Venus, as some wag had put it. And farther on, the canal became wider and we could see the domes of St. Mark's and the campanile, pointing above everything to that incredible blue sky.

What a wonderful square that is, St. Mark's . . . and those damned pigeons . . . and those four glorious horses, prancing on the balcony; then, of course, St. Mark's lion, high on his column, looking back—keeping his eye on the pigeons. The Palace of the Doges and the Bridge of Sighs, and once again the feeling of loss that those glamorous barbarians had moved away, and other times (even if for the better) had forever exiled the pageant of nobility.

St. Mark's is a curious building. It would look dreadful anywhere but where it is. As for the interior, sheer genius went into its plan. How was it possible to keep so much light out, and to create that obstacle course of marble, bronze, and alabaster! . . . I can guarantee that if they made thousand-dollar bills of alabaster, I'd refuse them. Here is the one material over which man cannot triumph. On second thought, perhaps there's one other . . . platinum. The only possible recommendation for these two products of nature is their rarity.

There were two painters on the grand scale who knocked one down: Titian and, again, Tintoretto. Guardi and Canaletto certainly tell us the everyday story of their day in Venice, but Titian, in those majestic portraits, and Tintoretto, in his attempt to populate the Doges Palace with the Heavenly Host itself—sacred and profane—they were the genuine echoes of the glorious past. And Tintoretto had another quality that was almost his alone: he could paint flight. He could make a human being soar through the air, light as a bird, light as light.

Venice was almost too much for a sixteen-year-old, falling in love with art, and the hotel by the station, on the sewer canal, was *altogether* too much. So I got permission to leave the tour and go to Florence a day ahead of schedule. I took the night train alone, and naturally I went third class. My seat was in an air-tight compartment with four vociferous Italians who started to eat after five minutes on the way. They ended up a fifty-variety sausage meal by munching on buds of garlic. It had once been said that my mother put garlic in everything but the ice cream, but even with my background I had never had my nose rubbed in it to this extent. One thing it did do. I passed out from the fumes about midnight and didn't awake until I made my escape in Florence at six the next morning.

Florence! This was to be the high point of the whole tour. Arriving alone at dawn, I'll never regret or forget. I had a light suitcase, so I decided to walk to the hotel, which was not next to the station for once, but on the Arno itself. Oh, God . . . what a city. How beautiful, how clean, how shining, how romantic. I walked along, clearing the garlic out of my lungs and letting my eyes feast on the city. Then suddenly I rounded a corner, and there it was . . . the Duomo, Giotto's Tower . . . and the doors . . . the doors to heaven, surely. Giotto, Ghiberti, Donatello, Brunelleschi—thank you!

Only the Duomo was open at 6 A.M., so I went in. The interior was all space. Compared to St. Mark's, it's as light as all outdoors. The proportions are so satisfactory you can breathe them, and the fact that it's uncluttered gives you a churchly feeling instead of the attic attitude so many famous churches have assumed, after generations have discarded their dead and memories there.

I just walked on, and I was still almost alone. I remember that I was indeed alone when, around another corner I came on the great square, the Signoria, the Loggia, and the Uffizi. There, across the way, I saw "David," gleaming in white marble. I didn't know, or care, that it was a copy. It was Michelangelo's first hello to me, and I answered back—openmouthed—and then "Perseus," Cellini's boy with the Gorgon's head, and around the base those lovely little nudes.

The only Italian I knew was the name and address of the hotel, so I said it to someone who appeared, and did I get an answer! It sounded like the first canto of Dante, but a finger finally pointed in a vague direction so I said *"Danke Schön"* . . . for some unknown reason . . . and went that-a-way. I think I used German because, subconsciously, at just that moment, I didn't want to be an American tourist. I wanted to belong to the world. I wanted to be at home in Florence.

The hotel people spoke English, and, being the first of our tour to arrive, I got a wonderful room with a little balcony—around the corner of which I could see the Arno and across from which I could look into what surely must have been Lorenzo the Magnificent's home. Of course, it wasn't. But it was a palace, and so romantic I couldn't believe my eyes. I fell asleep on my little balcony and woke up two hours later, panting with heat. The sun of Florence is hot, but how mysteriously cold you can get—and how quickly—in the first convenient shade.

What did I want to see first? What did I want to see alone? Through what glorious door would I make my first real entrance into the Renaissance? Should I go say a prayer in the Duomo or go up and survey the whole city from the Piazzale Michelangelo? I suddenly remembered I had a friend in Florence—Andrea del Sarto—dead a good many years but very much alive to me since he first introduced himself in our minister's house at home through his "Madonna of the Harpies." Now, where did she live? . . . The Uffizi! . . . There I would start my journey; there I would say hello to an old friend and meet some new ones.

Florence! . . . The Duomo! . . . The Uffizi! . . . These words, names, places are exclamation marks in themselves . . . you have to put dots of wordless wonder after each one. There is nothing else to say. The Uffizi! . . .

Has anyone ever gone through those doors, blasé, disgusted, bored, and not been lifted—"sent"—immolated—within a matter of moments? I haven't been there for twenty-seven years, but I'm "sent," just remembering it . . . sent into the greatest world of art, sent back into a civilization of art and excitement that has never had an equal.

First off, in the Uffizi I met a portraitist who let me look, through his eyes, into the eyes of the people of the past: Bronzino. There they are. The Medici, the men, the children, and the beautiful Eleanor of Toledo, in a gown so sumptuous she had herself painted in it—and buried in it. Bronzino is not a deep, psychological portrait painter, but his pictures are true memorials to his sitters. If you want the future to remember what you look like, dig up Bronzino and have him "do" you! . . . Hard, crisp, elegant, real—descriptive of his sitters and of his portraits of them.

I was in the flood. I was drowning in the world of art. I was sailing on a shell with Venus. I was a witness to the Holy Family. . . . And then, suddenly, I came upon a room . . . and there she was. My own personal Madonna.

I know now that del Sarto was not the greatest painter—far from Browning's "perfect painter." I know he was soft, overblown . . . I know that in the lists of greatness, he's nowhere near the top . . . but there *she* was!

Oh beautiful, serene, soft-eyed, and glamorous—she's not the Virgin Mother, not the Woman of Sorrows—she's the Queen of Goddesses, a woman to worship as a woman. She is beautiful, and she's in love with all mankind. Especially with me.

Only three things have ever caused me to weep, for beauty's sake or for art's sake: the Madonna of Andrea del Sarto, the first time I saw John Gielgud play *Hamlet* in London, and Kirsten Flagstad's Isolde. I'm always open to let them flood again, but for my tear ducts it's apparently got to be a special thing to make them flood . . . and anyway, I hate it. It hurts and makes me embarrassed, even if I'm alone.

And there I was, standing in the Uffizi with a watermelon in my throat and two painful jets of warm salt water spurting out of my eyes. At that moment the whole world could have walked into that gallery, and I wouldn't have been able to cover up. Then I heard a soft voice, over my shoulder, say: "Come over here. I'll show you the one that makes me cry."

I blew my nose, blotted my eyes, buried as much of my face as I could in my handkerchief, and blurted out a feeble: "Sorry . . . something in my eye."

The voice said: "Yes . . . beauty."

It belonged to a woman who must have been the mother of my Madonna, a lovely, comfortable, middle-aged Saint Anne. She took me firmly by the arm, led me out of the room and down the hall, and brought me up, still, in front of one of the most beautiful little pictures of all time: the "Annunciation" by Leonardo da Vinci.

"That's the one that makes me cry," she said. I looked at it for a long time, and when I turned around to thank her, she was gone. Secretly, I was glad I didn't have to thank her, but I always will be grateful for the knowledge that someone else could behave just as cornily as I did.

A collection like the Uffizi deserves to have (and has had) many books written about it. On that first visit I learned one very important thing about museums: you can't see everything. You aren't expected to like everything, and you don't even have to try. What you've seen and didn't grasp will come back to you another time—fully charged —to be plugged into your receptivity. What you have seen and reviewed, what you have discovered for the first time, will always be there. You can't lose it. Furthermore, the aforementioned books on the Uffizi, as well as all other documented art data, will always be there too, ready to help focus your memory. After all, had it not been for my sister's abandoned book, *Apollo*, Signor del Sarto and his Madonna might not have been familiar friends in an unfamiliar land.

Florence has a million other treasures: the tomb of the Medici, with its incomparable architecture, and the unbelievably great sculptures of Michelangelo; Fra Angelico; the Self-Portrait Gallery of the Pitti Palace, where you can see the artists as they saw themselves; the Bargello, with its Donatellos . . . treasures beyond belief. But Florence also has shops and the Ponte Vecchio. This bridge town, hung over the river, is enchanting, and for pure romance nothing can top it.

I had saved a small amount with which to buy Mother and Dad a present, and Florence would get that money, my economic chauvinism stemming from gratitude for its being so beautiful. And I was determined to get it on the Ponte Vecchio. I shopped and thought of silver, of leather, of everything sold on that bridge, but nothing really said "buy me." Back and forth I searched, and finally found it . . . a little bronze fountain figure. Twenty-five dollars. He was a cutie, holding a fish out of which the water squirted. There are hundreds of figures like this, but I'd never seen them, and somehow I felt sure that the shopkeeper's information about its being modern was just to spoof me— that this was an original Donatello-Verrocchio, undiscovered until now by *me!*

I bought it, lugged it to a packer, sent it home via collect freight, and sighed with delight that I had found a treasure in Florence and that my parents would have it forever—in the Middle West of America.

They received it in good order. The collect freight was sixty dollars. Then my father was forced into building a pool for it to fountain into. This cost two hundred and fifty dollars. The entire family spent two years, dragging rocks back from the Ozarks, to make the surrounding rock garden. The final blow came when Mother decided to import three hundred and fifty dollars' worth of rare bulbs from Holland to set the whole thing off, and as a background two mature willow trees were brought in, employing six workmen for three days. Then I decided, with Mother's permission, to grow water lilies. What I didn't know, but soon found out, was that they must be planted in rich, preferably fresh, cow manure—under the water. This murky operation caused the death of twenty-five high-priced, fan-tailed goldfish and yearly saw me up to my armpits in fresh cow dung, having spent the two previous days catching the replaced goldfish, who multiplied over the years to a final count of three hundred and two. Some years later, after the death of my parents, I decided I must keep the Florentine fountain. I dislodged it from its Million Dollar Park to send it to California, where once again a pool had to be built for it and flowers planted, and to date only two rather sad goldfish have survived to revel in the splashing waters.

After Florence almost anything would have been an anticlimax. But anyone who doesn't fall in love with Rome should have his heart examined. The names with which people label cities sometimes stretch the imagination, but Rome really does seem "eternal." You can't help feeling that it has always been there . . . and always will be. At sixteen you damned well better feel that way, or the rest of your life will seem kind of impermanent. There has to be one eternal place where men will always live and worship.

Tour 22 and our leaders leaned rather heavily on two aspects of Rome to take care of our curiosity about it—the Forum, those few remaining monuments to its ancient glory, and the Church.

By "the Church" I mean the glories of Renaissance Christendom . . . the churches of Rome. There are enough of them to satisfy anyone of any faith, and, indeed, they house greatly some of the greatest art.

Mother had told me her favorite story about a little Protestant lady who, on being told that the candle at the high altar in St. Peter's had not been out for a thousand years, pursed her lips and extinguished it, saying, "Well, it's out now."

I had thought this very amusing, but when I walked through the doors of that Great Temple, the impact of its importance dispelled any kind of humor spiritually, if temporarily. There has never been anything so perfect as the scale of this church and of everything in it. The cupids holding the holy water, who seem so tiny when you enter, are my size when you reach them, face to face; the soaring canopy and twisted columns of Bernini's great altar; the dome of Michelangelo; the tombs; the chapels and the chandeliers . . . perfection of proportion.

It was after many minutes of awed silence that it occurred to me: here I was, before the candle that hadn't been out for a thousand years. Mother's story crossed my mind, and I sincerely hoped that little lady (if she ever did exist) was safely home in Iowa, happy there, and that nothing on earth could ever bring her back to Rome to repeat that sacrilegious act.

The love of art may not be the surest way to become a millionaire, but one thing it teaches you is worth more than anything in life . . . tolerance. And more than tolerance . . . understanding.

Rome is the Church. Wonderful, gay, living city that it is, the wonder and majesty around which it throbs is the Church. It was the only place in Europe that to me, at that age, had not been deprived of its nobility by the passage of time, or social or political change. The kingdom of the Catholic Church remains, in all the world, the only realm that has the possibility of permanence. Other faiths will last as long, but none will ever again be able to house its monarch in such magnificence.

I never would have believed it, but Rome turned out to be the high point of the whole trip. And besides the above lessons it taught me never again to go anywhere with a mind at half-mast. You're only celebrating your own death if you do. Man has created so much beauty for so many different reasons—for everyone to enjoy and be a part of— that to shut yourself off from any section or second of it is a waste of time that hurts no one but yourself.

I was so moved by Michelangelo's "Pietà," I wondered how any work of his could top it. Even the "David" in Florence, heroic and masculine as it is, was pushed aside by the femininity and strength of this young Virgin and her dead son. When I was told that he had done it at the age of twenty-one, I realized that I had only five years until I reached that age, and I had no talent toward it at all. Somewhere (and it may have been there, standing before the statue that summer) it came to me that I was not going to be blessed with creative genius, and it may also have been at this moment that I made up my mind that, as long as this was true, I had darn well better compensate for it by becoming the most receptive human being I could become. I knew for sure that I liked art, and I'd better know everything I could about what I liked. I became an audience, then and there, for the drama of the eye. And once you accept that fact, it is almost impossible ever again to be bored with life. You have a built-in recipe for the cure of that most dread disease: boredom . . . the living death. All you have to do is open your eyes.

When you're young, there are lots of dreams of "doors" . . . at least there were for me. Being the time when things are opening and shutting with more vigor than ever again, youth has the door as a symbol. But there's one door that, once you've entered it, undreaming, you will dream about all your life . . . the little insignificant door through which you enter the Sistine Chapel.

Was it done on purpose? Did the architect plan it that way—that you should leave the ordinary world through a little door as you enter the heaven of Michelangelo's creation? . . . I don't know, but nothing is made of it in the tour of the Vatican. No guard suddenly stops and says: "Through this little door is another world," or "Don't let the size of this door fool you . . . you are about to be hit over the head by a giant on the other side."

But that's just what happens. Open it, and there you are, an immediate witness at the "Creation of Man." There you are, being judged by Christ in all His glory. There you are, a midget, standing at the toes of a titan. If you entered the world of art, alone, by the back door, as I did—this is the front door, and once you open it you're in for keeps in the greatest company you can have.

There's no point trying to describe it. Everyone knows how long it took him to paint it—the incredible difficulty of working directly on the moist plaster, put on daily, just enough for the day's work; how he held the composition in his mind all those years; the thousands of sketches, cartoons, that must have gone into the preparation; the incredible story he had to tell—the Sibyls, the Prophets, the Nude Youths, the Ancestors of Christ, the Miracles of Jerusalem—the accidents and personal torments that beset him . . .

There's no point in anyone's saying that this is the greatest, or the second-of-ninetieth-greatest work of art . . . work of man. . . . Nothing can describe it. But when you've seen it, your eyes never forget it. It may slip your mind for years, but one day something great will cross your vision, and immediately your eye will compare it to this ultimate experience of art.

Then there's the "Last Judgment." Again, no words to tell its writhing, suffering, ecstatic story. . . . There it is!

And the "Moses," in another church, that eternal visualization of the lawgiver. One almost suspects there was an eleventh commandment: "Let no man see Moses as he was until Michelangelo is born to see him as he will be forever, in the eyes of man."

There is, however, some solace in the "Moses" that it is only a fraction of a greater plan. Michelangelo was human, after all. The great tomb he planned, of which the "Moses" was only a small part, with the "Slaves," was never finished. He couldn't quite people the world by himself. But he did leave something for others to do, and the second great sculptor of the Renaissance did the rest . . . Bernini.

At sixteen the fountains of Rome seemed very frivolous, compared with the Sistine Chapel. I keep referring to those sixteen years, but after so many have been piled on top of them, I have to keep reminding myself that, in these chapters, I'm writing about those reactions, and not my older—*much* older—ones. What it boils down to is another proof of the living quality of all art. It is never static. What surprised you yesterday, you take in your stride tomorrow. What seemed frivolous at sixteen is very profound at forty-five. And that was the case with

66

Bernini's sculpture. But I know now that Rome is not complete without either of these masters. Rome without Bernini would be as empty as Rome without Michelangelo.

Naples was an obvious letdown after the Eternal City, but Pompeii was much more exciting than ancient Rome. The ancient parts of Rome—the Forum, the Coliseum—are grand and impressive, but in Pompeii you really step back into the period immediately after Christ and feel a part of it, not only because of the fantastic state of preservation, but because the real charm, the real reality of any period—old or modern—is not to be found in the capital, the great city, but in the typical smaller cities. I doubt if walking through the ruins of New York would possibly tell us as much about America as would the ruins of Cleveland or Kansas City or Seattle.

Pompeii is wonderful, and, of course, at that time, for a boy of sixteen the "feelthy" frescoes of Pompeii were really "jazzy." And for a young blond girl with a slight southern accent . . . very good for the powers of suggestion and attendant *un*decorum.

We were nearing the end of Tour 22. The train sped through Pisa, where we could see the Leaning Tower lean, and through Genoa, where we could see boats that reminded us that before long, we'd be on one and on our way back home. And pleasantly enough, the tour gave us the seventh country in the form of that minute monarchy, Monaco. It represented the complete escape from the world of art. There's none there . . . only the amazing ingenuity of man's triumph over a hill, rising out of the sea. He has covered it completely with as mad an assortment of houses of pleasure and peace to be found anywhere on earth.

Finally, two days in Nice, and then to Paris, the boat, and home. I spent those two days in Nice not in the pursuit of the beautiful (though she was very pretty), but in the study and exploration of the human body. Since I had dedicated myself to the world of art, I could hardly do better than to study seriously art's greatest source of inspiration—the female form.

ONE OF THE MEANEST THINGS LIFE DOES TO A BOY IS require him to become a man. Everything is so fresh in youth, and though I've seen a few young people who were bored, generally they are curious and alive to change—especially if they know how to see.

But seeing is a much-neglected course in most of our schools. In fact, visual education is a little like sex education in America. You pick up what you can, impelled by natural passions. Either that or it's unappetizingly clinical. The schools teach us what to look at, if at all, but almost never *how* to look at anything.

My education was started in a very progressive school, instigated by my mother and a group of other mothers who, en masse, had revolted against what was dreary in their education. The only trouble was that the teachers, trained at that time in progressive education, had indeed progressed from strained formality in teaching, but their informal approach bordered on impoliteness. We were all charming children, I think, and a good majority went on into a progressing world as artists, writers, actors. But what we have all had to fight was a leaning toward the amateur—in our professions, if not in our desire to be professionals, or in our hope of seeing differently and being different. Fortunately, there was just enough formality of teaching left at that time for us to be spared the abandon apparent in progressive children of this present day who are "let go" altogether, without any correction and certainly no manners.

This school gave us a whimsical appreciation of art and nature, sadly unrealistic, and most of us had to retrogress a class when we went into the higher realms of learning. I, for one, went from there to a very formal boys' school, the prime and only aim of which was to get me into college. From the manly athletic masters of that preparatory school (with two exceptions), I got nothing of the art of teaching, but I got "learnt"—and I did get into college.

There were no pictures around. In fact, there was very little beauty at all, except for the ever changing grandeur of the Missouri landscape, which was fast being encroached upon by the lava flow of suburbia. The fresh musk odors of the countryside were superseded, once you entered the hallowed halls, by a mixture of perfumes: one, the clean, clinical scent of that brown sawdust which takes everything with it on the janitor's broom; the other, the smell of stale sweatshirts and straight disinfectants, intended to keep our feet from becoming athletic while our bodies were being made so.

Even the buildings, the planting, the study halls were without inspiration. Music, that most tolerated of the arts in America, was injected into us, for it was a mark of culture, and, I suspect, it was meant as sort of an inoculation, intended to build up our tolerance to the endless, dreary concerts our parents inflicted upon themselves and which would, in turn, be inflicted upon us—unless we had the good fortune to escape that little social world they lived in, and expected us to.

In the way of the visual arts, it had nothing at all to offer. Sculpture was confined to those pneumatic brass or gold-plated athletes who adorn trophies and whose relation to life is first cousin to wedding-cake figures.

The only pictures were school pictures. Endless pyramids of pimpled boys were pulled together cleanly for that day of days, each year, when we progressed from one class to another, culminating with the somewhat more compact and higher pyramid of graduation day, less pimples, and a mutual look of: "Look! We made it! Where the hell do we go from here?"

Textbook illustrations are a miracle of verisimilitude. They are apparently selected by a board of educators whose determination it is never to let the illustration inspire the text; never to let it amplify, intensify, illumine, or even really illustrate it. These pictures are, with few exceptions, the work of the lowest grade artists of their periods, or if a known artist's work is reproduced, a process of reproduction is chosen to abnegate any subtlety or genius in his work, and to reduce it to the stature of the lesser artists. Portraits of famous men and women are in a technique that can only be known as "familiarity." You can tell at a glance that this composite of all high-browed balding men with goatees is William Shakespeare, and most of the rest of literature's great are the same picture with a change of wig, beard, nose, or eyebrows. The great events of history have one thing in common from Homer to Warren G. Harding: they all look as though they happened yesterday and were posed by the same group of actors in different wardrobes. This historical stock company is utterly uninspired, striking the same poses on any ground, and the siege of Troy, Caesar crossing the Rubicon, or Columbus landing in the New World—all have the familiar background of a badly painted, not too theatrical set. The final miracle (which some artist must have spent years figuring out) is how Dante's nose would look from all angles. You never fail to recognize him, even from the back, since his hat is merely his nose in another pose.

I don't think anyone with artistic leanings (what an unbalancing phrase that is) could have surmounted the obstacles of that one-track preparatory school. It never even made the nod to the visual arts that the progressive school had done. I guess little boys are not expected to have curiosity about the female statues that our little progressive girls had shown toward the males, since we never visited the museum. But I must say, in my own defense, as much as I felt the need for the visual excitement of the arts, I was able (or forced) to sublimate it, and I think I became a good specimen of the standard young American male, pointed in the direction of college.

Something must have still been showing, however, for Mother and Father were persuaded one summer (before the European trip) to send me into the wild, wild West to a boys' camp. They never came out with it openly, but I think they hoped against hope that I would learn to see things as things, the way other boys did, and not as experiences. My best friend was a boy named Freddie. Freddie was a curious boy, interested not only in being a boy but in knowing offbeat facts. A friend of his family was an archaeologist, and Freddie and I were caught completely in the undertow of his fascinating work. We were just drowning in the magic of the American Indian, which was this man's field, when our parents decided to ship us West for the summer.

The West in those days was still a long haul off, and while we knew our home town, St. Louis, had been the shoving-off place for many of the great western expeditions in the century before us, that all seemed long ago. But the West still had its mystery, and indeed it was not yet the commercialized West of today, Tucson and television.

So off we went, a group of incipient delinquents. Our parents deduced that if the western legend "Where men are men" held credence, then surely the geographic change would make boys boys. As a matter of fact, we were as average a group of spoiled kids as you could find. There were tough ones, determined ones, frightened ones, and in Freddie's and my case, adventurous ones. The two of us took to the West more like Ruggles of Red Gap than Paul Bunyan. We wanted it to do something to us—maybe not the same thing our parents hoped for—but that it would change us was sure.

As we hit the bleak outpost in southern Colorado which was to be our summer home, within two days we had created in our imaginations a territory surrounding the camp site, complete with Indians and buried treasure.

Using our few hours, free from supervision, to explore our imaginative land, we discovered gullies and ravines, small to be sure, but to us, comparable to the Grand Canyon. And one day up on an unexplored mesa, while Freddie was panning for fool's gold, I unearthed a genuine Indian burial ground.

So far in my life, nothing had been more exciting or more personal. All previous experiences had been, at best, secondhand through some adult help. But this was mine—and in my mind comparable to the discovery of King Tut's tomb. When I proudly arrived back in camp, deportmentally late, with my loot (a perfect skull and three fine bowls), I became at once a hero and even more of a curiosity.

Things had been a little rough for Freddie and me. We didn't take to the horse as well as we should have, but this made up for it. During the next week one of the counselors helped me finish the dig. The site proved to be of the great last period of the Mesa Verde civilization, dating from the twelfth century, and my fame was made. Photos appeared in the home-town paper, and though perhaps not in the eyes of the world but in my own, I was an amateur archaeologist from that day to this.

The lure of the American Indian has never deserted me, and I truly believe my interest in them and in their great natural art is the continuing impetus that has made me want to devour all creative work and has put a premium on my occasional recognition in contemporary art of the same ingenious genius of primitive man.

When I returned home with my treasures (and apparently the summer in the West had only strengthened my determination to be an artist or an archaeologist or something in that direction), I had a sneaking hunch my father took out a little more life insurance, positive that he would have to support a non-commercial dreamer, even beyond the grave.

Actually, they were pleased as punch. My survival of that summer, with exactly the same convictions and interests I had had before it, was like a declaration of intentions to them. It was the cincher in their doting minds that, while I might never make Dun & Bradstreet, I might make *Who's Who*.

Father suddenly became more interested in my interests than in his interests *for* me, and we shared many a curiosity for the rest of his life. One day toward the end of it he confessed that he had been trapped in the business world by the world of business, which was the whole world's business in his day. He would have loved to say to hell with it, but the hell of it was that any other life only meant lack of success, and so he had to give in to his success as a man of business and forego the chance of being a man of the world.

As I've said, the prep school afforded little artistic expansion, but I was chosen to illustrate our senior yearbook with far from deathless sketches, and though I was not one for being on committees, somehow in my last year I was appointed one third of a committee of three to select the gift which our class would present to the school. I was, and still am, a glutton for this kind of responsibility, never taking it lightly. I thought immediately of some work of art, fool that I was. My friend, the one art dealer, had a superb set of lithographs by Joseph Pennell. Pennell was a friend of Whistler's and a fine American draftsman, and since this series of huge plates of bridges, building, and construction included several of our home town, what could be more appropriate? Simply framed, they would at least lend some variety to the dreary school halls—a relief from the scattered pictures of presidents, principals, and students.

I presented my idea to my committee. They roared with laughter and voted two to one to give the school a cement bench, which was predestined to crack in half during one especially hard winter, a few years later.

When I got back from Europe, I had only one year left before going to college, and, inspired by the trip, I determined to become an active artist. In that one year I learned a fact that I wasn't about to admit for five years . . . I had no talent at all. I tried painting, sculpting, and woodcutting, to no avail. My greatest humiliation was a portrait I did of Mother, which she loved because I did it, so she had it expensively framed and prominently hung in her living room. For many years it reminded me that none of the great painters' talents had rubbed off on me, despite my love for their works. Shakespeare alone could describe that portrait: "Weary, stale, flat, and unprofitable." Nothing

I could say, however, would persuade Mother to take it down, and only when it was finally willed to me could I perform the kindest act of all and burn it—keeping the expensive frame, of course.

But one thing this lack of talent taught me. Appreciation. When you try to do something and can't—and admit you can't—you learn a healthy respect for it and for those who can. In the achievements of others I learned to see what I'd learned I could not do myself, and the greater the achievement, the more humble I became before it. And frankly, I have never regretted being unable to draw or paint, because if I could, I might not be quite as receptive to others. But because I tried to do it and discovered my limitations, I am perhaps more tolerant of all kinds of art than one who hasn't tried—or has and won't admit his limitations.

I know an awful lot of amateurs . . . Sunday painters, they call them now . . . and it seems to follow that the less talent they have, the more intolerant they are of talent in others. The one painter I knew as a child was a lady who sat near us in church. She painted polite little pictures of flowers, crammed into dumpy little vases, set on the damnedest rag bag selection of fabrics. Mother even bought one of these to give as a wedding present to the daughter of someone she didn't like very much. Years later, when this lady found out that I was supposed to know about art, she sought me out for a chat, backstage. Her first words were: "Now, don't tell me you like modern art, Vincent, because if you do, we won't have a word to say to each other." Being polite by preference, and having sat so near to her in church for so many years, we did have a few words to say to each other, but not about art. I learned a long time ago how to get out of that one . . . we talked about *her*.

St. Louis was an easy town to keep up with when away from it—artistically, at least—for it always made news by the violence of its reactions to art. Two occasions, I remember, demanded and got national publicity.

The City Art Museum is uniquely supported by a little tax called the mill—a token coin which represents a tenth of a cent. The levy doesn't hurt the taxpayer very much, and it certainly helps the museum, which derives a great part of the benefits from it.

Despite this unsubtly hidden though unimposing tax, the good people of my home town are vociferous in their disapproval of its use. While I was still in high school, the museum had the chance to acquire a very fine El Greco portrait, possibly a self-portrait, and they paid a fine figure for it. No sooner did the news break of this good fortune but a long line was formed around the City Hall with placards that demanded to know who the hell this Greek was, and how come he got so much money for painting a picture of himself!

The other event was even more delicious, for it involved a very ancient bronze tomb sculpture of a charming Egyptian cat. It was, at the time of purchase, considered to be the finest Egyptian animal bronze in America. The museum's board and director took great pride in announcing its acquisition to the public, bringing forth another storm of protests and parades around the City Hall.

I believe the price of the cat was $14,000, but its fame and publicity made it worth much more. On a visit home several years later, I was standing with the director, Myric Rogers, admiring the cat, when a lady came up to us and asked if this was *the* cat. Mr. Rogers said it was, and the lady, beaming with delight said: "Oh, I'm so glad I saw it. Now I can go back to Kansas and tell my husband I've seen the fourteen-*million-dollar* pussycat!"

But for all the opposition, the City Art Museum was acquiring some fine things, and for the few who picketed, there were many thousands who populated it. Today it is a very great museum and, along with the superb zoo and the outdoor summer opera theatre, one of the real prides of St. Louis. What makes all this exciting is that art can and does demand so much attention. To those brave men and women who have weathered the storm, and to those who actually gave their lives to create the same storm that would purify the materialistic smog of America, we all owe an enormous debt of gratitude. It has come to a point now where you cannot study any field of art, with the possible exception of Japanese, without reference to American museums.

Father once made a remark, while listening to the Yale-Princeton game on his superheterodyne radio, that left a lasting impression on me. The announcer kept referring to the teams and the spectators as "Yale boys" and "Princeton boys." Dad finally stomped out of the room, muttering: "My God . . . when I was there, we used to call ourselves Yale *men*."

I had always known I was going to Yale. In those days you didn't have to have straight A's or come from Alaska to make an eastern college. An average student, especially one with a father alumnus, could expect to make it. So I had taken it for granted, except with one twist: I looked forward to it. I wanted to be a "Yale man," and I knew exactly what Father meant about the "boys" remark. I looked forward to this four-year journey that would make me a *man*. The attitude, so prevalent in our country, of wanting to be forever young, even then had escaped me; for I had always shied away from immaturity, in my immaturity, wanting above all things to be mature—to be ready for the new through acquaintance with the old. Everything in our culture is aimed backward. The arrow points to youth, and it's hard when you're young to find your direction out of it.

Twice in my life I've anticipated a great cultural experience, only to discover that one should never look forward to culture. In going to Yale, I thought I was on my way to the Athens of America. Great paintings and statues would be everywhere; the buildings would be classic, as befitted the alma mater of my father and brother and, particularly, as befitted the college where I was going to spend four years, then graduate a cultured, *gentle* man . . . I hoped.

That was the first time. The second was when I went into the theatre, positive that actors must be the most interesting and interested people in the world. . . . But more about that later.

First, let's take Yale. Not as an educational institution, for it's a great one, but as an example of the diversities of American architecture and taste . . . which may give some insight into my wide-eyed disappointment upon arriving there.

Physically, Yale is a grand example of how one period of architecture can be piled upon another, creep up behind it and on top of it, and end up by putting the false fronts of Hollywood movie lots to shame, for they at least are admittedly settings for make-believe. But Yale (and many another college) is for real and earnestly wants to give the impression of stability and permanence, architecturally and culturally. In fact, they proudly reproduce their architectural mutations on plates and ties, napkins and towels, for old grads to weep over.

On the Old Campus the original New England brick buildings remain intact, with all their old charm showing through the inevitable ivy. The sun, when it appears, gleams on the tiny warped windowpanes, which age has turned to amethyst. Inside, the rooms are economical and low and would indicate that Yale men have grown in stature—at least physically—since Nathan Hale lived there. Incidentally, he still lives there for all Yale men, in the noble statue whose expression summarizes the sentiments of us all—that we regret we have but one life.

All this has a cozy, if uncomfortable, charm. It wasn't long before our more immediate forefathers brought forth upon this continent a style of architecture, dedicated to ugliness, discomfort, and gloom, and to the proposition that all men are created to live in a tomb *before* dying. These mid-nineteenth-century dormitories still house many a Yale man, and will for years to come, I hope, since their destruction would require the atom bomb. They are built to last to the last Yale man. They are brick, with a façade of real stone (ingeniously made to look like imitation stone), and they all bear someone's name—whether in honor of or as a memorial to, I can't remember.

The entrances are rather like the gates of hell: high, wide, and sometimes handsome. Inside, the lofty ceilings let in more light than where Nathan Hale holed up, but it is the light of a prison, for the walls are painted two tones of gray or tan, and in the bleak New Haven climate it is impossible to tell whether you are inside or out. The stairs are marble . . . Vermont marble. They always are, all over the East, to the point where you wonder if there can be anything left of Vermont in Vermont.

The doors to the rooms are high and solid and so heavy and tightly hinged they almost refuse to let you into the chambers themselves. The living room is well proportioned but absolutely refuses to be made livable. In my day, no matter what you added in the way of furniture, pictures, drapes, or rugs, the effect remained the same . . . you were living in a substantial cardboard box. It could not be turned into a home, and maybe that's what the architect had in mine: home is where the heart is, and here, you were supposed to develop your brain.

But because of the solidity of their construction and their ability to house a great many students imaginatively, comfortably—home-away-from-home-like or not—they will remain.

During my stay at Yale one moved from one building to another each year, so that he got a taste of each kind of architecture. Fortunately, we were spared having to live in the war memorials which, in order not to offend any race, creed, or custom of any soldier, sailor, or marine to whom they might be a memorial, were architecturally conglomerate.

From the simple brick oblong that housed Nathan Hale and his classmates, Yale moved, with the rest of America, through the Greek revival, Roman revival, and stopped short with an abortive, obscene, yellow-stone style called, surreptitiously, "Romanesque." But of all the styles to invade New Haven, the Goths conquered most completely. All styles stood in abeyance while icicle surmounted icicle, to the tip of the highest Gothic-inspired spire.

The fact that the original Gothic architecture rose, plan upon plan, unto the third and fourth generation, and that the craftsmen were given almost free scope to memorialize the life of their time and themselves in stone, did not deter the architects of Yale. Borrowing a Butter Tower from here, a cloister from there, and arches from everywhere, in a few short years they piled together the whole huge mass of Harkness Quadrangle with the aid of rivets and steel. Yet today, with the aid of a vile erosive native weather and enormous plantings of ivy, this homogenized Gothic edifice has, indeed, come to look almost genuinely Gothic—that is, until you spot the steel window casings, tiled bathrooms, and young gentlemen, crew-cut and Brooks Brothers-bedecked, hard at work assimilating culture inside those crenelated, stony walls.

But the Italian-American stonecutters who worked on Harkness and the other Gothic piles at Yale did have their way with the great tradition and left some charming portraits of their families and friends in the sculptural decoration—and at least one left a mystery, which took the top brains of the university years to unravel. I believe it was my friend, Fritz Liebert, who, strolling into his office in the library, came upon a stone inscription that intrigued him. In Gothic type, it read: "He was born with a gift of laughter and a sense that the world was mad."

Fritz pointed this out to fellow librarians, who all tried to guess the origin of the quote. Great minds suggested Aristotle, Dante, Shakespeare; but Fritz (or someone) finally came across its origin: it is the opening line of Rafael Sabatini's famous romantic potboiler, *Scaramouche*. Hardly a fitting author to be immortalized in stone on the Yale library, but obviously the favorite work of the stonecutter who put it there. Please don't ask if he ever read beyond the opening line . . . they may make another version of it in the movies, if you do.

Not content with having re-created the style of the thirteenth and fourteenth centuries, the university planners looked to other times to simulate, and the results were fascinating, not to be duplicated until Walt Disney took it upon himself to lead the boys and girls of America from Prince Charming's palace to Buck Rogers' rocket in the wink of an eye at Disneyland.

When the university was finally able to acquire (or clear) the land across the street from Mr. Harkness' Gothic memorial, a problem arose in someone's mind: how to make the new college building show a proper face to Harkness, but inside, at heart, be more American? The vogue for Gothic was on the wane, but you couldn't just ignore it. There it was . . . and greatly beloved by all who had ever lived in it or walked through it. It would be too severe a blow to any Yale man's aesthetic sensitivity to leave Harkness' gloomy cloisters and be confronted with something entirely different. So the façade of the new building had to be Gothic; but two steps inside the arch, and there's old Virginia . . . red-bricked, white-trimmed, and quaint to the last Georgian pillar and round hall window.

All of these styles—Nathan Hale, Georgian, Gothic, Roman, Greek, war memorial, nineteenth century, nothing-style dormitories, plus isolated (thank God) examples of Swedish Modern and Bastard Bauhaus—are concentrated on an implacable modicum of land called the campus, almost incapable of growth because of the city which surrounds it. The only hope of expansion I was ever able to foresee was, believe it or not, in the Egyptian style cemetery, across from the cafeteria.

I take Yale as a perfect example of the visible changes of taste in America. It is neither better nor worse than most colleges, and it does represent the spirit of our country—ever on guard not to lose its identity with the lands of our origins across the seas.

In my time the art school at Yale was one of the Romanesque monstrosities, producing a rash of Grand Prix de Rome winners, particularly in sculpture. Each year I'd go see the annual exhibition of Yale art students, and there was one outstanding fact about the output: you couldn't tell one year from another. The Grand Prix de Rome statue was identical, year after year, and belonged to a school of art best described as "Museum Façade Classic." They were stone men, or women dressed in stone; they had no particular bodies underneath, no particular costume, and, whatever the material they were supposed to have been sculpted in—they all looked like they'd been done in soap. Inspired by these winners, I put my hand to a female nude which, after several unsuccessful attempts in clay, I actually did in soap . . . Ivory . . . and then used it.

Yale was not particularly artistic. There were groups who wrote well, and the wit of the witty magazine was awfully charming, if a bit limited to Yale humor. But the years just before my stay had produced the editors and founders of *Time* and *Life*, and that was hard to live up to.

My life in New Haven was greatly enriched by the acquaintance of James Thurber, who lived outside the town and to whom I became enormously attached—not only as a writer, but as a draftsman of great ability. Thurber invented the caricature of the modern man, lost in a world of women and dogs, and made us realize, almost for the first time, the importance of the cartoonist in American society.

The great political and humorous cartoonists have made a very real contribution to our culture. In the midst of a period of America taking itself too seriously, they have made us look at ourselves and laugh—or think. They have been an escape from the overwhelming burden we all feel in our industrial prowess, and surely they must be ranked among the greatest American artists from Nash, in the nineteenth century, to Thurber, Fitzpatrick, Helen Hokinson, Al Capp, to the culminating genius of Schulz and his wonderfully witty world of "Peanuts."

Remember Milt Gross and "Nize Baby"? His serious drawings were almost comparable to Van Gogh; Dr. Seuss' comically gloomy and Bosch-like animals; Rube Goldberg, who envisioned the I.B.M. with his delightfully idiotic machines; "Mutt and Jeff," "Krazy Kat," the "Toonerville Trolley" . . . all these were before the comic strip turned to "soap"—"soap operas," in their case. . . . Then there were Bill Mauldin and the other wonderful war cartoonists who, seriously or comically, did so much to lighten one of our darkest periods.

The Gallery at Yale had some marvelous things—silver, furniture, American paintings by Trumbull and Samuel F. B. Morse, *and* the Jarvis collection with its mighty Pollaiuolo and charming Piero de Cosimo "Lady and a Rabbit." Also hidden away for the curious knocker-on-the-door . . . a superb collection of prints, especially Rembrandt . . . and you could visit it, unhampered by crowds. . . . No one ever came to see it.

One of my favorite Yale stories happened only two years ago. In an attempt to liven the Gallery's exhibition policy, the directors decided to put together a show from the collections of Yale graduates. I'm told it came as an atomic surprise to them that some high percentage of the top collectors of America were Yale men. The Whitneys, Stephen Clark, Robert Lehman, Averell Harriman, Wright Ludington, Conger Goodyear, Henry Luce, and on and on.

The part I love most and sincerely hope is true (a friend reported it to me) is that when the lists of what they owned had all been sent in by the alumni, and the committee had made their choice from the literally thousands of superb paintings, drawings, etc., they found themselves short on eighteenth-century French material. But a late-arriving list supplied all and much more than they could ever need.

From Newport, Rhode Island, came news of the unbelievable collection of this material, owned by Mr. Forsythe Wickes of the class of 1898 . . . hundreds of eighteenth-century French drawings of the very highest quality, which many of the directors had imagined could only exist in the Louvre or Bibliothèque Nationale in Paris.

I was also told that from those submitted lists they could put on a comparable exhibition every year for ten years and still not exhaust the supply. Which goes to prove that old Elihu Yale left a lasting mark on all his namesakes, for when he died there had to be six consecutive auctions to dispose of his fabulous collections of curios, gems, musical instruments, and nine thousand paintings.

Lessons, lessons! We never finish learning them! I missed so much at Yale, I'm sure, just because I didn't know which way I wanted to go.

The drama school was in a state of flux those years, the great Baker having taken his final curtain call, as they say in Variety. I went over to see about it as a possible way to try out one of my secret schemes —to be an actor. But it seemed sort of precious, and also, while I knew that someday I'd have to take a crack at the theatre to get it out of my system (or to make it my life's work), the drama-school climate didn't appeal to me at all, and never has. I think there's only one way to learn any of the arts, especially the theatre and the art of acting, and that is to act—to do anything you can to be before the public—and not necessarily the pre-sold public that makes up the universal drama-school audience.

But I definitely needed some sort of extrovert activity, being a confirmed one, so the Yale Glee Club came along as a solution to all my problems. I loved to sing, and I loved to have a good time, and a glee club is the perfect place for both. I made the club, all right, but was never socially ambitious enough to be a soloist. Anyway, we still had Lanny Ross and some other mighty fine tenors and ambitious young basses who fit the job perfectly.

Yale was a place where it was one hell of a help to be from an *Eastern* prep school. They'd scouted those schools and knew all the top boys in them long before the boys got to New Haven. So it was no small job to push your way from the Middle West into any of the top social or athletic endeavors in the East.

The glee club traveled and sang in competition with other clubs, and one summer sixty of us went on a tour of Europe. It was a riotous experience from start to finish and, more important, gave me another chance to have a peek at the art treasure houses abroad . . . a very small peek, I fear . . . snuck in between rehearsals, concerts, and hang-overs. But what a ball! Girls galore, beer and wine, and the marvelous companionship of college men, off on a spree!

I submitted a cartoon to the comic magazine, which was accepted. It showed a freshman, riding on a train, going to New York—writing home: The caption: "Dear Mother and Dad. The first few days were hell, but I'm beginning to find my way around, now. . . ."

For one lovely moment I thought I was going to step into Peter Arno's shoes (another Yale man), but the next half dozen drawings I submitted were not only dull in wit but in draftsmanship. So I was doomed to appreciate, which indeed I did. There were some very clever cartoonists in the class of '33.

Courses in freshman and sophomore years were practically a re-prisal of the last years of prep school, and only one course (which everyone took because it was easy) proved to be inspiring: the history of religion. It inspired me because I had always felt that art and religion were inextricably tied together, and here was the proof of it. And it went much further to show me how most acts of faith are works of art—music, writing, singing, painting, sculpture, and architecture—reaching their peaks in their assimilation into religion. From the Assyrian, Egyptian, Greek, Roman, Medieval, and Renaissance to the present day, many of man's highest attainments in art have come directly from the dictates of either his own faith or the faith of his nation. They carry over from one epoch to another, so that the iconography or language of any art form bears traces of all the others.

There is a oneness in the purpose of all art, revealing, to those who understand, that that purpose is the edification and instruction of the human mind in the richest secret of life. Through his art, man has a chance to repay the Divine Power who put him here—coin for coin, what he has cost—and to show the deepest gratitude for being alive.

I learned, too, the beauty of our language, and that speaking it beautifully is (as they say) an art in itself. Too few of us take the trouble to be universal in our speech. We may become worldly in our tastes, but we remain suburban in our accent and rural in our enunciation.

Among the best-remembered people in everyone's life are those few teachers who inspire you to think—who send you off on an unexpected tangent into a brand-new area of exploration. They are able to make what they teach to all their students individual to some. They manage to fit themselves and their knowledge into what you want to know, and once that excitement has been turned on, the light can never be extinguished on that particular subject. You will always be interested in it and always overjoyed to know more and more about it.

My two secret ambitions—to be an artist or to be an actor—were keeping their secret, even from me, during the first years at college. Little glimpses kept coming through that made me sure one or the other would eventually become a fact. But Yale was not the kind of university that set itself out to create artists or actors. Rather, its aim was to give you an all-around education and, by the simple act of having created a Yale man with a diploma, make you a possible leader in your community, socially or otherwise—if you cared to chance the otherwise. But the Yale man of the twenties and thirties went out into a pretty secure world, if he didn't stray too far from the world of Yale-type men, in spite of the depression.

Today things are very different. With the enormous growth of educational facilities in state and private institutions of learning that were then considered far below Yale, the supremacy of the eastern colleges is being challenged every year by others, all over the nation. They offer wonderful educational opportunities to men who cannot afford eastern tuition fees, or who simply have no interest in, or need for, an eastern background.

But whatever opportunity a student has, financial or scholastic, whether he makes it into Yale or the University of California, Hawaii, Alaska, or Texas, his most direct and lasting inspiration is apt to come from some individual teacher.

My Shakespeare course at Yale was taught by a handsome, somewhat pedantic, dignified man named Carl Young. He didn't miss much in his exploration of that universal genius, but he approached the bard as literature, rather than theatre, and the one thing I missed was the magic of performance. Mother and Father had subjected me to the theatre at an early age—and especially the theatre of Shakespeare. I'd seen Sothern and Marlowe; Fritz Leiber, Robert Mantell, and Walter Hampden—some good, some great, some mediocre, but always, through their interpretations, came the majesty of those words of the great poet.

It was not until Mr. Young came to *The Tempest* that he allowed himself to impart to us the spirit of Shakespeare and not just the word. He took flight in the beauty of that play, and took me right with him. He showed me a "brave new world," one that I knew I must try to be a part of, but I also knew that it would take me time to find out how to enter it.

During the years that we were not allowed to elect our courses,

I kept up with my art interest by frequent trips to New York. I confess that, during these trips, I wasn't fussy. I could be easily lured from art pursuits if I made a good debutante party or just went from one speak-easy to another with the boys. However, I did manage to see and learn a lot, not only from the museums but from the dealers. With very few exceptions they treated me like the most potential customer ever to enter their premises, and I found them extraordinarily knowledgeable and willing to share that knowledge.

There is something very "firsthand" about the knowledge that comes from actual trade in a commodity. A lifetime dealer is a lifetime guarantee of the real thing. Of course, they can make mistakes, but so can the scholars, and the dealer is much more apt to admit this.

I got myself seriously in hock to one of them one year. It is difficult in college, on whatever allowance you're allowed, to make ends meet. There's too much fun to be had, and there are too many new worlds that charge admission. It just goes. So when you see something you really can't live without, and it costs more than twenty tickets to the movies, you're in real trouble.

One of the dealers had a self-portrait of Alphonse Legros, the great, neglected French etcher of the last century. It was a sepia drawing, in profile, of that beautiful old man, whose looks and technique were close to Leonardo's. It was a very reasonable one hundred dollars. I put down twenty-five and for the next four months went on a once-a-month, one-week fast of the Waldorf Cafeteria's delicious barley soup. I still have the Legros, but barley soup I can't drink more than once a year.

Another less satisfying debt I got into was for a small bronze version of The Vine, by Harriet Frishmuth. She was a very popular sculptress in the thirties and, as I see her now, a logical visual outcome of the poetry of Elinor Wylie and Edna St. Vincent Millay. Many museums still have examples of her work, though they have been relegated to the garden spots, and, at the moment, their charm has superseded their artistic value. However, I daresay they are more popular with more members of museums' women's committees than a Lipchitz or Henry Moore.

Change of taste, which is one of the most fascinating aspects of art history and about which little is written, takes place throughout our lives often without our realizing it. Those years in college can leave us open-minded or can close our minds forever, depending on how we want to grow. If we think of graduation as the end of learning, we are apt to be stuck with a taste that becomes old-fashioned, almost at once. But if those years whet our appetites to see, to read, to realize that everything is forever new, our tastes must change and become richer for that change.

The twenties and thirties were the great years of print collecting, and it was so competitive that editions of contemporary etchings were sold out before they came off the press. Frank Benson was one of the most popular etchers and did some beautiful airy compositions of ducks, resting or in flight. These items almost became objects of barter, for you could double your money if you were lucky enough to be on the artist's or gallery's list of patrons. Today the great print makers of that period are little sought after, but there will be a revival of interest in John Taylor Arms, Muirhead Bone, and perhaps even Frank Benson.

I've often wondered if all the suggestive jokes about "come up and see my etchings" had anything to do with this. I doubt it. But that expression was really run into the ground and may just have made others as self-conscious as it did me, when I was collecting them.

The point is that the taste for etchings is not the same, and again the American artist has suffered, for the impressionist prints still bring big prices. There are still collectors, however, who are taking advantage of this lack of interest and are making important purchases at very little cost. One day they will become sources of real interest to students, and when the pendulum of taste swings back (as it always does) they will be of great value.

Carl Rollins was a fine printer and teacher at Yale. My roommate, Ted Thomas, was a friend and fan of his and got me interested in typography, a great and noble art. I have Mr. Rollins to thank for introducing me to a museum, often skipped by even the most interested people—the Morgan Library. Set as it was in that time, amidst other old New York mansions, many of which are no more, it seemed to me still to be a home, and, had I not been taken there, I never would have dared go in.

J. P. Morgan spent his life and a great part of his great fortune collecting books and manuscripts. After you've seen that collection, you feel the only thing that's missing is the original manuscript of Genesis. On my first visit my reaction was typical. I fired up to the challenge and went in hock again for a first edition of something or other, which—upon coming to my senses and realizing that if I planned to collect anything, it was going to be pictures—I unloaded on a rich classmate at a slight profit.

One lesson that was taught me (which I still regret wasn't learned sooner) was offered by Herman Liebert, a classmate, dear friend, and, at the moment, distinguished librarian and scholar at Yale. "Fritz" came into this world for one purpose, and I suspect he knew what it was at birth. Where his mother ever could get the little wigs he *must* have worn as a baby, I'll never know, because I'm sure he demanded, at the age of two, that he be dressed like Dr. Samuel Johnson.

I met him the first few days of my freshman year, and the first thing he uttered was a long quotation from Boswell. How a boy of eighteen could have managed, in an eastern prep school, to sustain an interest in the eighteenth century, I'll wonder at all my life. But here was a complete scholar in his own field, entering Yale. He was so fascinated with the Johnson circle that he seldom spoke of anything else, and while he was enormous fun and always stimulating, many of his close friends (especially me) were put off Johnson forever.

I finally learned my lesson, just last year. Under the seat of a plane, I found a paper-back copy of Boswell's *The Life of Samuel Johnson* and roared and rolled and rocked myself from New York to California in the delight of this discovery. I can't stop reading Boswell. . . . The moral? Let yourself be infected before you build up an immunity to greatness!

I scraped through those first Yale years, grade-wise, and assumed the dignity of a junior with a pack of fun behind me but still no purpose up ahead. That year proved a revealing and exciting one. I took my first formal art course—creative art, that is—and when I saw what I could do to make a charcoal drawing of a plaster cast look like a child's rendition of Frankenstein's monster, I gave up, then and there. Scheme Number One, to be an artist, was out. Scheme Number Two, the Actor Plan, I had the good sense not to bring out into public view. I just studied that art with all the pocket money I could get together and, singlehanded, supported the local movies and the Shubert Theatre. I think I can honestly say I saw every movie, good and bad, made between the years 1930 and 1933. And I didn't miss many concerts, plays, or revues, either. The result was a determination to one day find out if the actor's life was to be for me. I didn't know how I'd go about it, but I knew I'd have to try it on for size.

Admittedly, I was slow, but I never really went to Yale or let it come to me until my senior year. Then, out of the blue, there were a hundred classes I wanted to take on a hundred subjects. Out of that same blue had come the overwhelming realization that I had only one year of grace left before the big world would gobble me up forever. I felt like beating myself for all the time I'd wasted . . . until I looked at the past three years and knew how much I had really got out of them and the life at college . . . the people I'd met . . . the things I'd seen. It didn't look quite so bad, after all. Perhaps I was in the same spot as all the others. I didn't want it to end any sooner than it had to, and until it did, I was determined to make the most of it.

I elected two history of art courses, and they proved to be just what I needed to cinch what I had learned, up until now, on my own. Basically, they only added dates and extra facts to the knowledge I'd already acquired through my long curiosity and open eyes. They clinched the deal between art and me, and I accepted the fact that whatever I would learn from art would be about man, and what I would learn from man would be his art.

Here the teachers were more than adequate, catching fire occasionally from the visual material they were discussing. But still they were talking about reproductions . . . great material, secondhand . . . and it was only when they could use living material from the gallery collection as illustration that you were able to make firsthand identification with the work and the personality of the artist. However, the old Chinese saying that "One picture is worth a thousand words" was never more applicable to anyone than it was to me, so slide after slide slid me further and further into the land of pictures.

Even if the professors were not André Malraux, Roger Fry, or Herbert Read, they transported me from the most average student onto the dean's list, which gave me privileges to cut classes.

But the time for that nonsense was over, and I wanted to miss nothing. It was a great year, richly rewarding, and by the time commencement rolled around, I felt ready—if slightly underarmed—to enter the battle of the world outside. What's more, I no longer worried that my mind was still open as to what road I'd take. I even thought it rather smart of me not to have a definite plan. This way, I could learn more and perhaps find the right road, in time, then go straight to my destination.

One thing was sure. Whatever life would offer in the way of a profession, a business, a *life*—I'd always have that special sphere in which to spin: the wonderful circle of the arts. Thanks to museums, galleries, and books, some of the best things in life would always be free for me to wander in . . . wherever I went . . . whenever I wanted to.

THERE COMES A TIME IN LIFE WHEN YOU KNOW WHAT YOU like and have to make up your mind to like what you know, or at least have begun to know. In other words, you must determine in what direction your knowledge is leading you, thus far.

I was in exactly the same position as a great majority of my contemporaries at that time—young American men, graduated from college, but minus the conviction that they had learned anything specific. The way to a goal was nebulous, as was the goal itself. Most of us discovered that education, purported to be for life, was not for living. Too, the depression of the early thirties limited the market place for educational wares, the young college graduate being caught in the precarious middle of a national economic crisis. From this shaky vantage point we pondered the possibility that America was only for the man of business. How, in this era, could one hope to make his way in the arts?

Abstractly, I knew that my adult life had to be in the arts, but how, I hadn't the slightest inkling. In some way I wanted to apply my education, self-taught and school-taught, to making a life and a livelihood . . . as an artist.

The history of art made more sense to me as the history of man than politics, anthropology, or anything else. I guess I have to admit I was one hundred per cent picture-minded, for it was through illustration that I was able to grasp the meaning of any subject, and I began to realize that, although I had always loved the arts, I had not understood the possibilities of their application to everyday life.

However, I did understand that a sure way to discover how much or how little I knew was to have to teach what I'd found out to someone else. Although I certainly wasn't trained to be a teacher, and I wasn't at all sure I could teach, to clarify my own feelings I determined that I'd like to try to help others *think*—to pass along what I *thought* I knew.

A friend of my sister's learned of an opening at a boys' school in New York City that would be preceded by two months' counseling at that school's summer camp in the Adirondacks. It was a perfect opportunity to find out a lot of things. I took the job, which paid very little but gave me a chance to use what I had learned. What it really meant was moving quickly from the student's approach to learning to that of the teacher's. I made wonderful friends among the faculty, who helped me translate what I knew into the language that could help others know for themselves.

Two remarkable people, Marc and Cecil Baldwin, who have remained close friends, gave me the keenest insight into the teacher's philosophy by letting me share in their dedicated and lively excitement at being privileged to inspire young people in the desire to learn. They were both more than distributors of prefabricated knowledge. They were prophets of what education can mean to students who would let themselves be made aware that the truth can make you free and that freedom from ignorance is the highest good to which man can aspire.

The two months at camp, under their knowledgeable guidance, helped me to be ready for what I have since come to know as the highest calling. Even though it did not end up my life's work, I have often since found myself in the role of enthusiasm instructor, if nothing else . . . enthusiasm for the unalterable fact that the mind is the government, the home, and the temple of man.

Being in strict fact only an apprentice teacher, the headmaster scattered me throughout the curriculum to see what I could do and to discover where I fitted in. I was able to persuade him to let me try out some ideas I had on visual education. I wanted to go into each class in the school and illustrate, through the visual arts of the period being studied, what that period looked like.

For instance, in the Latin course I showed the students what Cicero and his contemporaries looked like through the magnificent school of Roman portrait sculpture. Where de Maupassant and Zola were being read, I let them examine the visual report of their time through the eyes of the many superb nineteenth-century painters, some of whom were intimately connected with the writers, like Zola and Cézanne . . . Baudelaire and Delacroix.

The experiment was successful, or at least the students said so, for many of them had no idea at all that the periods they were studying had any "look" at all. They thought of them as something in the past, which had little connection with the reality of any era. Of course, they studied the tongue of the past but not the eye.

In the school I had an art appreciation class and tried to give them an idea of the problems involved in seeing pictures by explaining artists' problems . . . how almost all of them, in their time, were bucking the past to be "modern" and how many of them succeeded only through great trial to create something new. Perhaps this was the most significant contribution I was able to make, and as is always the case when you teach others, I taught myself something, too. Few people stop to think that the great creative minds of every and any period are always competing with their immediate past—to present the day they live in as something new and worth representing to their contemporaries and to the future.

Periods of discovery about yourself are seldom fun. It's tough to realize how little you know just when you think you ought to know a lot, and that period immediately after graduation from college, when you suddenly realize for the first time that "commencement" means beginning, and actually you are just beginning to learn—to live—it comes as a terrible blow to your ego. You become aware that all you really learned at college was *how* to learn and that continued learning is the true key to all existence. That is its real importance.

My year of teaching taught me that whatever I was going to do or be, I had to know more. And I was lucky enough to realize that I wanted to know more about the history of man through his art.

My Yale graduation present was a check for $1100, accompanied by a letter from my father saying that this odd amount would buy one junior membership in the country club at home. But there was a postscript to the effect that if I used it for this purpose I would be disowned. I don't think Father ever thought for a second he would have to disown me; he knew too well I was too curious about life to lose it in a locker room, and yet, in an endearing way, he meant it. It would have hurt him deeply if I had settled into a life that never could have supported me and in which perhaps he suspected the only support would have had to come from him.

And it was true. I could not have withstood the ravages of that charming little social life I would have inherited by being his son. If I were going to settle down into complacency, it would have to be only after some severe wing clipping had completely domesticated me.

I took the graduation check and bought myself two years' further education in the place where, at that time, the amount could be stretched furthest—London.

The Courtauld Institute of the University of London offered a superb volume of courses in art history. The tuition was $200, and I had been informed that I could live nicely on $75 a month in a boardinghouse, or "digs," as they call it—with meals. Third-class passage to England, off season, was cheap, and so with what I had saved I could possibly eke out my master's degree in the next two years.

London appealed to me enormously as a challenge, for I hadn't had time to like it when I was there before; but I felt that by living among the British they might warm up a bit, and for my part, I was determined to get to know them. And indeed I did. The sixteen months I lived in London was a time I'll never forget for all the best reasons. I learned a great respect for the English way of life and their devotion to learning, but especially for the way in which they have been able to make the arts an integral part of their whole activity, of their social structure.

They live with the arts completely. The theatre, for instance, which in this country exists only in New York, is a part of the entire British character. Philosophy and poetry still have their number-one seat there, and if they don't measure up to the rest of Europe in the visual arts, it is because they like what their painters have produced and see in it an expression of themselves. They are as ready as the rest of the world to take umbrage against someone radically new—like Epstein —but as they know him better and see his place in the scheme of their culture, they honor him with knighthood. We in America would be more apt to neglect him until after his death. Whoever coined the phrase of "giving honor where honor is due" must have been British. They honor their artists and make them part of their present history, not their past.

For two years in a row I had the delight of being entertained at the Epstein openings in the Leicester Galleries in London—and I mean entertained. That grand Anglo-American was at his shocking peak in 1935. The second year was the best—the year before a huge blockbuster Christ had incensed the gallery pussyfooters, and so this second year they came, they hoped, slightly better prepared. The front room contained the rows of superb heads, sultry models, and juicy joyous babies. Then came the second room and a by-this-time almost acceptable group of stones and bronzes, including a couple of past shockers, but around the bend was "Adam." The groans, the screams, the giggles of delight were heavenly to watch and hear—for here was Adam, man enough for any man and way too much for any woman— the great ape-father of us all, a suppliant to warmth, head raised, arms bent, fists clenched, in need of self-identification, so lately had he come across from animal to man. The ladies screamed, but Adam prayed to God for strength. With all his shock value he was finally accepted, too, but I have yet to see a photo of "Adam" which did him justice. He has been edited into a profile from the wrong side.

The Courtauld family was of vast wealth and early in the century had built up a magnificent collection of French impressionists. They gave many of them to the great museums in London, the National Gallery, and the Tate and kept a few choice ones in their superb Adams house on Portman Square. This they then gave, complete with pictures, to the University of London to be the College of Art History.

London University is made up of dozens of this kind of gifts and therefore has no center and no campus. It's scattered all over the city, and consequently each college has its own entity. You live in London, and you attend the University of London.

Home House, as the Courtauld's gift is called, was built by the Adams brothers for the Countess of Home and was never altogether completed. But the main floor where the classes were held was considered the greatest example of an Adams interior in England. The entrance had the most magnificent double stairway that twisted up to the fourth floor—and the living room was Adamic perfection. An enormous oblong room looking out on the square, it was painted the subtlest of Adams greens with four monoliths of red granite, one in each corner. The far end of the room harbored a subtly sculptured white marble mantelpiece.

In this startlingly beautiful room hung these great paintings, "The Card Players" of Cézanne—a single portrait of one of the card players, and a "Mt. Ste. Victoire" by the same man; a Modigliani nude, "Wheatfields at Arles" by Van Gogh, Lautrec's "Jane Avril Leaving the Theatre," Daumier's "Don Quixote," and a tender and beautiful unfinished Madonna and Child by Fra Bartolommeo.

This was our classroom. A little distracting, to say the least, for the lecturer, who not only had to project to be heard, but in his choice of slides and illustrations had to compete with some of the best and most exciting pictures of modern times. I missed many a pearl of wisdom with my eyes riveted on that luscious and seductive nude of Modigliani's. His nudes are all either fresh from love or awaiting it, and the answer to this question was a matter of important speculation for many of the male students. One picture I forgot to mention hung between the windows, an enchanting "Ballet Rehearsal" by Degas. If it hadn't been for the brilliant array of lecturers delivered to us that year by Mr. Hitler from the shores of Europe, I fear the competition between them and the pictures would have been too steep.

But Hitler was beginning to throw his weight around, and the first blows were felt by the great museums' directors and art historians, as well as the modern German painters. They could see the handwriting on the wall and left in droves, coming naturally to England, which is always ready to welcome distinguished scholars. It is extraordinary, I think, that these seemingly harmless, erudite men were thought to be such a threat to Herr Hitler. But actually they were, for their whole philosophy of history, based on the creative acts of men, was in direct opposition to the Fuehrer's determined indoctrination of the German people that all art, except state-inspired German art, was decadent. Of course they were dangerous. They had been teaching and writing for years that freedom in art was the true expression of democracy and that it was the one creative commodity which transcends barriers of race, creed, color—or politics.

It didn't matter that everyone in the know knew that, while Hitler was banishing other than Fascist-inspired art from the museums, he was, with the other hand, making millions marketing it in the auction rooms of Europe. Even more directly contrary to his credo—Goering, his right hand, was collecting it—by confiscation or just plain theft.

It was an exciting time for art—a proving time of its great power and lasting worth. No one can dictate the ideas of men and get away with it—and I feel sure if there is to be an undoing of the seemingly limitless power of the Soviet Union, it will be through this same mistake. You can't make men worship, paint, write, or compose according to an ideological principle, unless it be the principle of freedom of worship, image, thought, and inspiration.

I took as my subject for my projected M.A., "Dürer and the School of the Danube," and I was assigned to Mr. Campbell Dodgson as my master. Mr. Dodgson had been for many years the keeper of prints and drawings at the British Museum and was, without question, the outstanding authority on Dürer and the whole German Renaissance School.

He was a monument to scholarship in every way. You had only to see him walking down the street to know he was someone special. He shot like a bent arrow from one place to another with the determination only the British have—on their feet—to get where they are going. He had no age, but you suspected he had been born old, like a dwarfed Japanese pine tree, and just got more beautifully gnarled as the years went by. He knew so much of Dürer, having written more about him than anyone else, next to meeting Dürer himself, I couldn't have done better than to have Campbell Dodgson as my guide to get to know that genius. His name proved to be an open-sesame for all my research, both in London and all over the continent.

Dürer was a prolific artist, and great works of his are in most every museum in Europe, especially his drawings, which are among the finest ever done. They are scattered everywhere, and since great drawings are rarely hung in museums, you have to ferret them out of the boxes where they are kept to protect them from the ravages of time.

With Mr. Dodgson's help I managed in the next six months to see most of Dürer's lifework, and I ended up with a feeling of intimate friendship with that great man. Since then I've tracked down many other painters' works almost as thoroughly, but the intensity with which I pursued Dürer I have never repeated, so perhaps that explains my near idolatry of the man. What seems to assure his greatness to me is the fallibility of his painting. He never completely mastered the whole of art, but he certainly came close. There are so many moments of absolute truth in the best of them . . . and very few falsehoods.

The Courtauld lectures covered all fields of art, and the concentration on Dürer was only the way to the M.A., but the real fascination of that year was London itself. It is not only rich in the inherent vitality of all great cities but richer than most in its dedication to being the most cultured. For very little money you can take an active part in it. You can hear the greatest concerts, standing in Queen's Hall, for seventy-five cents, or for the same price you can queue up for the best seats left in the theatre, fifteen minutes before curtain time.

The most glamorous thing the British of all classes do is to buy the idea that art is for everyone and that you can pay as much or as little for it as you want or can afford. Americans are apt to look upon it as the prerogative of the upper economic classes, which of course it is not. However, the rich of all nations today make us feel that perhaps it is, what with their fantastic boosting of art prices beyond any true worth.

I lived in the museums, though it wasn't until I got to New York and had the economic leisure of a successful play that I learned to use them completely. They were my dessert after a feast of studies. I fell in love all over again with pictures, and I think I learned an acceptance of all art of all periods, then and there, through the great treasures in British collections.

People are always asking me what my favorite painting is. There is a great Tintoretto in the National Gallery I couldn't leave alone those two years, and I got so familiar with the collection I could afford to visit just this one picture time and again. It's "Origin of the Milky Way," and while I don't know the whole mythological tale (who is doing what to whom), Tintoretto pictured the essential story with perfect clarity.

Venus lies tilted on a cloud and Cupid, hurled by Mars through the air to kiss her breasts, strikes stars from them on contact, and the Milky Way is born. The composition swirls and squirms, and, most miraculous of all (as I'd discovered in Venice years before), was Tintoretto's ability to give the feeling of flight. You become aware of his mastery in surrounding the figures with air and not just making them hang there like moored balloons. He enabled them to move and fly, without wings. Somehow it's easy to grasp the idea of a human flying with wings, as in the case of angels, but without them, most painters achieve blimps. Not Tintoretto. By his magic they lose their earthly anchors and they soar.

Among the other gems in the National Gallery is the great Van

Eyck "Arnolfini Wedding," as charming a picture as exists and an achievement technically unparalleled in its time—and since.

Because of our Courtauld connection we were allowed backstage in the museums, and one of the most harrowing days I ever spent was watching a restorer shave off the wood panel behind a priceless Rogier van der Weyden, right down to the paint, and then transfer it to canvas. The public doesn't realize that many of the greatest masterpieces have been saved from cracking, flaking, or just complete disintegration by the genius of modern restorers and their sensational techniques.

Up until this century paintings seem to have survived by sheer luck. They have been abused and neglected to the point that you wonder how we have any left. But somehow the philosophy of art enjoyment has changed, and while everyone knows the enormous value of great paintings (and that alone might be reason enough for preserving them), there is more to it than that. Perhaps our two world wars have taught us a keener appreciation of them—since we seem to hold human life of such little value but cannot deny the inestimable worth of human achievement.

The Tate Gallery is devoted loosely to modern art. Actually it dips back into the eighteenth and nineteenth centuries, and when I was there in 1935, it was no more contemporary in what it exhibited than twenty years before. There are superb Gauguins and French impressionists, but what really makes it a must are the Turners and Blakes.

I don't know why, but I always think of Blake and Turner as twin mystics. Blake has always been considered such, but I've never felt that others thought Turner a mystic too. And yet I never see those great, late, mysterious landscapes and seascapes—in which nature, the elements, and the implements of man commingle—that I don't feel his divine power and sight, and almost divine ability to portray them with such heavenly excitement.

Turner and another great English painter, John Constable, surely deserve credit for the whole impressionist approach to the outdoor observation of nature. We know that Delacroix, the father of modern French painting, was enormously influenced by Constable. It is told that when painting his early "Massacre at Scio" he saw a Constable and was so impressed by the concept of the painted sky he struck his out and added another, inspired by the British master.

William Blake could only be the product of England. There is something practical and quotable about his mysticism that is British. Those heroic Michelangelesque figures in his drawings and engravings still look like idealized Englishmen, blond and athletic. His foolish virgins are poetical English ladies, and his poems are idyllic landscapes filled with the weird humor Lear was to turn into such delightful nonsense later on. There is a good humor about this kind of mystic only England could breed. I love Blake, but I always want to smile at his semi-serious, well-bred naïveté. He is a charming prophet, if nothing he ever said was particularly prophetic.

But Blake was a devotee of the eye and had things to say about the imagination involved in the visual experience which have stayed with me. He once said: "Some scarce see nature at all, but to the eye of the man of imagination, nature is imagination itself; As a man is, so he sees; as the eye is formed, such are its powers."

It must take a very old and secure race to give birth to such men and to the extraordinary men of unpublicized good will who exist all over London. There is hardly any field of art or science to which some individual has not devoted his life, collecting all the pertinent facts he could lay his hands on. At one point in my studies I needed desperately a more complete research than I could find through the Institute library or even in the museums. I needed a cross reference on those admirable "little artists" who surrounded Dürer and his school and who founded schools of their own elsewhere in Germany and Austria. Men like Wolf Huber, Urs Graf, Beham, Aldegrever, and Albrecht Altdorfer. I went to W. G. Constable, the distinguished head of Courtauld, with my troubles and without a moment's thought he wrote me out a little note and put it in an envelope with a name and address not two blocks away.

Two days later I presented the letter to Sir Robert Witt's secretary, who led me courteously to the basement where I found hundreds of steel filing cabinets filled with every article, reproduction, or mention of the artists I wanted to know about. A lifetime of careful study had gone into this library, and there it existed for anyone with the interest to use it and live with it. I went there at least once a week for seven months, and although I never met Sir Robert, I was deeply grateful to his patience and scholarliness for having made this available to me and to others. There are dozens of libraries like this, belonging to wealthy men who have taken their hobby seriously enough to be able to be generous with it.

London was a marvelous place to hunt for undiscovered treasure. Besides having the best bookshops in the world, there were wonderful print shops where you could still make fantastic finds in prints and occasionally drawings. While casing the old bookstores near High Holborn, I came across three fine drawings, obviously from the same notebook and by the same hand. They were mannerist sketches after Andrea del Sarto's Sant' Annunziata frescoes—the paper and watermark proved that they were possibly done contemporarily with those frescoes, and a mysterious collection stamp indicated that they were from an unknown royal collection. They cost two dollars apiece, but they proved to be worth much more for the adventure in which they ultimately involved me . . . trying to find out who did them.

The most eager people on earth are those who think they have a "treasure" and want to prove it. I have never let the search for the author of these drawings go for more than a few years at a time. When I've seemingly forgotten all about them, the desire to find out will once again grab hold of me, and I'm off on another hot trail. I may have seen a drawing reproduced in a book that has certain similar traits, and I track down every known reproduction of the man's work until I'm satisfied he is not the right one. About ten years ago, between planes in Chicago, I was visiting the Art Institute as usual, and the late, great Carl Schniewind, curator of prints and drawings, showed me a wonderful pen drawing of Paolo Veronese. There was the same mysterious collection stamp. I told him of my drawings, and together we searched to identify the owner of that stamp—nothing. But again I felt assured that if a drawing of the quality of the Veronese was in the same collection, mine must be good, too.

I may never find out—but, then, I may, and when I do, whichever way it turns out I will have had great fun and learned a lot in the process.

I bought the edition of Dürer's Drawings, put out by the Albertina, with Campbell Dodgson's introduction. Nothing can equal these reproductions. They are so good, in fact, that the Albertina itself shows them as originals to the casual unauthorized visitor. I have held them alongside the originals, and it is almost impossible to tell the difference.

A few years ago I saw a water color by Constantin Guys, for sale in a very high-class gallery. It looked familiar to me, and on closer inspection I realized it was an Albertina facsimile. The dealer honestly didn't know it, but I was grateful for the intaglio stamp they are legally obliged to use; for the Albertina, having achieved such remarkable reproductive technique, could fool almost anyone into believing them originals.

With Mr. Dodgson's magic key I was allowed to unlock the unbelievable storehouse of drawings in the British Museum. And through another instructor we were permitted to see the collection at Windsor Castle—the Leonardos and the newly discovered Poussin drawings, which were being found continually between the pages of old books in that library. It seems Charles the Second was a great drawing collector but also something of a hoarder. He hid his purchases in books. I hope this story is true, for I love to identify that lively king with all the rest of us who, affected with collectionitis, have to sneak things in and hide them from our more practical mates. I like to think of Nell Gwyn stamping her foot and saying, "It's all right to buy me a new spaniel, Charlie, but stop bringing them drawings home."

For all their incorporation of the arts into everyday life, the British keep on producing some of the worst painters in the world, and they support them, too. The height of vogue in London, 1935, was a water-colorist named Russell Flint and a portrait painter named Simon Elwes. Flint developed a style best described as Spacial Calendar Art.

Golden brown nudes, as slippery as Russell Patterson's, loll and bask on long stretches of damp sand. Elwes had a genius for making every English woman over sixty look like the Queen Mother and all under that age like English ladies, whether they were or not.

The annual exhibitions of the Royal Society were something to be seen. They were tradition, rampant on a field of paint. The good painters like Sutherland, Nicholson, and Spencer hadn't come on the scene yet, and I don't know if they ever made the Royal Society or not, but the fuss kicked up by Sutherland's wonderful portrait of Winston Churchill would lead me to think not. Whoever made the crack that "Winston paints good like Eisenhower should" should also think up a jingle about Sir Winston's blind spot about modern art. I may not agree with Mr. Churchill's approach to art, but I suppose I should defend with my life his right to paint—though from what I've read, the old boy does have some humor about himself as a painter, and it's a good thing, too.

Christmas of my first year I took off for Vienna to see the Dürers at the Albertina, and incidentally I had an invitation to go skiing in the Austrian Alps. Third class from England to Austria is a long hard trip, but when you're young and tolerant of discomfort for the sake of adventure, you can "take" anything. But those wooden seats come very close to taking you; they definitely leave a lasting impression.

This was winter 1935, a time of ferment in Europe. Hitler was on his way wherever he was going, but for the innocent American, safe with his passport, there was outwardly little trouble showing. Once in Vienna, settled snugly in a little pension behind the Karlskirche for a dollar a day including breakfast and a quarter to get up and down in the lift, the whole rest of the world could have blown to bits. And I had the greatest protection of all—a passport of equal importance: I had a letter from Campbell Dodgson to Frau Dr. Hilda Spitzmueller at the Albertina, one of the greatest collections of drawings in the world.

The building itself is an eighteenth-century palace, the former town house of a famous family. It is formal but handsome because of its spaciousness, very serviceable as a museum, or rather a study museum, since few of the treasures are on display. But with Mr. Dodgson's letter and the friendliness of Dr. Spitzmueller, I was one of the family, and every weekday from 9 A.M. to closing time at 5 P.M. I was allowed to pore through the thousands of master drawings which are carefully kept in uniform boxes in the storerooms.

First off, I was shown the great Dürers: "The Praying Hands," "The Violets," "The Rabbit," the superb heads in black and white ink on blue paper, Dürer's little Christmas card of the Christ Child holding the world, made on parchment in Venice and sent home to his Agnes in Nuremberg, the sketches for his paintings and engravings—so many of them I suddenly realized that, had I not seen them, I would have only half known his genius. After about two days of this the *Frau Doktor* asked me if I wouldn't like a little change. So one of the attendants set six large boxes in front of me. They were a group of sixty drawings that had been selected for a special exhibition somewhere and would be gone the rest of the time I was there, so I should see them.

What a thrill. They were sixty of the finest drawings in the whole Albertina collection, ranging from Schongauer through the whole German Renaissance. Then six great Rembrandts, Fragonards, Rubens . . . too many to list but everyone a masterpiece. It was truly the history of drawing in one very easy-to-take lesson.

I crammed as much as I could into my head from the Albertina during my stay there, and if I've forgotten a great many of the drawings individually, I'll never forget the quality and quantity of that collection. Once again I blessed the instinct in men of taste and wealth—or whatever it is that makes them build up and preserve these treasure hoards of art. For the student they are invaluable, for under one roof he can see what would take him years to track down in separate collections, and to be able to view a great cross section of one artist's work at one time is the only way to get to the very heart of his talent, to see him as a fully rounded creator.

But much as I love drawings, Dürer and all, I have to admit Vienna had other charms. The Kunsthistorisches Museum with its Brueghels, Correggios, Tintorettos, its magnificent collection of antique gems; the Hofburg which contains the regalia of the Hapsburgs, though this is always kind of depressing. It's as if they put all of John D. Rockefeller's money on display. True, the jewels are superb examples of ancient and more modern craftsmanship, but a crown demands a head to wear it, and pearls and diamonds lose their brilliance off a lady's throat.

But of all Vienna's charms, the one that came as the biggest thrill to me was the baroque, the rococo. Not since the great days of Greece has there been such a perfect marriage of art and architecture, and while Vienna is not the center of this form, it has some very fine examples of it.

Michelangelo is credited with being the founder of baroque, and if it needs a definition I suppose he will do. The great Chapel of the Medici in Florence is a perfect example of classic derivations, applied to the high Renaissance and ending up something completely its own style. The dictionary defines baroque as "extravagantly ornamented." High baroque is hardly that, and people are apt to confuse it with rococo, which carried it a step further. From the dictionary again, rococo is "tastefully florid ornamentation."

But to get back to the Medici chapel, it is almost severe at first sight, and only when the elaborate patterns of marble come into focus do you notice the involvement of design and subtle use of color. Then you notice, too, superimposed on this, the twisted muscular figures of "Night" and "Day" and the contorted "Thinker" or portrait of Guilio de' Medici.

Michelangelo died in 1564, and the news spread rapidly that he had given birth to a new idea in architectural decoration. By the next century Bernini was to redo Rome with his marvelously inventive fountains and churches that led directly to further ornamentation and the real rococo.

In Venice, for instance, one of the greatest artists of all time— Giovanni Battista Tiepolo—broke through the domes of the churches to let in heaven with his grandiose compositions of sky-borne pageantry and his infallible technique and draftsmanship. The formal and almost classical picture-book technique of the Sistine ceiling now becomes an actual vision of things going on above. The architecture is tricked into joining the decoration so that you can't tell where one leaves off and the other begins.

In Vienna the triumph of this form is the library at the Hofburg. The whole design is created to give the illusion of a long, narrow, apse-like room with columns springing upward and outward so that the ceiling seems to be twice as spacious as the floor.

Then the Karlskirche is a progression from this. A classical façade, in front of which are two enormous twisted columns which writhe into the sky, and the interior all white and gold and blue with a madonna swooping out of the largest gold sunburst this side of heaven.

This was my introduction into the achievement of the baroque and rococo, and while I have never had the chance to discover it completely, I never fail to take it in wherever I find it. Recently I've made its acquaintance again in the thrilling invention of the Mexican churches, which have an added charm in the almost primitive technique with which they approached this highly sophisticated art.

I left Vienna to seek more Dürer and to see some of the background of his astounding talent. I say "astounding," for I don't believe any artist before or since has, singlehanded, brought the technique of his country's art from one period to another. In fifty years Dürer transformed German art from medieval to Renaissance, and to understand this achievement one really had to go to his birthplace in Nuremberg. I had been there as a boy, but I wanted to pay tribute now that I was trying to make myself at one with the great man. Most especially I needed to see some of the surroundings, to feel the Romanesque and Gothic background into which he was born and from which he, like all artists before and after him, had to break out to be contemporary.

I revisited Nuremberg, and this time, with Dürer and his friends having become such a rich part of my life, I saw it with new eyes. Again the truth that the more you know about something you like the more you like it. Walking around the town you could imagine it at

Dürer's birth, a fortress city still caught in the isolated identity of medieval times. And knowing that, you could imagine what a challenge it was to the budding minds of Renaissance men—to open those gates and let the wonderful sensation of the reborning world of Italy come in. How hungry they must have been for new ideas, new ways of doing things, and especially of seeing things.

Dürer as a young man went to Venice to see for himself the great awakening that had taken place there. He met the Bellinis, he copied Carpaccio, and it was probably there that he first contacted the disease of curiosity that was to infect his whole life. There wasn't going to be enough time to see everything and do everything and try to change everything, but what time he had would not be wasted. When he returned home, the great volume of his work was already in his mind and nothing could stop him.

It always comes as a surprise to people when they find out that those great engravings of his were sold in the market place, usually by his wife, as mementos of Nuremberg or as religious pictures to be framed and hung for devotion in one's home. Nowadays we think of them carefully framed and hung in museums, or to be come across at the great dealers for great prices; and while many of them brought good prices in his day, especially as his fame grew, they still were done to be sold to the general public—almost as we buy post cards. A couple of centuries later two of the greatest Venetian painters—Guardi and Canaletto—were indeed no more than souvenir painters of the scenes of Venice. Just as we will buy some glass from Murano, in the eighteenth century the tourist would bring home a Guardi.

Gothic art, which was so much a part of Dürer's background, had in its past as strong an influence in the Romanesque, and I remembered suddenly that not far from Nuremberg was the town of Bamberg where artists worked in the twelfth and thirteenth centuries, whose influence was felt throughout Europe in the great Gothic sculptures. And so one bitter day I took the train to Bamberg to see the great cathedral and especially to pay tribute to that equestrian masterpiece, "The Rider of Bamberg." This statue I had seen illustrated a thousand times, and now I would see if it, too, would amaze me in the original by being a thousand times more exciting.

Bamberg must have been an important town in its heyday, but arriving there in midwinter and walking from the station to the cathedral, you almost felt it was a ghost town. Maybe the populace lived away from the old city, as so often happens today in our towns here, for there was absolutely no one around that day—or out of doors, in any case. The cathedral (with its "Rider") is equally famous for its exterior carving, and now I was about to see it. The street turned and there it was, the greatest monument of Romanesque art—scaffolded from street to tower with tons of wood—not a single sculpture visible. After all those centuries against the wind and rain, they were checking it for repairs . . . on my time!

Much as I approve of the preservation of great works, my disappointment was acute. But then I thought of something. If I could bring it off, it would assuage my disappointment a thousand times. If I could climb those scaffolds I'd be among the very few who'd ever seen the sculpture as the artist had when he created it. I would be closer to the original than anyone could ever be, standing below and staring up.

I went inside to see if some attendant could help me or give me permission. The church was deserted, and there stood the "Rider," majestic on his horse; there were "St. Elizabeth" and the "Virgin," so famous. But I could only give them the quickest glance, because I was determined to see that Tympanum and those glorious saints and kings and queens who surround the door. No one was there. I walked around, echoing my frustration with my heavy shoes, when as quietly as if one of the stones had come alive, a little old, old lady rose up out of the choir stalls and continued her dusting.

My German is adequate—I always manage to eat, and I have learned to read that strange language they have invented for the tongue of art; but my attempts to get through to this old *Frau* that I wanted to climb the scaffolds on the church, even if she could understand them and my frantic physical contortions in trying to picture my desires to her, even if she knew what I meant, from all appearances she thought

me simply mad. When she said anything at all it was one word—
Landamt—but mostly she shook her head—*Landamt?*—I'd never heard
the word.

I left in dejection and, being cold and hungry, thought I'd try to
find something to eat. This time when I walked down the street, the
city was all at once alive. Could one tourist have brought all these people back from the dead? I found some food and had a glass of delicious
hot Italian vermouth and life looked better. Then I thought I'd try
that word on someone. Quizzically, I looked at the waiter and said
"*Landamt?*" He pointed down the street. Well, that meant something,
so I started the way he had pointed and on saying the mysterious word
to several others got pointed farther and farther until at last I stood in
front of the city hall. There over one door was the word—*Landamt*. So
I walked in. Slowly, in the meticulous German or French or whatever
you use when you're afraid speed will lose the attention of your foreign
audience forever (as well as your train of thought) I explained that I
wanted to climb the scaffolding of the church. Without an answer,
whoever I was addressing wrote something cryptic on a piece of paper
and handed it to me. I thanked him and left directly for the cathedral
and climbed directly up the scaffolding where I lost myself face to face
with those beautiful people of stone for several hours.

To this day I don't know what was on the paper. No one ever
asked to see it and no one questioned my right to be a hundred feet
above the street, crawling over that façade. I left Bamberg that night,
intimately aware of the magic of the Romanesque. I saw the whole of
it, inside and out, alone and silent—a perfect communion with a place,
an art and an age. . . . And when I finally had time to study the
"Rider," he was just one more masterpiece in a forest of them.

I have read that the sculptors of Bamberg could have been the
teachers of those of Chartres. Gothic sculpture follows directly the
Romanesque, in time at least, but the Gothic masters somewhere along
the line must have revolted at the realism of the Romanesque and
produced a more stylized and sophisticated vision. "The Rider of Bamberg" is a triumph of realism, and so are many of the other works in

that cathedral. How typical again that the pupil discards the teacher to say something in a new way, or a decade rejects the vision of the one before it to have its own expression or, as sometimes happens, it may go back for inspiration to a style discarded by its immediate predecessors.

I stopped in Frankfort to see the Dürer drawings there and to see the copy of his great Heller Altarpiece which is all that's left of the original, burned many years ago. There I was given that marvelous facsimile of the notebook which he took on his last trip of exploration to the Netherlands. These pages are scattered all over Europe, but the Pressler Verlag in Frankfort has put them back together, and you can follow Dürer step by step to Holland.

Art is always the immediate, the contemporary report. And so it was with Dürer; the modern man, emerging from the highly stylized Gothic into a realism that harked back to the Romanesque.

The story goes that word had come to Nuremberg that a whale had been washed ashore in Holland and Dürer had to see it. He set out on this long journey and on the way kept visual notes of the trip. He met Lucas van Leyden and drew him as lovingly as he put down a captured fox or the water front of some little town. Apparently the whale had washed away, or rotted most likely, for there is no record of it. But on that trip he caught a fatal illness, and, returning to Nuremberg, he died in the city which he had helped to lead from its ancient age into the modern world.

Until you live in England it's hard to understand the British attitude toward spring. But once you have lived there, their ecstasy over this natural change is completely understandable. English winters are certainly one of the circles of hell. The North Pole is less formidable than the cold that creeps into your heart itself and through everything you can get on your body. The British have gas meters in their houses, and one of the reasons there are so few suicides from gas in England is that the shilling you must put in it to get gas runs out before any harm can be done. Also, their stoves give off only enough heat to keep you from freezing to death—they never warm you.

So when spring does finally break through the icecaps and the crocus braves a bonnie head into the cruel March wind, the British are overjoyed. I don't think they would ever admit it, but somehow for a moment they let their souls shine through. It isn't that it's not "business as usual," but they let up a little in the precise decorum of their lives. The regulations relax and everything seems gentler. For a month or two you can see the source of that great river of poetry that has flowed from this nation from its beginnings, and then the springhead disappears once more under the tall grasses of a short summer . . . and back to the cold and rain.

During those months when everything relaxes, even the curriculum of the schools and Courtauld's became less demanding and less interesting. So I chose that time to take my second dare in life, to see if my other scheme would work—the theatre. I tried out for a bit part in the tiny private Gate Theatre, got it, and two months later won the lead in the premier production of Laurence Housman's *Victoria Regina*. It was a hit. The American impresario Gilbert Miller saw it and bought it for Miss Helen Hayes to do on Broadway, and I was hired to play Prince Albert, opposite her.

I left England with deep regret but with great elation, too. I was on my way to Broadway and what I hoped would be the purpose of my life—to entertain.

NEW YORK, NEW YORK! . . . IT'S A WONDERFUL TOWN!
So goes the lyrical description, and no red-corpuscled young man who's attended Yale would argue the truth. The short commuting distance between New York's home town, Manhattan Island, and Yale's home town, New Haven, Connecticut, makes it easily possible, in fact imperative, for every fun-loving fellow to meet the big city, head on.

Of course, one's youthful geographic acquaintance is more often made with—well—*isolated* sections and the inhabitants therein . . . the jaundiced-eyed hotel clerk, to whom the name "Smith" no longer brings a smile but a yawn; hot and cold running girls; and (in my day) that tinseled street, now dedicated to the parking lot . . . West Fifty-second.

During my weekend pilgrimages to the great city I left off being a Yale student and became a student of life—the high life of a metropolis where every glittering light bulb flashed out a message of haste . . . hurry up and *live!* The frenzied voice of that era was shrieking "Life is short! . . . Take it in great gulps!" (Prohibition gulps, of course.)

As for my interest in art, there was no waning, just a kind of categorizing. I would gulp New York life, since it threatened brevity, while art could be taken in slow sips, its longevity assured. Consequently, it wasn't until I'd graduated, gone to England, and returned that I really got to know New York, city-wise and art-wise. The combined stimuli of working in the theatre and actually living in the wonderful town made me realize that the "gulping" period was merely a tryout. Now the curtain was up, geographically and artistically, and I was well armed to be an avid audience for all the arts.

Victoria Regina opened the day after Christmas, 1935, and while not as great a critical hit as it had been in London, it seemed destined for a long run for many reasons: the presence of Miss Helen Hayes; Mr. Gilbert Miller's superb production; Rex Whistler's sets, and to my intense delight—*me!* I had made a hit, and it looked as if this was my destiny and the answer to all my vocational wonderings.

At twenty-four, to be Helen Hayes' leading man! Let's not kid. It was pretty damned exciting, and two weeks after the opening, when Jules Bache gave a party for Miss Hayes and invited me, I knew that the world was not only my oyster, but there were pearls in it, too.

I had no idea of the Bache collection except that it was supposed to be fabulous, so I left the theatre that night, starry-eyed with expectation. I walked up to number 814 Fifth Avenue, rang the bell with newborn confidence, and was admitted by two butlers. The door opened into a marble vestibule, hung with Botticellis. I took that in my stride, but just as I was about to hand my coat to the butler, I saw a drunk totter down the stairs and catch himself on a *picture!* Being me, I didn't care if he broke his neck—but what was the picture he was swinging on? . . . Goya's "Don Orsorio"! . . . the little boy in red with a bird on a leash.

I don't remember the butler catching me as I staggered back, almost in a state of shock, but somehow I managed to mumble an excuse and went back out into the cold night air. About an hour later I got up nerve to tackle it again, made it, climbed the stairs to the party—straightening the Goya on the way—and joined the famous, rich, and happy guests who I wished would all get falling-down drunk so I could see those pictures. They didn't, and I didn't, and it was many years later before I had the chance to see them where they are now . . . unencumbered by drunks, at least . . . in the Metropolitan Museum in New York.

While the excitement of being in a hit was high, it was soon to wear thin. A long run becomes a job, and though the challenge is there every performance, there is the rest of life to be lived—the life of the hours of light. One thing I soon found out was that being established in a hit show affords one a marvelous opportunity to learn, to study, and to take advantage of the greatest asset an actor has: his welcome by the world at large. Incidentally, taking advantage of the erroneous public notion that all actors are rich and can afford to buy to their hearts' content is another formidable foot in the door to many an adventure often denied the unpublicized (but much more often well-heeled), just plain public.

So, while I was being the nighttime-and-two-matinees Prince Albert to Miss Hayes' Victoria for two years, I took advantage of the above assets and entered the New York art world by the front door, with very few assets in my pocket. I went in with many a great personage on my arm, or mine on theirs. Miss Hayes, Mr. and Mrs. Gilbert Miller (her father was Jules Bache), Beatrice Lillie, and many others who knew of my interest and either wanted to share it with me or have me share theirs. The dealers in the art world were courtesy itself, and of course their incentive to be co-operative with these personages was very keen. If Miss Hayes bought something, or even liked it, the whole world of her acquaintances knew it and was influenced, more or less, by her preference. On the supposition that actors are artists and therefore must have taste for the other arts (and the better the actor the better the taste), the dealers would show their wares to us with the joyous knowledge that even if nothing was sold for cash, the actor has what the dealer strives for—an audience. What an actor does or buys is news.

As a matter of fact, Miss Hayes was very astute in her likes and dislikes, and barking up her artistic alley was well worth their while. When she liked something, she said so, and when she didn't, she had enough charm to leave the painter or dealer not exactly thinking she *did*, but alive with the hope of her conversion.

Over the years I've learned that there are dealers and dealers. There are those who frighten you to death with their façade of knowledge and their stock. Then there's the one who follows behind you as you view the exhibition, making sage comments about the work or trying to help you see in it what he or she sees in it. Some have a ghastly habit of telling you who else has had the good sense to secure one of this artist's work, and if you don't get one, you're an idiot, because so-and-so —who obviously knows more than you do (or has more money)— bought *two* the day the show opened.

The dealers who pay you compliments on your taste are pleasant, to be sure, but a little embarrassing because you are suddenly left with the feeling that if you don't buy something from them, you have no taste at all.

There was one great dealer who had me completely buffaloed. I was scared to death of him, because I'm very forward about asking prices of things. With his answer he always gave me a look that seemed to say: "What the hell are you asking for? *You* couldn't possibly afford it." And most of the time he was right.

One I knew seemed to hate to sell anything, and I often discovered the best piece in his show was sold—to him. This always infuriates me. Why does he show it if he wants to keep it? And I'm like everybody else. I always want what's already been sold . . . it's so safe and so economical.

The dealer who drives me into a state of drooling idiocy is the one who slowly, with the timing of a master torturer, brings one treasure after another before my starving eyes. He happens to be the smartest one, however, because at the end of an hour I'm a complete pulp, lying on the floor screaming for him to send them *all* to me and to send me the bill!

Most of all, I enjoy the one with a chip on both shoulders. He stands in the middle of his gallery with a prophetic look of annoyance at your trespassing. He knows if he is showing a new artist's work that the press will be great, that all the pictures will be sold, and that you will not be among those advanced viewers who will have the sense to know what *he* does. He hates the customers for many reasons, but mainly because he's a customer, and just because he has money doesn't mean he knows a thing about art—or what he likes—or what he should have.

The kindly, friendly, fatherly dealer gets nowhere with me at all. I always end up feeling I'm too young to own pictures and that I should put in another fifteen years of intense study before I even dare to enter his establishment.

All foreign-born dealers are worth their weight in theatre tickets. The majority have titles, like "Doctor," and know more about every period of art than all the art historians put together. Their knowledge of the obscure is encyclopedic, and they can dismiss, with a volume of derision, your favorite work of art. If you have the temerity to express an opinion or to disagree (God forbid), your name is mud—even if it happens to be on the bottom of a check, paying him for something.

In foreign lands the dealers have the perfect solution to the whole problem. They're never in. My wife and I once lost three precious days in Paris, because we saw in a window an African carving we had been looking for for years. Three persistent days of inquiry ended up with the news that it was August, and of course they were closed for the month. Oh, the French! How wonderful is their contempt for money when year after year, at the height of the tourist season, they go off on their bicycles to the South of France!

Don't get me wrong. I couldn't live without dealers . . . but their eccentricities would make a book in itself—and has, in the case of Lord Duveen. And I was to know, firsthand, the cause of these peculiarities when I became a dealer for a short time, some years later. It's the customer, not the dealer, who's really odd! Having been both, I'd better write that book about myself . . . which I'm doing.

For the most part, the galleries have always been wonderful to me. Mr. Carrington and Mr. Collins at Knoedler's were as instructive by their generous interest in my art phobia when I was at Yale as any teacher I ever had. Antoinette Kraushaar and Frank Rehn had opened their stock for my inspection, suspecting, I guess, that whatever stock I ever bought would be more likely to come from them than Wall

Street. But still, they did this when I was a student, with no likelihood of being a collector. They did it because they wanted to share their love of what they dealt in with anyone whose interest was genuine.

But some of the galleries were not so easy to get at, and those were the ones to be assaulted now, in my new position as a "hit" actor. Miss Hayes got as big a kick out of her position as they did, and she included me in the wonderful adventure of seeing the best in the best places. We would play games of what we would like to own, after a day's tour of the galleries, and George Macready (playing my brother, Prince Ernest, in *Victoria*) and I took over that game when, one day, Miss Hayes succumbed to a lovely little Renoir of a girl in a white lace hat.

It was rumored she had paid twenty-five thousand dollars for it, though whether she did or not, I never had the gall to verify. It was a hefty figure for those days, but cheap on today's mad market. George and I were impressed with the power of twenty-five grand and hypothetically took the same amount into Fifty-seventh Street to see what we could buy or what we *would* buy, had we had it.

We played the game very seriously and, using our fame as the Victorian Brothers, hounded every dealer on the street and even several of those elegant ones who didn't need Fifty-seventh Street as an address.

The results were not only a great "collection," but by today's values over a quarter of a million dollars worth of art. For the twenty-five thousand we *didn't* have, we "bought" two great Modigliani oils, a Cézanne water color, a Van Gogh drawing, two enormous and brilliant Soutines, three Picassos, and a Seurat sketch for "The Grand Jatte." Apparently, one of the ways to be a great collector is to be rich at the right time.

Not long after we opened and it was evident that this was the greatest triumph in Miss Hayes' long career, she was toying with the idea of having some painter immortalize her as the young queen. In vogue at that moment was Dietz Edzard. Helen asked me to see an exhibition of his with her, and told me of her desire. We went through the four rooms, filled with his button-eyed ladies in frilly hats and frilly dresses under frilly parasols, and on the way out Miss Hayes thanked Mr. Edzard and the dealer, then turned to me and allowed as how there was no need to have him do her, or Victoria, as he already had—a hundred times.

It was great fun being with her, even if I didn't have the money to buy what I wanted. At least I could have the pleasure of trying to sell someone else (who had) on the idea of owning a good painting. While selling them the idea of buying Soutine or Modigliani was hardly being avant-garde in 1936, still the diehards resisted some of the greatest modern painters. However, I did succeed in convincing one person to go out of her way to see something, if not new, at least new to her.

I am one of that group of people who, on seeing Beatrice Lillie's name on a billboard, begins to chuckle. There is a wickedness to this lady's wit that absolutely kills me. One evening Miss Hayes asked me to Miss Lillie's apartment. I chortled all the way over in the cab, delighted with the prospect of actually meeting my comedic heroine. And I was not let down. She *was* a delight, on or off the stage. Her apartment was conventionally luxurious and warm, but the art she saw as belonging to her was the most incongruous thing I'd ever seen, for I had a theory: a person's taste in art reflected them (or at least some facet of them), or it should.

Her pictures were heavy, British, and dull. Perhaps they did reflect Lady Peel, a side I'd overlooked, or a Beatrice Lillie never seen by the public—and that I was part of that public, I had to admit. But shouldn't there be something light or wicked or gay? I'd have even settled for a "laugh, clown, laugh" type painting, with which so many comedians surround themselves.

The evening was a plodding delight . . . plodding because I was determined to find something hysterical in every word she said, and when I left, laughing and scratching, I felt like an idiot because really she hadn't been that funny. So I decided to walk home. It was a long walk, but if you don't like walking anywhere else in the world, you have to like walking in New York. The route home led me down Fifty-seventh Street (as any route did), and I found myself still upset that Miss Lillie was so humorless in her picture possessions. Before I knew it, I had appointed myself a committee of one to remedy this condition.

It stayed in the back of my mind for months, and I knew it was a tough job since humorous pictures are hard to find. Funny ones are a dime a dozen, mostly relegated to greeting-card art, but real humor . . . who had it? Brueghel? . . . Longhi? . . . Picasso? Very few. There is joy in many paintings, even by the greatest, but downright humor is rare.

Then one day I saw it. In a gallery window sat the most charming Modigliani in the whole world. It was a little blond boy, pudgy and arch, with blue eyes which gave you the feeling that you were looking straight through his empty, fat head to the sky on the other side. I found myself laughing out loud, standing in the street. Since someone might come upon this scene and think me a little idiotic, I walked on, trying to pull myself together. At the corner I suddenly clapped my hands a loud whack as the idea in the back of my mind and what I had just seen merged like a clap of thunder. This picture belonged to Beatrice Lillie. It was a wicked comment on youth, the kind of comment she might make on a particularly repulsive little English boy.

I called her and told her about it and begged her to at least go see it. It made me laugh, and I wanted to share that laugh with her. She promised and she kept her promise—and she bought it. She got a good buy, but actually I think she bought it because she had to admit it was amusing, but not because she really liked it. This proved to be the case. Several years later (ten, to be exact) we met when she visited a movie set where I was working. I had almost forgotten the Modigliani, but she came over to say hello and reminded me of the incident. She thanked me and said, "Dear me, it's worth a lot of money now, isn't it?" I allowed as how it was and that it hadn't even begun to hit its top. Miss Lillie listened to my predictions of the future art boom and said, pertly, "Well, that may be, dear—but I still don't like it."

Another ten years have passed now, and a friend, returning from London, told me that backstage of *Auntie Mame*, Miss Lillie's dressing room is the talk of the town. It is completely decorated to surround a certain painting which hangs, spotlit, at the end of her room, like the star it is. . . . Modigliani's Little Blond Boy and Beatrice Lillie share equal billing—backstage, at least.

But if French art was slowly being accepted in 1936, American art was rapidly being rejected. The innate snobbery of our art-buying public—always looking to Europe for a cultural rub-off—was closing eyes not only to what was going on contemporarily, but the interesting schools of American art of the immediate past were being neglected, too. The Ash-Can Group—the Eight, representing fine painters like John Sloan, George Bellows, Ernest Lawson, George Luks, and Maurice Prendergast, were having a tough time retaining the public interest, and their prices were either remaining status quo or dropping.

Only one school of art, if you can call it a school, was having momentary success: the Social Scene Painters. William Gropper, Philip Evergood, Tschabatzov, Burliuk, and a few others were making their comment on the birth and growth of fascism. It was the time of the W.P.A., and the Spanish Civil War was in full swing. Every young artist worth his salt took a serious interest in what turned out to be World War II.

I bought a Gropper oil called "The Defenders." It was a powerful picture with the social wallop of a Daumier or Goya. Unfortunately, none of the aforementioned American painters ever reached the master stature of those two greats—not as far as craft was concerned.

Most of them have fallen into neglect today, but I, for one, believe that someday, when we're ready as a nation to look at those grim times in their proper light, some of these men will come up for reevaluation—if not as great painters, then as great commentators and strong draftsmen.

My own collection, small as it was, was going off in every direction at once. I bought a beautiful Vlaminck flower piece. It cost me $400, and I was very proud of it. I showed it to my sister once, who studied it with great care, having come a cropper several times before with me on the subject of modern art. Finally, she shook her head and said, "Oh, how I'd love to loosen that arrangement. The man knows nothing about arranging flowers." She was pretty near right. That tight style Vlaminck had set his hand to later became a stencil of stultified dullness. From the brilliant pictures of his Fauve period, he took to the mud and dirty snow, which has become his signature and—now that he's dead—his fortune.

The Vlaminck hung next to the Gropper, and to this incongruity I added the beautiful self-portrait of Alphonse Legros in sepia crayon. It has the delicate nobility of a Leonardo, and even though he is practically unknown today, I still worship this drawing. Then there was a George Bellows crayon of "Girls by a Lake," a few etchings by Goya— and, as if I felt I had to justify my belief in Modigliani to Miss Lillie, I acquired a pencil sketch of Adam, by my favorite. It has another humor . . . different than Miss Lillie's Modigliani . . . more naïve but absolutely charming. The father of us all stands naked in the Garden, with birds and dogs and nature all around him. Everything is as it should be in Eden, but Adam sports a lush mustache and a gallant little Vandyke beard.

For the young collector there is nothing better than the graphic arts. Etchings, lithographs, and drawings can be had comparatively cheap, and often their quality and their message is finer than the so-called more important works. Those marvelous Daumier cartoon lithographs were very cheap—two and three dollars—and a Goya "Capricho" could be had for twenty-five. Even the Modigliani drawing of Adam was under a hundred. The great posters of Toulouse-Lautrec had not yet found their place on the wall of every American home and were to be had for ridiculous prices. One rare one I got was originally the cover of Clemenceau's book, *Au Pied du Sinaï*. It cost forty-five dollars then, but one sold recently for seven hundred and fifty dollars, and another, of the café singer, Lender, has gone up to fourteen hundred dollars.

The type of American painting most popular at the time was exemplified by Alexander Brook and Eugene Speicher. For Christmas,

Miss Hayes gave me a small landscape by Brook, and though I hate to admit it, a few years later I traded it in for something else . . . more permanent. I wanted something first-rate by which to remember such a first-rate person. Anyway, it hadn't been her choice, really, since I had admired it on one of our gallery tours, so I felt no regret about the trade and have, as my remembrance of this great lady of the theatre, Lautrec's theatrically lit lithograph of May Belfort, holding her little black cat.

There were many American artists whose work I liked and wish I could have acquired. Foremost among them was Franklin Watkins, a fine and imaginative poet in paint. I wonder what's happened to others, like Mervin Jules—and I regret never having made myself buy a Kuniyoshi. What real dignity and charm that man had. Joe Jones gave real promise, and Arnold Blanch and Doris Lee could always be counted on to be a hit with the public. I later bought Miss Lee's funny, sexy "Noon"—two lovers in a haystack—but, unfortunately, it left me one time when I had a desperate need for cash.

Every exhibitor had a brace of modern masterpieces that were reasonably priced, and many of them which Miss Hayes and I saw on our tours are now the treasures of the great museums. One day, at Valentine Dudensing's, we joined Margaret Sullavan to look for the first time at a new shipment of Picassos. The *pièce de* was the famous woman looking at herself in a mirror, now in the Museum of Modern Art.

It was a shocker, and still is—though we're all so used to it we've forgotten how startling the first look seemed. Helen and I were a little prepared for it, having been around so much, but Miss Sullavan took it big—almost as a personal affront. She was pregnant at the time and really reeled back in horror at this daring composition. She collected herself finally and half jokingly remarked that she hoped it wouldn't mark her child. She's Irish, you know. . . . I never knew the outcome, but she had a baby girl some weeks later, and I've always had an enormous curiosity to see that child.

After *Victoria Regina* closed, apparently the gods thought I'd had enough success for a while, and so I dove into a period of trying to prove myself a lasting actor. I did everything that came along, from stock to soap operas. It was an impoverished period, but what money I did make continued to go into collecting and the study of art. Just before we closed, Miss Hayes had advised me to turn down a million-dollar movie contract. She had hated the movies, for all her success in them, and couldn't bear to think of anyone she liked being a part of them. Besides, she felt that I should learn my business where an actor should . . . on the stage.

It was hard advice to take, but at this distance of twenty-odd years, I guess she was right on all scores. What kind of collector (or actor) I would have become with a million bucks is hard to imagine now, but I like to think I would have been as interested a one as some difficult years, financially and professionally, have made me. Perhaps the million would have made it too easy, because gathering things the way I have, when and if I could afford them, has forced me to know what I'm buying . . . that I'm not just buying anything I like . . . and I never could afford to buy what other people said I should like.

I had many adventures, meeting painters, but one of the most hysterical happened while I was sweating out a flop in New York, a year or so later.

To the million crazy things actors are asked to do, the good people who run charities have contributed more than their share. The Kosciusko Foundation gave a ball at the Waldorf-Astoria in the winter of 1938 and asked me to play George Washington in a pageant of the life of the great Polish-American and friend of our first President. They sent a make-up man to the theatre, where I was transformed from the Hungarian butler I was playing to the Father of Our Country. The make-up and costume turned out classically George Washington, and I was off for the Waldorf in a taxi, a little self-conscious in my tricorn hat and white wig.

It isn't easy to sneak into a large hotel lobby, dressed as George

Washington, without attracting a little attention . . . even in New York . . . but I made it quickly to the elevator, only to be curtly refused admission or elevation. The operator insisted I use the service elevator, on the grounds that I was an entertainer. After a limp insistence that I was indeed the Father of My Country—and a well-known actor on a mission of charity, to boot—I gave up and took the service elevator to the ballroom on high, where the pageanteers were impatiently awaiting me, ready to march to Valley Forge, forthwith.

Across the whole end of the room was a very impressive mural on paper of one of Kosciusko's exploits, done by the winner of the Foundation's art award. I met the fellow and was amazed to learn he was only eighteen years old. His name was Bernard Perlin. During the next few weeks we became good friends, and I found out that his prize for the mural was a trip to Poland to study. Also, it came to light that he was just able to live in New York until he would leave for Poland (and very frugally, at that), so I proposed he do some tiny murals in my tiny bathroom in my tiny one-room apartment for a tiny fee, which proved a help to him.

I was gone a great deal of the time while they were being done, but Perlin had a key, and occasionally I would come in and find him standing in the bathtub, my Siamese cat curled around his feet, painting away on his mural of Adam and Eve, a subject we decided was appropriate for a bathroom—why, I don't know.

When I got married, I outgrew the apartment, and of course the murals, having been painted directly on the wall, had to be left behind. Perlin went on to become one of the top artist-correspondents for *Life* magazine in World War II. He turned in a brilliant series on the war in Greece and was decorated by the Greek government for his front-line report of their heroic struggle. Since then he has become one of our leading magic realists, and his work was chosen to represent that facet of American art at the 1958 Brussels World's Fair.

I never knew what happened to the murals until I met Imogene Coca, years later, who had rented the apartment after I vacated it. She and her husband, in an attempt to renovate its shabbiness, had had them neatly painted out. And thus was lost an "early work," if not a "masterpiece," by Bernard Perlin.

There were exciting discoveries to be made those years. Marsden Hartley was still living, and while he had a fine reputation in his lifetime as one of the top American moderns, the emphasis on French art was so great that there were still many of his finest canvases for sale. I'm grateful now, as I look at these virile Maine seascapes and fishermen (almost all of which are now securely in the best museum collections), to have had the chance, through Hudson Walker's Gallery, of seeing them, all together. I never bought a Hartley. Either I didn't have enough sense or, more probably, enough money. . . . I wish I'd had one or the other or, preferably, *both*.

Somewhere else I've talked about looking at pictures with the possibility of adding them to a collection. It's not a bad idea to play this game with yourself, even if you're not a collector. I do it with pictures, or things I know I can't possibly afford. It gives you a very personal approach to the object, and you know for sure, when you come out of the one-sided argument, whether that work represents your taste.

I once had a funny and strange experience with this game. There was a gallery in New York that handled the output of the three great Mexican artists, Orozco, Rivera, and Tamayo. Tamayo was still a young man, and the gallery sold him for very little. His style wasn't completely formed yet, but you could see the intensity and humor that were to make him great. Rivera was still a master, and only here and there could you begin to see the signs of his later degeneration into an almost completely decorative artist.

The great man was, and is, Orozco. It's just possible that he ranks with the great muralists of all time. Savage and political as they are, his murals carry a wallop like Michelangelo's wallop. There's nothing serene here. The walls burst with declamatory violence. In Guadalajara, where the major part of his work exists, you can enter into a contemporary experience in art, second to none in the Americas today. The great murals have been there many years, now, but the public reaction to them is still alive. It's like a story out of the Renaissance.

Argument still goes on about them, and violently. The ones in the city hall still come in for abuse, verbally and physically. There are many places on them which need repair where the public has defaced them out of political outrage, and the present city government does nothing about it.

These murals are as alive and as much a part of the life of the community as Orozco intended them to be. They haven't yet fallen into the language of the land like older, controversial works of art. It's exciting to be so near one of the reasons of art—the instructive, educational reason.

And the greatest murals of our time are those in the orphanage in the same city. What majesty of concept, and what perfect use of architectural space. I would like to be around when the controversy has calmed down and Orozco takes on the aura of "Age and Acceptance" —when the criticism has turned to praise, as it always does eventually in the arts, especially if the one criticized has spoken with historical purpose.

But back to *my* experience with Orozco. . . . There was an enormous canvas of Zapata in this gallery, seven feet high by five wide. It was a magnificent oil, much in the technique of the murals and with all the power. The "Zapata" stands in a cave entrance, daylight behind him, and the people (represented by three tortuous figures) beg him for deliverance. The blues, browns, and reds are superb, and it speaks eloquently for the freedom of the Mexican people. It moved me very much, and word had it that Orozco himself considered it his greatest easel painting—which, indeed, it is.

I used to visit that gallery three or four times a month, and to make myself welcome I bought presents of silver and Mexican folk art, and I even furnished my one-room apartment with some rustic Mexican chairs, all for sale at the same place. Alma Reed, who ran the gallery, knew from endless conversations and gulps of praise, that I adored this canvas, and so I suppose she assumed that I would like to own it. Anyway, one day she asked me if I would make her an offer on it. My heart sank. What the hell would I do with a seven-by-five-foot canvas in a one-room apartment? Besides, I had reason to believe the picture cost around five thousand dollars which, since I was working in the newly founded Mercury Theatre with Orson Welles for a hot one hundred and twenty-five a week, I didn't have.

My original point—that if you look at a picture long enough, you know whether you would like to own it or not—was pointing right at me. So I told Mrs. Reed that all I could muster was seven hundred and fifty dollars, and much to my horror she said "Sold."

The transfer was made. For my seven hundred and fifty dollars I was delivered what seemed to me then, the largest painting since Tintoretto's "Last Judgment." But there was one wall in my one-room basement apartment on Fifty-third Street near Sixth Avenue that would just hold it, and there a carpenter and I managed, with toggle bolts and screws, to get it to hang.

Orozco, being a mural painter, always foreshortened his figures somewhat, to be seen from below. Since the walls of my place were about seven foot six, there was no way of hanging the picture except from floor to ceiling. The best view of it was from a lying position on the kitchenette floor some twelve feet away, and there one day, to my amazement, I found six ardent Orozco fans whom Mrs. Reed had told about my purchase, standing in line to lie on the floor for a proper view.

The end of this tale and the moral: I learned to see Orozco, all right, but I soon realized that unless you have the space for a picture of this size and excitement, you shouldn't own it. When I went off to summer stock that year, I lent it to the Museum of Modern Art, who, in turn, lent it to the Chicago Art Institute, to whom I finally sold it. It looks wonderful there, and it should belong to the public. Orozco was a public painter.

I missed lots of opportunities as a collector, either from lack of funds, guts, or taste, but I don't think I missed many as far as my art education went. I have never had the slightest qualm about pricing anything. Why should I? The dealer doesn't know but what I may be an eccentric millionaire's eccentric son who's an actor for laughs. And so I rode right in, even to Wildenstein's, and without batting an eye took those banker's figures their super-stock brings. It's a wonderful way to find out what's in demand and what the world's taste is up to, year by year; for in the art world, money means any one of three things—popularity, quality, or rarity. Of course, the highest prices are asked for those masterpieces which are all three, plus being unobtainable, fashionable, and great!

If I could offer any advice to a would-be collector, it's to learn prices. In this way you can never go broke and never be taken. You will always be in the happy state of knowing what you can afford and, even more, what you can afford to like.

The vogue of primitive art was late hitting America. For one thing, it smacked of the sea-captain days, not too far back in our culture—the day of the "curiosity," brought back from strange lands. And for another, while it could be beautifully camouflaged in a Victorian interior, the decorations of the twenties and thirties were not about to introduce something so ugly and inexpensive into their cautious creations . . . à la Lady Mendl.

The Europeans, on the other hand, had long appreciated the originality of the creative primitives, and the great moderns, like Modigliani, Picasso, and Braque, quite frankly, were very much influenced by them.

In New York at this time (1935–42) there were few galleries that showed much of it, and you had to be very "advanced" to dig it at all. But fortunately, I had read enough and knew enough advanced people to want to advance into that field myself. With the help of those few dealers and the Museum of Natural History, I was able to get a start at learning its appeal. I've collected it and studied it for many years now, and have come to some conclusions as to why it has come to play such an influential part in our lives and the lives and work of our artists.

If the appeal of so-called primitive art needs any explanation, this might do: in our hectic, complicated living we yearn, not too secretly, for the simple life. We see in a people devoted to the simplest kind of life—seeking food for the day and living in a traditionally dictated pattern of religion—the kind of life that would cure the ulcer and relieve the headache. So in their art, which somehow gets done within these stern dictates, we see a genuinely creative release.

Then there is something in the fascination of the abandoned image of worship. Most primitive cultures, carving in wood or modeling in clay, make new idols and masks for each season, each festival, the old ones having served their purpose and having been turned over to the natural decaying processes of the jungle or desert, to the termites and the tempests. Thus, when one of these idols is snatched from oblivion, it somehow represents a moment of worship, brought to a standstill for us to wonder at.

When I say "so-called" primitive art, I mean the confusion in our minds about the word *primitive*. We think of it as meaning "untrained," "simple," etc. Well, most true primitive art is anything but untrained, and far from simple. Anthropologists define primitive art as the art of peoples without a written language, but their art is, in a sense, their language—hence the definition is invalid. And it is almost always rigidly disciplined and rigorously appreciated. The artists of the South Seas, Africa, the American Indian, all held the high regard of their society. They were revered for their talent, much in the same way as we regard the priest as an interpreter—an envisioner of deity. They alone could make visual the unseen thoughts about their gods. What their people dreamed of their deities, they brought to conscious recognition.

Understanding the appeal of primitive art has a great deal to do with understanding modern art, cubist art, abstract art. It was the "discovery" of this art of simple people that helped bring about the modern Renaissance, just as the rediscovery of the art of Greece and Rome was a primal cause of the Italian Renaissance in the fourteenth or fifteenth century. All contemporary art stems from it, or from our scientific discoveries—either directly or indirectly. This desire to return to the simplicity of life . . . to the original vision, as it were . . . and to explore the heart of nature, even to the atom, has perpetrated the creative urge of our time.

If we take the progression of modern painters and see their preoccupation with the primitive, we'll see how, having absorbed it into their work, it was passed on into the work of others until now, it is part of the living language of art that speaks to anyone who'll listen.

It was during one of those frantic summer layoffs when actors charge into summer stock to pick up a few bucks and a lot of experience that I made the acquaintance of primitive American art. Skowhegan, Maine, has one of the oldest stock companies, and I was pleased to be asked to be their leading man for a few weeks. In the rare intervals between rehearsals I couldn't wait to snoop in the antique shops which, twenty years ago, still had antiques and not the junk they have now, which all looks like something that should be confined to a church bazaar.

Willard Cummings, whose family had one of the best collections of Early Americana and who lived in Skowhegan, was a budding young portrait painter and a rabid enthusiast of the primitives. So I had a good guide into that fascinating world and we went on many happy hunts together.

My first find was a board I saw nailed on a barn to cover a leak. Rubbing a wet finger over the dusty surface, I revealed a hand, then rings on the fingers, and a turquoise bracelet on the lace-cuffed wrist. This detached extremity was holding a large red rose, around which stylized butterflies hovered, waiting to come in for a sniff.

I learned from Bill, whose excitement was as keen as mine at my find, that it was a sampler which the early painters used to show their prospective sitters what could be done with and for them. They would do the head and clothes, then inquire which type of hand they would like, showing them several of these samplers. It's unfortunate that in some cases they didn't do it with the heads. Some of our forebears were pretty grim-looking customers, and an idealized head or two might have come in mighty handy.

Edith Halpert of the famous Downtown Gallery has done an enormous job of putting this early material into its proper area of importance. She has discovered artists, forgotten for many years, and has given the world an appreciation of the real talents and charm of these neglected men. The weather vane and ship figure have fallen into place as examples of our first sculpture. Anyone who has missed the naïve charm and great power of this period should take a look and share the rightful pride we now have in our early native craftsmen. To Edith Halpert and to Mrs. Watson Webb and the great du Pont collection at Winterthur we will forever be indebted for our knowledge of American arts which, but for them, could have disappeared in the destruction of neglect.

Bill Cummings did a portrait of me that summer that still amuses me, for it is much more what *I* thought I looked like than what *he* thought I looked like. It is the actor, par excellence . . . all ham and a yard wide. But nothing could part me from it, even though it's a person I hope I never meet again.

I made my first pass at Hollywood the summer of 1938 and was cast as Constance Bennett's leading man in a small turkey called *Service De Luxe*. The only reward I had from this venture was an expensive wardrobe which took me the rest of the year to pay for and which immediately went out of style, leaving me with a full-dress that looked as though it had football pads in the shoulders.

So it was back to New York and a long run with Laurette Taylor and Florence Reed in the all-star revival of *Outward Bound*. I may have been learning my trade as an actor, but none of these ventures were teaching me how to make up for that lost million-dollar contract. Knowing Miss Taylor and Miss Reed almost made up for it, for truly two greater talents never faced a footlight. And then, being in New York again, even if on dietetic wages, I was free to study and to revel in that endless stockpile of art, about which only New York can boast: the Museum of the American Indian, the largest and finest collection of one culture in the world; the Hispanic Society of America; the Morgan Library; the private collections I still had access to, and the ever bulging galleries.

Even if you're out of work, New York is a wonderful place . . .

although, just as you get to know it, street by street they tear it down, rip it up, and throw it away. Then they replace it—sometimes for the better, sometimes for the worse—but it is always fascinating! Occasionally, a whole section will move or, as in one case, a whole trade. My deepest regret is the dying out of Fifty-seventh Street as the "Avenue of Art."

What fun it was to go from gallery to gallery in those four blocks between Fifth Avenue and Third Avenue. But now, to see all of the exhibitions, you have to cover what's left of Fifty-seventh Street, tramp up Madison Avenue, then off on the side streets for miles. Art has added a new dimension: exercise.

One place in New York which will stubbornly stay put is the Metropolitan Museum. The façade neither deteriorates nor gets finished. The floor in the entrance hall cracks a little more each year, and that flight of stairs gets longer and steeper. But the Met's the Met, and it is curiously a complete reflection of the city itself. They are always tearing it up and rerouting you through it. Your favorite object can disappear for years behind a wooden wall, and your favorite painting travels like a salesman. But the adventure is always there . . . those ecstatic masterpieces . . . and the building . . . as ugly as a bank vault . . . and as useful.

Although I've been a museum-goer since I was a little boy in St. Louis (and, as you've gathered, I didn't miss many of them in Europe), still it was in the Met that I really learned to use a museum. I learned that they are not just to visit but to *use*—to live in, almost. If your feet can take it, any museum can become a whole world.

At one time, I was to play in *The Duchess of Malfi* with Orson Welles . . . a strange play, wherein the characters are difficult to pin down. The play is Renaissance throughout in feeling, and the men are Renaissance characters, par excellence. Where to look into the face of the Renaissance . . . to see for myself the hauteur, the elegance that supported these egos in a time of so many highly competitive personalities? Well, it was in the Met that I discovered the character of the character I was to play. Coming up those endless stairs one day,

I met the fellow, face to face, in that elaborately simple and intriguingly magnificent portrait of a de' Medici prince by Bronzino. What a thrill of recognition! Like discovering the secret of a great performer, which can never be fully explained but which, being in on even partially, you can't resist trying to reason out . . . performance after performance.

There are so many worlds to visit in a museum . . . the world of each artist, which he has reported with such love, such care and often, such humor or irony. It is a chance to let someone else see for you—a chance to live in someone else's world in some other time. Everything we know of the past, we know through the mind of man, expressing himself in art. In a museum you can see, and actually be alive in, the Venice of the eighteenth century with Guardi, Canaletto, or Longhi. You can be behind the scenes at the ballet with Degas or live with Daumier the political turmoil of his disturbed nineteenth-century industrial revolution.

Goya can give you a clearer, deeper picture of eighteenth-century Spain than you could ever get visiting there. Or if you want to know the Spain of a century before Goya, it's pictured for you, with the greatest virtuosity, by Velázquez.

You can even enter the highest realms of the spirit through the visionary eyes of El Greco, Fra Angelico, or William Blake, or wander through the whole mysterious scenery of a dream, vividly awake in the prisons of Piranesi. You can travel from heaven to hell on the jet stream of Hieronymus Bosch's brilliant imagination; or witness the Crucifixion, the fall of Icarus, as they would have happened in the time of Brueghel.

I used to think Utrillo was playing Paris for all it was worth, almost to the point where his pictures became the American idea of Paris. But a few years ago my wife and I arrived in that dream city, and as usual I was so excited I couldn't sleep. So I left Mary a note and took a cab all around the city at 5 A.M. It was all Utrillo. The mottled walls, the whites, the grays, the peeking vistas of familiar buildings and parks around the crooked streets, the signs, and even the large, broad beams of the French women, going to work—all of it was Utrillo, as surely as all French children are Renoir.

Painters take places and things unto themselves and make them their own by loving them so much they see not only as nature is, but as man incorporates his ideas into nature. Arles is Van Gogh; Aix, Cézanne . . . and, in a rarer case, St. Francis is Giotto. We, as audiences, can love the scene or the saint through their eyes. Today, letting the great photographers—Cartier-Bresson, Weston, Elisofon, Steichen—be our actual eyes, we can look for the painter to portray the mood of our age, the philosophy; for he, too, is content to let the photographer tackle reality.

The Met is one of the most complete museums in the world for the student or even for the person who wants only to see the famous masterpieces. Heaven knows, they have enough of them. . . . Every once in a while, I like to "do" the Met completely, pretend I've never been there before, and follow the arrow around the history of art. I start with the Egyptian, Assyrian, and all the early cultures, then move into Greece and Rome, up to the Byzantine and Gothic into the Renaissance. Then I have lunch.

With my belly full of museum cafeteria food that is meant to do no more than fill it, I start with the late Renaissance, amble into the modern, and finally into the art of our time. The latter used to be difficult to find at the Met, and one had to supplement the historical by going to the Museum of Modern Art or the Whitney, on Eighth Street, for American art. But the new Contemporary Wing at the Met is really superb and enormously vital . . . a perfect exclamation to the history of man . . . so far.

Then, sometimes, I look only at the forms, and I never fail to be amazed how continuing they are throughout history. They really only change as civilizations change their tastes. The early Greek goes right into the Gothic, and the Hellenistic straight into the Renaissance. Early Greek . . . Gothic . . . modern. Hellenistic . . . Renaissance . . . romantic.

Another time, I just look at color. Of course, you can't do this with sculpture, but in the painting galleries, it's great fun to move swiftly and see how vivid the color was in opulent periods, how somber in times of stress and change. At least it seems so to me . . . the clarity and purity of the color in a Veronese and the somber brilliance in a Daumier.

Sometimes I go through merely inquiring into the personalities of the subjects: see how seriously some of them took themselves, while others saw life as a wild experience of joy. Look at a Roman portrait sculpture, and then at a Frans Hals or, in the same country, an Ostade, full of joy and humor; then contrast the serious merchant princes of the early Rembrandt and the static, enigmatic faces of Egypt. Yet within the disciplined severity of their line, drawing, and carving, what a wide variety of expression—how vividly some personalities come across, depending on the artist's talent.

One of the great tangles that hurts the pleasure of going through most museums has recently been unraveled by the Met. Many of its collections—the Bache, the Altman, etc.—were given with the stipulation that they be hung as a *collection* and not put into random order as they should be, according to periods. The deed of gift specifies this, and it is often impossible to get around, but the Met has solved this wonderfully by joining the great collections in a labyrinth of rooms and halls, so that somehow you can go from period to period, from Altman, seventeenth century, to Bache, seventeenth century; from Altman, sixteenth century, to Friedsam, sixteenth century.

The Havemeyer collection, which possibly enriched the Met more than any gift it has ever received, fortunately was allowed to be scattered into proper places, and, strangely enough, in this way it's much more of a tribute to the Havemeyers—for, nine chances out of ten, a masterpiece in almost any period in any room will be one of their gifts.

I think my favorite museum, however, is the Frick Collection. The Met is so vast that, even for a hungry art lover like myself, it's a pretty big meal. But the Frick is just right . . . not too many pictures and almost all of the highest quality. Its greatest invitation is extended through four of the most wonderful paintings in the world: two Rembrandts, a Titian, and a Bellini. To me, the most beautiful male portrait I have ever seen is the Titian in the Frick. It is all romance, all Renaissance, all man. I don't suppose we'll ever know who he was. I don't really care. I like to think that perhaps Titian saw him walking in the square and was so struck by his manliness, his clothes, by the romance of this creature, he broke through the crowds of ladies who must have surrounded him and dragged him off to his studio to sit for him.

The Frick Rembrandt self-portrait is, of all his self-portraits, a true monument to his honesty. No painter saw himself more profoundly, nor in so many moods. In this, he reached his peak, and a monument it is. Beyond just being a picture, it has the solidity of the Pyramids, the anguishing beauty of the Parthenon. Rembrandt looks beyond himself in this picture to the very secret of life . . . to the reason of man . . . to his soul.

My young son Barrett, coming to New York for the first time at the age of sixteen, without the usual parental nudge was more profoundly moved by this Rembrandt than anything he saw—and my feet will attest that he saw everything. I was impressed by this, for if a boy, not too given to art, could see in that great face something that touched his almost untouched emotions, I knew that Rembrandt's reputation was founded on rock and was not like many painters whose fame rests on their sphere of influence, their output, or their appeal to sentiment.

Another of his paintings there used to have the most romantic title in the world: "Death on a Pale Horse." I don't know who dreamed that up, but it was a great idea. Before a ruined castle in a landscape of rich gloom, a noble young man, arrogant and aware of his beauty, rides a proud horse the color of pearls. Why not Death, leading us to the end of our days, to herd us into oblivion? Well, they've changed the title now to "The Polish Rider." Those clinical art historians, I'm sure, couldn't support this wonderful frivolity where the master was concerned. What a pity—but it couldn't matter less. Just look at it and think what you like. To me, it will always be "Death on a Pale Horse."

I've said a dozen times a dozen ways that one of art's greatest joys is that it allows you to see through another's eyes, his mind, his heart. But it isn't often that the genius of two men is blended so that the one can tell the story of the other with such distinction that the report is comparable to the act. When it occurs, art reaches new heights. Bellini has done it twice for me: once in his "Agony in the Garden" and in the Frick's "St. Francis in Ecstasy." Sometimes you read a passage by a great writer, and you know what he says and how he says it will always be, for you, the only possible way it could be. Less often a painter will describe an event in a way that fits into your interpretation of that event so perfectly that it becomes the event itself. This is how it was, and where it was, when St. Francis had his triumphant ecstasy. Perhaps it's only for me, but then, that is another joy of art . . . it is always personal. No one can ever take from you your identification with a work of art.

I'm sure it must sound as if I spent my entire life in museums. I often think I have. I love them. To me, they are fun . . . the kind of fun I like . . . stimulating, provocative, intriguing. But they mostly house the art of the past, and that's only half of art. The other half is equally as much fun, and that is seeing the art of the present and getting to know the artists.

But I was most concerned those years with trying to clinch a position in the theatre, and I took on every possible assignment to round myself out in an art that I had already learned could not be one-sided. It is many-faceted, this job of being an entertainer, and I discovered one facet that has kept me active and excited for twenty years: the lecture platform.

If you ever want to find out what you know on any subject, accept any offer that comes along to speak out publicly on it. I had received much publicity about my art interest and was asked to speak about it in colleges around New York. I took on all comers—first, because it demanded that I sum up my knowledge by looking back at it and looking forward in it; and secondly, I wanted to learn how to impart to others the excitement I had from the arts in general. I didn't want to be a pedant. I'd heard too many of them, feeding their sedations to eager audiences. I wanted to make the whole adventure of art alive and awake.

I spoke everywhere on everything and have ended up with the satisfaction of being in love with my lecture audiences and hopeful that they love me, too. I try to create in a lecture an exchange of ideas (even though I'm the speaker) by taking subjects, the questions about which I already know, so that I try to come to the audience as an "answerer," not a lecturer . . . as a listener, not a speaker.

Nothing I have ever done has been of more value. Before you dare open your mouth, you have to know what you're talking about. Your wits have to be sharpened before each encounter, to be able to feel from the people out front, as you go along, the questions they will ask you later. You have to be on top of your subject and let yourself be the medium through which you make your revelations. You are the poultice to draw forth the inquiry that must follow if the poultice is to be effecting or effective.

With all the activity I was able to drum up in the theatre, on radio, and as a lecturer, there was still, in the back of my mind, an intense desire to live in the West and to take another crack at the movies. I was not ready for it, or it for me, because somehow one more journey to Hollywood proved just as unsuccessful, and I came back again to do the long and highly successful run of *Angel Street* in New York. I had been shopping for a good villain role, having been so identified with Albert the Good, and other "good" men, and I really hit the heel of heels in the evil Jack Manningham. Judith Evelyn, Leo G. Carroll, and I survived Pearl Harbor (which happened two days after we opened) and ran a long and exciting year on Broadway. Everyone in the theatre put aside his outside life to work for the war effort, and if actors had nothing else to recommend them as human beings, they must accept the crown of humanity for their efforts in behalf of all good causes—and their crowning achievement was their tireless effort for the armed services.

That effort took many forms, the most artistic of which was the

Stage Door Canteen. It was not only artistic, with its beautiful décor of paintings by all the best scenic designers in the theatre, it was enticingly theatrical as well. Never has such a cast been assembled to serve the soldiers soup, sandwiches, and sex.

My favorite night as a bus boy (that was my fun duty at the canteen—working three days a week in the kitchen, making sandwich spreads that should have caused us to lose the war) was about six months after it had opened. My fellow bus boys were Alfred Lunt and Philip Merivale. The GIs knew that everyone there was supposed to be famous, but one of them, inquiring of me who my helpers were, had never heard of them.

Another asked me who those dames pouring the coffee were supposed to be . . . Helen Hayes, Katharine Cornell, and Jane Cowl. . . . Never heard of them. Then, like gangbusters, through the front door came Linda Darnell and Betty Grable. The house broke into a roar! Soup, sandwiches, stage stars . . . who cares! Sex! *Wow!*

I had another movie offer toward the end of the first year of *Angel Street,* and I knew I would have to accept it. I hated to leave a successful play for the insecurity of a movie career, but as I look back on it, I think it was most certainly the desire to be an American and not a New Yorker (or even a Californian) that has always made me eager to get on with the delightful duty of knowing my country; and to this day, I feel that the West, with the least to offer culturally, has the most to offer, American-ly. Everything has been tried or accomplished in the East, and the accomplishments live or die according to how much life is left in the people who are alive to enjoy them. For instance, museums in the East, while housing great treasure and even sometimes well endowed, have a terrible time surviving the apathy of the too-satisfied public, in proportion to the public pride taken in them. I have met Bostonians who are well acquainted with the brilliant achievement of the Fogg Museum in training most of our top art historians and museum directors, and yet have never taken the trouble to go to it or to support it with gifts, membership, or money.

And so it was to California that I was bound to go, not only because I loved the West but because, for all my love of the theatre, I was still a Missouri boy whose original theatrical contact was with Pearl White, Charlie Chaplin, and those other fabled creatures of the "Silver Screen."

I took some of the money I had saved during *Angel Street*, along with several pictures, and did a little fast trading before leaving New York behind me. I managed to trade a Bronzino portrait, plus a little cash, for one of the few real gems of art (which I still own) . . . a small Goya oil on ivory, done in the last year of his life, with the wonderful title: "Old Man Looking for Fleas in His Clothes." It is two inches square and incomparable in its grandeur—its monumentality.

With this and a wonderful water color of a picador by Constantin Guys tucked under my arm, I left New York. I must say, when I unwrapped them on the train, I felt that Fifty-seventh Street was right in my pocket, and I'll always be indebted to Kirk Askew for showing me these treasures and helping me have them.

The trip to the coast with Goya, Guys, and a seven-year contract with 20th Century-Fox was further heightened by the presence of Clare Luce and Charles Chaplin on the train. Somehow we made contact, though they were worlds above me in theatrical rank, and the trip was a delight with my two distinguished confreres getting into polite political disagreements, and Mr. Chaplin, at the drop of a reminiscence, acting out his famous routines in the club car.

As I left them early one evening to catch up on some sleep, a lady at the other end of the club car stopped me and said: "Who's that delightfully funny white-haired man? He's almost as good as Chaplin."

Hello, Hollywood! Good-by, New York!

The Gallery

Y THIS TIME, IF YOU'RE STILL WITH ME ON THIS VISUAL
excursion, you must be saying to yourself, "Where the hell are the
pictures?" So am I.

An art book (which this really isn't) without pictures? And to
have to wait this long to find them? *Really!* . . . Well, when I started
all this, I dreamed of a book lavish with illustrations of every point I
wanted to make and everything I had ever seen. But I've been cured
of that by a lot of pills. The hardest one to swallow was the cost involved, but the bitterest was the realization after looking through my
library that most general art books do nothing but reproduce, over
and over again, the same masterpieces. I guess there just aren't that
many great works, so they have to repeat them over and over again,
or else someone has the idea that the public won't believe you unless
you give them a diet of publicly approved masterpieces. Well, who's
to say what is and what isn't . . . or what was and what will be?

It's not that the masterpieces are in any way soft food. Far from
it. But anyone who loves good cooking knows that the delicacies are
often the little-known or the side trips from the accepted, everyday
menu. The real meat of art appreciation and enjoyment is often the

142

undiscovered, the unknown, the newly discovered, or those delectable tidbits we rediscover for ourselves.

So with a conceit born half out of a desire to do something different and half out of a will to justify a large part of my life's intention, I've hit upon the idea of illustrating my "art book" with art from my own collection: things, sculpture, drawings, paintings that I have found intriguing enough to put out a good living for, or that my wife and I have chosen to express our idea (to ourselves) of what we want to look at and live with.

Another reason for this is that throughout the story I have consciously referred to works of art almost everybody knows. So far it has been my reaction to great works and great names, and I hope I have come to some conclusions about unknown names and less important works, too.

I will never fail to be impressed (or sometimes unimpressed) by the masterpieces, but it is those things I have made up my mind about, and am willing to make an effort for, that really belong to me. In our collection are objects I consider masterworks, and I don't care who agrees with me. But whatever I think, I could never put across the one real point of this tale if I didn't make the whole story personal—even the illustrations. I have wanted to say only that art is so much a part of my life I would love to have it become a part of the lives of others who perhaps never thought of it as other than an outside experience; who have never let themselves become involved in and with the creative act of other men and women.

I have chosen the following objects because of their quality, their personal involvement, or their story. And I've left out some things I love very much because they don't reproduce well, or lose face because of absence of color. They represent almost forty years of endless excitement in their acquisition, and endless learning by having them so close to my sight. They have become as familiar to me as my front door, and the ones I open up to you now are doors I am never apt to close behind me.

Speaking of doors, our old (1928) California-Spanish house has

143

a very impressive front door at the top of a long flight of steps. Once inside that door, you're in as uselessly beautiful a room as you can imagine. It's a type of room that, over the years, has shrunk in scale as well as nomenclature. Once it was known as the "great hall," then, a size smaller, it was called the "entrance hall." A few decades and it became the "front hall," later it dwindled down to a cubbyhole entitled the "vestibule," and today it is a nameless space between two closets where the door itself has just enough room to open without banging the opener in the face.

Our hall, I think, comes under the heading of "great entrance halls." It is thirty feet square and twenty-three feet high. But enough of that. . . . Pretend you're opening our front door—and come on in!

Pretty damned impressive, isn't it? This is our great five-and-a-half-foot stone Huastecan sun god we found in a Laguna Beach storage warehouse. The story of how we got it home and into place I'm going to write for *Sports Illustrated,* as it's an athletic adventure of no small note.

But on with the illustrations. The next four tell a little story of the fabulous art of Africa. The first illustration of two objects represents two cultures— one from the seventeenth century, the other from the nineteenth or possibly even the early part of the present one.

In the foreground is a chieftain of the ancient kingdom of Benin, in bronze, about twenty inches high. I cannot think of these highly sophisticated figures as primitive, so superb is the technique of casting and the realization of this figure as sculpture.

The man on the horse is wood, and as a friend once said, reaching perhaps to compliment the piece, it has the compassionate arrogance of the "Entry into Jerusalem."

Infrequently do we know the artist in the great gallery of anonymity of African art, but in the case of the second illustration of this gigantic mask, we do. He was one of the last true Yoruba sculptors, uninfluenced, at least in this work, by the crushing pressures of the white world. His name was Bamboya, and he created this wonder of organized detail with a pocketknife and an adz about fifty years ago.

He has made a city and the story of that city from a single piece of wood. It weighs forty pounds, is four feet four inches high and seventy-five inches in circumference. There are fifty figures on it, and it was made to wear. The sinewy Yoruba boys wore it lightly as they danced and jumped onto six-foot platforms in their frenetic ceremonies.

The chief, with his tasseled parasol on top of which the smallest children play, rides majestically into the heart of his tribe. A guardian, who knows acutely the importance of the personage behind him, rides on the resigned, respectful horse, reining him through the crowd. Attendants fan him cool and keep the insects at a distance, while a dozen soldiers (see the detail) stand attention to see that all goes well. But little life goes on, even in the presence of the Important One. The mothers feed their children, the matron fetches water, and the children pause a moment to be properly impressed. But the procession still moves on.

Every collector must end up liking some particular school or period of art more than others. There, once again, is the personal affiliation, the plan that fits all your judgments together to make a certain work—or in this case the work of one tribe of African people—completely to your liking. I am inevitably

146

9

drawn to Yoruba sculpture. It is at once savage and sensitive, and sentient enough to reveal the great tradition behind it and yet always to be new. And it has soul—that extra rare quality in which the rules and traditions are fused with the personality of the artist and can be discovered in each work, fresh and individual.

The Yorubas, carrying on the great tradition of Ife and Benin, almost surpass the earlier masters, adding as they do a very real interest in movement, expression, and real-life vitality. The Benin sculptors, great as they are, seem almost self-consciously classic, while the modern-day Yorubas retain the sophistication and at the same time carefully guard their identities with their own people. It is classic folk art.

The other tribe that fascinates me is the Bambembe. The little (seven-and-one-quarter-inch) mother and child will do as an example of the monumental in miniature. What power! Like mother, like daughter! What serious humor . . . or is it imagination?

Next, let's take a little drawing with a big background. It is a study. for a famous painting in Perugia, and it is by Federigo Barocci. He is almost unknown to us in the United States, because for some reason the art plunderers of the past hundred years overlooked him, and most of his paintings remain in the churches and collections which have always been their home. It comes from the great collection of drawings assembled by Sir Thomas Lawrence.

Some might think it unimportant, but it was important enough to have been done by Barocci in preparation for one of his greatest canvases, and it is beautiful . . . no one can deny that. I like it for all the above reasons and one more: it never gets dull. It has the essential quality of greatness—it grows, not only in beauty with each viewing, but in importance as a work of art. It is a few essential minutes of a great man's life and work; it is a Gettysburg Address —or two lines by Shakespeare. They are enough, and so is it, to give us a clue to what made them great.

I don't really want to be bowled over by monuments in my own home. Imagine living with the "Last Supper" at the end of your dining room . . . I'd lose my appetite. But this "Angel of the Dead" from Myrina, for instance, will do for me in place of, say, the "Winged Victory." It's four inches high and as close to Greek perfection as I care to come to, at home. How light it is . . . how tender . . . If death sends creatures of such sweet dignity to take us off, I, for one, will go gladly. Or if an artist will make me one of these to put in my grave, I'll accept the myth and come with the angel back from the underworld to thank him personally.

151

Sometimes it happens that two contemporary artists, friends and ex-changers in their lifetime, move into the history of art at different speeds. One leaves the other behind. But time has a way of catching up with the laggard, and he may even eclipse the fame of the one earlier recognized. I'm betting that this will happen to Henry Fuseli, the friend of William Blake. Blake's fame as a poet, mystic, and painter, plus (I believe) the fact that he was British and that mystics and painters are rare in that land of poets, has caused him to leave his great Swiss contemporary far behind. Now art lovers are beginning to find in Fuseli's fertile imagination, and through his brilliant and virile draughts-manship, a quality they miss in the static and gentler Blake. This drawing of Prometheus is a great excursion in the art of drawing and will stand up to the work of anyone, any time.

This figure is my pet test case. I know where it's from, but it certainly isn't typical of its origin. It could be Gothic or a lot of things. Actually, it's—— But take a guess —what do you think? I'll give you a clue. It's made of stucco. I've seen experts go ten centuries out of the way on this one, then when you put them right, they use their best "Oh, of course," usually repeated two times, "Of course, of course."

The lady with the braids and holding the pomegranate is from Afghanistan, the fourth century A.D., the city of Hadda.

You've seen our entrance hall. Now here's a wall of our living room. Without this picture a verbal description of these objects would sound preposterous and would more than likely send a dozen top interior decorators into a state of shocked retirement. The large painting on the left is by Richard Diebenkorn, and is the one that hit Van Johnson on the head and which Mary titled for an inquisitive female questioner, "We Like It." Beneath it is a table, full of African objects including the Bambembe mother and child which you've already seen. A bowl of Mexican piggy-bank fruits and a wonderful Batak figure fill out the tableload. The big cross is seventeenth-century Mexican and is gold-leafed wood. The plant won't stop growing, so it's a good thing we got the photo this year while you can still see the cross. The Spanish chest, Mary bought with part of her designer's salary from *The Sweet Smell of Success* and is the best piece of furniture we own. On top of it is a god, the Father, from colonial Mexico. God Father sails through a nimbus of light with the help of a cloud and a dove. He holds in one hand the orb of the world and in the other an object I'm sure was meant to look like a scepter but to us more closely resembles a good panatela cigar. On his head he wears a triangle, representing his trinity, made of etched mirror. The little picture to the right is a crayon drawing by Modigliani, and beneath all this is a red and orange, black and white Navajo rug. It may sound savage, to say the least, but truly it proves how successfully all good art goes together to make an enchanting place in which to live and look.

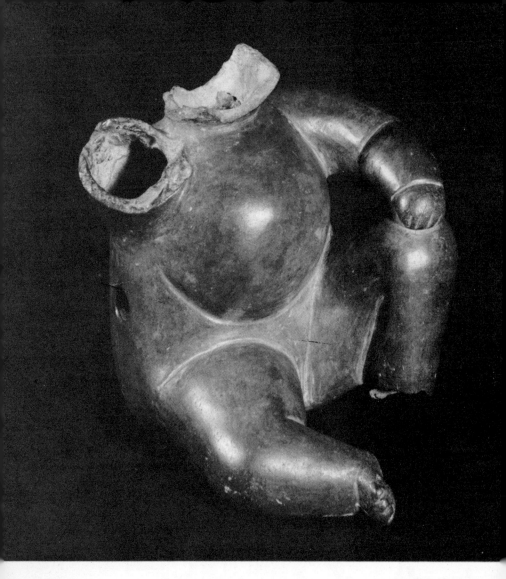

Of all the pre-Columbian fragments I've ever seen, this is my favorite. It comes from the early Olmec culture of Mexico and to my mind is sculpturally comparable to anything in the whole history of art. It represents a child. Could anything better express the rounded mass of infancy? There is structure beneath the flesh, but the flesh is the artist's first problem here, and how subtly the fold of it undulates to form a rhythmic pattern of childhood. Warshaw's "Skull" on the facing page and this two-thousand-year-old torso are equal triumphs in the representation of volume and man and abstracted reality.

As interested as I am in abstract art, I am touched to the mind by great draughtsmanship. Nothing can take the edge off a beautiful AND imaginatively drawn object. Howard Warshaw's "Baby Skull" is just that. You sense the mysterious volume and capacity for growth of this bone cave. At the same time, it is touchingly rendered, leaving no doubt that it is the skull of an infant. I bought this parchment fragment of humanity from an amateur American Indian archaeologist and presented it to Howard. He returned life to it and made it artistically alive.

Everyone with possessions plays the game of what you'd save in case of fire. New Year's Eve, 1958, we had the chance of playing it for real with a canyon brush fire that sent a hundred-foot wall of flame within two hundred yards of our house. After we had evacuated everything we could and finally were given the welcome signal that everything was under control, I emptied my pockets. Items: one nine-dollar jar of caviar, one traffic ticket—and this two-and-a-half by two-and-a-half inch oil, on ivory, by Goya.

A critic once wrote of this and the other miniatures painted in the last year of Goya's life: "There is a grandeur and a fantasy in these final expressions of his art, matched only by the late Titian or Rembrandt."

I can find no quotes on the aesthetic value of traffic tickets or caviar.

Does the pleasure derived from a work of art necessarily have to do with the artist's whole achievement? I mean, is it possible for someone to paint a picture or carve a statue that is excellent and appealing, and then do nothing else as good—or even nothing else at all? I have bought three or four things I love from student exhibitions or group shows and have never seen another thing by the same hand.

I was on the jury of a huge show in northern California. The quality of the work was exceedingly mediocre, and the job of making awards was very difficult, since almost nothing stood above the rank of amateur or, even worse, "arty." My fellow jurors passed by what to me was the only interesting thing in the whole show. It got no mention at all, but I liked it, so I bought it. I met the artist, a charming young lady, and gave her my own award in the form of

160

a check. My taste has been slightly justified by the admiration of it by several well-known painter friends, and it continues to hold my interest and the interest of all who see it. Her name is Eunice Bosson.

161

One of my oldest friends in Hollywood is Edward Carrere, for years the top art director at Warner Brothers Studio. Typical of our profession, these men who do such fine work in providing the settings for motion pictures are little known and often little appreciated. Ed has tried to break away from his craft on occasion, to do some work for art's sake and not just for the "business." He is technically a genius, who talks period and construction with his pencil as easily as other people say hello. But only when he had the chance to get away from it a few years ago on a trip to Europe was he able to see for himself. He did a series of water-color drawings of Italy that are really inspired and original in every respect. He found, at last, his own tongue . . . and he speaks well.

The next three pieces are all from Latin America—Mexico, Veracruz, and Costa Rica. They vary tremendously in size, date and, in one case, material. The first is the oldest and the smallest and proves one of my favorite theories— there's nothing new under the sun. This aspect of art has always intrigued me, especially when you come across ancient origins of what we think are modern miracles. This one's from Tlaltilco, in the valley of Mexico, around the second century before Christ. It is two inches high. In the family tree of art, it is well connected from the archaic Greek right down to Picasso, who would accept it, not as a fantastic ancient prank, but as a fact he could make his very own. By the way, the other eye is on the other side . . . Picasso can show all three.

The next item is a much more solemn mood of Mexico, but it too boasts art relatives of ancient ancestry and great note. . . . The seated scribes of Egypt . . . the serene Buddhas of the Orient . . . all find relation to this majestic clay figure from the Totonac peoples of Veracruz.

The last piece is from Costa Rica and is carved in volcanic stone, giving it a lively surface texture in contrast to its massive, sit-down weight. I'm told it's a musician, playing a flute, but I prefer to see him as a primitive ponderer, plotting the future of the world—a monkey, maybe, just about to be a man and not quite sure the change is for the better.

I can't resist following this last monkey-man with the first man—Adam. At least Adam, as Modigliani saw him, shyly sensual, is already sophisticated enough to know the world is his if only he could manage it alone.

There is an element in art that is often overlooked by the public—the element of fun. Either people are afraid to find fun in a work of art in the misguided thought that they might be making fun of it, or they can't let themselves enjoy the possibilities of humor in a profession that everyone takes dead seriously . . . but I've rarely seen anyone throw back his head and roar with laughter before a painting or drawing. If he does, it's usually in derision, and yet humor is one of the highest forms of genius which we do not deny to the poet, novelist, musician, or even actor.

The bronze figures reproduced above are by the wonderfully witty American sculptor, Gaston Lachaise. I find his vast nudes wickedly satirical comments on the wanton world of womanliness. I'm delighted by his solution of the titanic problem of making those broad-beamed balloon-busted babes sail through the air as lightly as the most ethereal angels. Modigliani's "Adam" opposite here has the same saving sense of fun, which makes the Original Man the father of mankind's acknowledged saving grace—humor.

167

More than anyone in modern times, Constantin Guys proves a lot of my feelings about art and artists. He actually was a reporter for the *Illustrated London News* and before the advent of photography covered the great events of his day—the Crimean War and the whole reign of Napoleon III. He also proved the fact that greatness in a work of art has nothing to do with size, technique, or medium. To my knowledge, he never did any oil paintings, and the majority of his charming reports on the life of his time are small and delicate washes or water colors. This picador is one of my prized possessions. I could not enjoy it more if it were life-sized and on canvas and by Velázquez.

William Brice, as I have said, is a favorite friend and favored artist. The pen-and-ink landscape below is typical of his vital and penetrating description of our earth. Like Albrecht Dürer, he sees beyond the appearance of nature to the original vision of all life as divinely created for us to enjoy.

This tiny sketch page from Adolph von Menzel's notebook is an ideal example of the immediate record a draughtsman makes of an event . . . as immediate as a camera could, and yet with so much more humanity. The baby crawls through her father's legs, and before the artist can catch it, it is on its way back. Only a master would state this little drama with such frankness and tenderness and admit that life is quicker than the eye.

There are so many pictures, pots, and just *things* I would have liked to include. Everything that we've collected has an importance in our visual lives, but they say you shouldn't put all your eggs in one basket—so before I let you out the side door, here are a few I can't resist sharing with you. Below are two Nasca pots from Peru, very old but very new forever in their humor and charm. Man and wife? Perhaps, but man and woman? Definitely . . . Look who's having all the fun!

The pot man, holding a pot (on the next page), is from the valley of Lima in Peru, too. If you can understand this and not understand the modern art of Paul Klee or Joan Miró, somebody's taking a sidelong glance at something and seeing nothing. That may not make sense, but neither does looking in the past and being blind to the present.

Below is a group of modern Mexican folk art figures, illustrations of children's stories and reminiscent of folk art of all time, everywhere. All art is the art of the people, but all people aren't always ready to accept all art as their own. Too much nonsense about who did what. Who cares . . . as long as whoever did it, did it good?

Those four titles on the next page are little illustrated stories by the Hopi Indians of New Mexico. Where does naïveté leave off and imagination take over to present us pictorial poesy at its simplest and its best? In the art of the American Indian is to be found grandeur comparable to any art anywhere. Maybe we should give it back to them, as the old saw says. At least they haven't lost the ability to see directly their own directions.

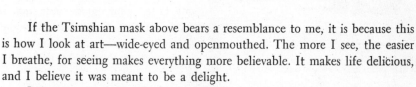

If the Tsimshian mask above bears a resemblance to me, it is because this is how I look at art—wide-eyed and openmouthed. The more I see, the easier I breathe, for seeing makes everything more believable. It makes life delicious, and I believe it was meant to be a delight.

It is so easy today, with every medium of communication serving us feasts for the eyes, to see the world as the best of all possible worlds; to see mankind in its true light as the creator of so much beauty; to surround ourselves with knowledge of art, man's highest expression of gratitude for the gift of life.

Art is, or can be, an everyday experience, and if you make it such, every day will have a beginning and an end that means continuance, furtherance, and futurity.

We have plastered our walls with our taste, some good some not so good, but ours. Dollar bills make dull decoration, and automobiles aren't made to last. Even light bulbs burn out . . .

But some night, or some dewy dawn, come over to our house. We'll give you a cup of coffee, and after we've worn you to a frazzle with the whys and wherefores of what we like, we'll let you out by the side door. We won't have to point it out to you . . . it's hard to miss a totem pole, twenty-five feet tall . . . but there it stands in our back yard for all the world to see. A totem pole in your back yard, Mr. Price? . . . Of course! Doesn't everybody have one?

Y OU CAN NEVER REALLY APPRECIATE OR UNDERSTAND THE business of art unless you actually run a gallery. Although I had always had the most pleasant relations with dealers, when I was a student and a budding collector, my lasting respect and admiration for them was born out of becoming one of them myself.

A year after World War II began I left the cast of *Angel Street*, and came to California under contract to 20th Century-Fox. My first picture for 20th was *The Song of Bernadette* which, being a religious film, the studio approached with typical lugubrious reverence. It took nine months to make, and the boredom of waiting for a call from the studio began to pall. My "Victorian brother," George Macready, and I decided to open an art gallery, since we were fairly immune from the draft, being parents and, for the moment, over-age.

We rented a little shop in Beverly Hills between a bookstore and a very popular bar, figuring correctly that we'd catch a mixed clientele of erudites and inebriates. Our stock consisted of the hodgepodge George and I had collected separately over the years, augmented by some of my more interesting items, which were converted into cash to buy others and to run the business.

The Little Gallery, as we named it, unimaginatively if literally, opened modestly in the spring of 1943, and we found ourselves an immediate success in attendance, if not sales. The wives of our friends used it as a shopping center, and we became expert baby sitters. The husbands came in later, after a few belts at the bar, and the talk was lively even if it seldom could be steered onto the subject of art. But we were the only gallery in the west end of town during the war, so we finally got our share of the art demands of the community, too. The rent was low, and for the first two months we just made it. But as long as we weren't *losing* money, and we did earn a living in the movies, The Little Gallery would survive.

It was the realization that we were rapidly becoming a rendezvous for New York homesick actors and artists that brought us to the serious endeavor to make it pay. Because we were primarily interested in showing young artists' work, we had the problem of charging off publicity, openings, and rent against the very low commissions we asked of our very low-priced artists.

Galleries usually take 33⅓ per cent of the sales price of a contemporary work. This is figured out by asking the artist what he wants for the work and then tacking the 33⅓ per cent on, and believe me, it takes a lot of twenty-five-dollar commissions on seventy-five-dollar pictures to pay the rent in Beverly Hills. Most of our profit had to go toward buying stock, and we combed the surroundings for inexpensive and interesting items, which seemed to be what our clientele wanted.

In our two years of existence let's say we never lost any money. We had a whale of a good time, and we did introduce some good painters who have since gone far in the art world.

We introduced Morris Graves, Paul Burlin, and John Whorf to the West Coast and gave first showings to William Brice and Howard Warshaw.

My discovery of (and meeting with) Howard Warshaw was one of the delights of my life. In the basement of another gallery I saw a funny little drawing—almost Steinberg in quality—and asked the name of the artist. I was told he was an eighteen-year-old animator at Walt Disney's. I asked to see more and was told by the dealer that he had little interest in Warshaw's work, but would I like to meet him? Yes, I would. Two days later a hairy, black, Teddy-bear of a man came into the gallery. He had the charm of a great puppy and an undiscovered intensity which gave great promise. We looked at his portfolio of drawings and made a date to see the rest of his work at home. The home work proved to be more drawings, all enchantingly macabre and much influenced by Eugene Berman and Dali, but the few paintings gave the same promise as his personality: that of hidden intensity. We bought as many as we could for our stock, and I bought one for myself, which I still love. It's a drawing of a lanky, seedy woman, charmingly bedraggled. She makes me think of all the mad heroines of tragedy, if they had lived to become mature women—Ophelia, Lucia di Lammermoor, and even Juliet. I've always felt those girls died young for a reason.

Howard took the money and went to New York to live, and paint us a show. We heard from him regularly, and an occasional painting would drift in by low-rate mail. A year later he and the rest of his first show returned to California.

It was a delightful exhibition. We hung the twenty-odd (and I do mean odd) dark paintings of dreary empty rooms and death-blue people and ghostly flowers on a background of old fish nets, draped on the walls. Scattered across the nets were roses, culled from every garden we could find them in. The roses, retaining their shape in death, were left there for the month's exhibition. It was a success— and from this distance, I must admit, more than a little "arty." But it was fun.

Our openings consisted of anywhere from fifty to four hundred people crammed into our little room, drinking the strongest, cheapest vodka martinis we could make. Everyone came, and one day I'll never forget brought Thomas Mann, Franz Werfel, Rachmaninoff, and Aldous Huxley . . . a pretty good cast of talent. Spasmodic customers included Tallulah Bankhead, Fanny Brice, Katharine Hepburn, and other assorted actors, writers, directors, and just people. Barbara Hutton, lost in the life of Hollywood, was a frequent visitor and, finally, a buyer who saved our lives in a moment of financial crisis.

Barbara, it seemed, loved Venice and had some magnificent Canalettos, and though she enjoyed our company and our gallery, she was honest enough to say we had nothing for her. But one artist who caught her fancy, if not her purse, was the delightful, tragic, and genuinely Bohemian John Decker.

Decker's charm saved us twice. We had an exhibition of his paintings, the best and least eclectic he ever did, and we sold many of them. "Ghost Town," which Thomas Mitchell bought, is to my mind his best work. Miss Hutton loved the pictures—and Decker—but just couldn't find the one that said hello to her. In the gallery one day she told Decker of her love for Venice. He allowed as how there was one picture he just didn't have time to finish for the show, but he thought it would be finished the next day and that she might like it. She promised to come back.

By noon the next day Decker was back and so was Barbara, and more importantly, so was the painting—a three-foot long, two-foot high painting of . . . Venice. Palaces, gondolas, the Canal shimmered from the canvas with the authentic light of Venice. Sold to Barbara Hutton . . . one painting of Venice by John Decker . . . as wet as the Grand Canal, having been done from start to finish in twelve hours' time.

Decker was very close to John Barrymore—in fact, so close that, until a pet parrot gnawed on Decker's nose, their profiles were two versions of the same thing: rough and smooth. He was genuinely a worshiper of Barrymore, the actor and the man, and at his final illness was with him night and day, recording tenderly the dying giant of the theatre. Finally, when Gene Fowler had finished his great memorial, *Good Night, Sweet Prince*, Decker's wonderful little head of Barrymore was selected for the cover. The original was in our show, and that greatest of all Barrymore fans, Tallulah Bankhead, bought it.

In celebration Decker gave a bang-up party for Tallulah. There were fifty guests, and, more surprisingly, there were four huge roasts of beef and lamb. No one could have that many ration tickets, but on inquiry as to how he got the meat, Decker led us all into his studio and unveiled an enormous canvas of a rather handsome, overblown blonde, entitled: "My Butcher's Wife."

Earlier I said my say about dealers, conceding that they aren't really to be held responsible for being a special, if rather odd, breed of men. It's the customers' fault.

Women head the list as the prime cause of dealers' disturbances. Being more on the prowl during gallery hours, they make up the largest attendance, if the least revenue. The gallery to them is part of their welfare work—to see how the young (or old) artists are doing. Ninety per cent of them have a quick semester's veneer of art history or appreciation, and from my experience they all must have written the same final exam on the subject; for, indeed, they don't know anything, but they are dead certain of what they like—which is practically nothing, too.

They are all interior decorators at heart, and the unfortunate artist whose palette differs from their color scheme can die of starvation, for all they care. Also, they have built-in tape measures in their hands and almost no picture is the right size.

Being the most practical of our species they love a bargain, and if they can't find it, they start whittling away at anything to create one. Prices were not meant for them and "no" is not to be taken for an answer. Their technique is superb, and time means nothing. If they see the tiniest chink in your armor, they'll come back for months to make a kill.

One lady customer of ours came every Thursday for six weeks just to "admire" a picture which she wanted for fifty dollars less. On the seventh Thursday she didn't show up, and we were half delighted and half homesick for the sight of her. After all, she'd been a steady customer. The day passed, and we closed with an uneasy feeling that all was not well. Nine o'clock the next morning, Friday, she was there, and the shock was so great she got the fifty off and proudly carried her picture home.

The uncertainty and frustration of their lives is another cause of distemper among dealers. One now-famous gallery owner years ago brought to California the "Guernica" show of Picasso's at great expense, and while it caused a lasting sensation among the initiated, not one thing was sold. Everyone agreed about its importance except the customers.

Artists drive you crazy in this business, too. Though the gallery is their major outlet, they treat it as if it were a great slot into which they pour the fruits of their genius only to have it come out pulp. No matter whether things are sold or unsold, they can always find something to gripe about. If things are sold, they feel almost as if you'd kidnaped their baby or if it's unsold, they are unappreciated and the dealer becomes a nurse and mother in both cases.

I've known galleries to put in as many as ten losing years to build up a certain stable of painters, and when finally some of them "came in" they walked out.

Finally, the one blow which cuts deepest is the collector, usually a new one, who can't make up his or her mind and after having made a purchase comes back for reassurance, or in some cases even returns the work and takes his money back, or much worse, leaves it as credit which he uses as a tormenting toy in all future dealings.

We didn't last long as dealers, partly because wartime rents wouldn't stay put, resulting in a threat to evict us from The Little Gallery. But mostly we were dying from success in our real profession. Both of us were "in demand," as the saying goes, and, lovely feeling though it always is for actors, it leaves little time for anything else. While our charming, practically volunteer helper, Barbara Wolferman, did her best to keep the gallery and us going, we finally folded our tent and noisily stole away.

It may not have been a great gallery, being definitely on the Bohemian side, but it was exciting, and I think we're still missed in the Los Angeles art world, which has grown grander and, I'm sad to say, a little duller.

Personally, I learned a lot. To buy well, to discover the hidden and unusual, and to be at ease in the business world of art. I loved the customers. Even the Great Names didn't bother me as sales prospects—all except one, that is. Every time she came in, I'd run upstairs and make Barbara wait on her, then I'd watch, trembling with excitement. To this day I've never met her, but she still makes me tremble . . . Garbo!

We split the remaining stock when we closed, and I found myself with a pretty ragged collection of stuff. But during our search for material I'd met one of the greatest characters in the art world and one of the most controversially exciting—Earl Stendahl. No one has put Earl into his proper place in the history of great dealers, but I must say briefly that without him, we would know much less of the tremendous variety and brilliance of the art of Mexico, before Columbus. He is a real pioneer and an astute businessman. He created many of the greatest collections of pre-Columbian art that are now beginning to enter our museums, and he is to this day the most adventurous spirit for a "find" I've ever met.

Earl was instrumental in bringing me together with the late Walter Arensberg, whose unparalleled collection of early cubist art now reposes (almost over my dead body) in the Philadelphia Art Museum. Mr. Arensberg had toyed with several local universities and museums to be the repository of his collection after his death, and recriminations are still alive on both sides of the argument as to why "this one didn't get it or that one turned it down." This is where I came in. In my innocence, not knowing the whole story, I called Walter and said I wanted to start a much-needed Museum of Contemporary Art in Los Angeles. Mr. Arensberg was excited and baited me with the hope that, if I could succeed, the Arensberg collection would stay in California where it damned well belonged and was greatly needed, too. Along with Richard Sisson, a young actor who had recently discovered he hated acting (or couldn't, or something) and wanted to be an art historian, I set out to round up all interested parties in the museum project. We corralled one of the nicest men in the world, Kenneth MacGowan, to be our leader. Then we drove herd on Fanny Brice, Edward G. Robinson, Sam and Mildred Jaffe, Jim and Barbara Poe, and a few other dedicated art lovers and good citizens, and before we knew it, we had $10,000 and an empty loft building next door to the old Romanoff's Restaurant in Beverly Hills.

Kenneth Ross, lately a director of the Pasadena Art Museum and a critic of some note, was pressed into underpaid service as our director, and a group of really volunteer ladies were hornswoggled into "manning" the room, the desk, and the minute library. An out-of-work carpenter built us some partitions, and Fanny Brice, during a preopening board meeting, took off her beige skirt and left it as a sample for the painters to use for color on the walls. The May Company gave us publicity by posing models in a hastily arranged corner, and we were set to open.

Through the generosity of the major modern-art collectors in Los Angeles and around the country, Ken Ross put together a superb show called "Modern Artists in Transition." The crowds poured in, the membership boomed (that is, the two-dollar, five-dollar, and ten-dollar ones), and we were a going (if slowly) Modern Institute of Art.

In two years we built a membership of five thousand, and an annual attendance of forty thousand, but by the end of the second year we were doomed to close. The public, especially the students, could not do without us. There were torchlight parades to protest its closing. Ten thousand students put their signatures on a petition which was sent along to all the big business firms and the heads of motion-picture studios; most of the original founders were bled time and again for additional contributions, but the good, rich people of Los Angeles wouldn't come through, so we closed.

Not only did we have trouble raising money from the people who could have supported it, but some of them were otherwise ungenerous, too. They would not loan things for exhibition.

I have a letter which I cherish from a famous actress who, on being asked to loan a certain painting from her collection (of almost nothing notable) said she couldn't possibly lend it and knew the institute would understand, since her entire bedroom (where the picture hung), even to the sheets, pillow cases, and toilet paper, was done around the colors of this painting. I finally got to see the painting, and the thought of that bedroom kept me awake many nights. Conversely (though I may be prejudiced, of course), the mere sight of that actress still puts me to sleep.

I was "out" more than I could afford and disgusted after two of the most laborious and exciting years of my life. What we did will be the foundation someday of a real big money-supported museum, but all the work and love and devotion those many wonderful people put in had left a bitter taste that many of them can't forget. Their resultant disinterest in Los Angeles as a cultural entity could hold it back in the future—though I hope not. It's a city that needs all the culture it can get.

During one of my rabble-rousing attempts to keep the institute open, I came upon the ideal message to Los Angelenos about their apathy for culture—a road map I found in a gas station to use on a trip from Los Angeles to San Francisco, listing the "points of interest" in each city. San Francisco: three museums, ten public parks, a great zoo, public concert places, the aquarium, etc., etc. Los Angeles: Forest Lawn (a cemetery) and the La Brea Tar Pits (a hole in the ground).

I wish it was with this thought we could leave Los Angeles—but it is the most exciting city on the face of the earth, and the excitement stems from the fact that it's an open field for everything. Other cities have solved the problems, or partially solved them, or at least done something about them. But not Los Angeles. The public is there, and the surrounding communities pulse with the energy and endeavor: Long Beach, East Los Angeles, Claremont, even Pasadena. But in the center is the big city where no one believes he lives—or (is it?) believes that he's *alive*.

The remnants of our Modern Institute group are all presently working for U.C.L.A., and the art department there, somewhat restricted by the red tape of a great university, is doing a brave job. We have imported energetic and creative men like Frederick Wright and Gibson Danes, but sooner or later we'll lose them if they dare to go too far in the right direction. Dr. Richard Brown at the County Museum is making the right noise to break that $14,000,000 mausoleum apart and get an art museum where the paintings are not separated by stuffed animals and prehistoric bones from the La Brea Tar Pits. Still, Forest Lawn has more living visitors than the museum, and its copies of the "Last Supper" in stained glass, some undistinguished imitations of Michelangelo's "David," and the nudes of Canova draw more praise than the museum's superb new Goya.

San Diego has the finest zoo in America, but the Los Angeles Zoo is not much more than a home for retired Metro-Goldwyn-Mayer lions.

Nevertheless, Los Angeles is my "Home, Sweet Home." I chose it, and, as goes the cliché, I've made my bed—but I'll be damned if I'll lie in it or, worse, culturally *die* in it!

So it follows that I am one of a small group of people—the same people who persistently collect, lend, and encourage interest in the arts, to which at least a small segment of the population responds with real vigor.

Even if the closing of the Modern Institute was a costly heartbreak for all of us, we all learned a lot from the experience. Dr. Karl With, who succeeded Kenneth Ross as our director when he became City Art Commissioner, proved to be a real inspiration. He came from the Cologne Museum to America to protest Herr Hitler's assertion that anything he didn't like art-wise was degenerate.

How important direction is! To the actor, the director is the audience. He is the rudder from curtain to curtain; it neither rises nor falls without him. To a museum, it's the whole lifeblood, and, believe me, most of the museum directors I've known give their lifeblood to the post they occupy at the moment. My admiration for them is unbounded, for I've seen firsthand what a good one can do and how little can be done with a mediocre one. I don't think I could ever summon up the kind of altruism they display on each job. They collect works of art, encourage collectors, raise money, plan exhibitions, do all the paper work, and nine times out of ten they buck a board of directors who either couldn't care less about art or who cover up their lack of caring (to say nothing of their lack of knowledge) with all sorts of biased beliefs of what they think good or bad for public consumption.

I remember an incident not long ago when an exhibition of the giant German expressionist Max Beckmann's work was opening at a trustee top-heavy museum. The wives of the trustees were given a preview of the show and were so startled by the strength of Beckmann's pictures they confused it with ugliness. They took out their revenge by refusing to pour the tepid tea at the opening that night. A gayer group heard of this and volunteered to take their place—if they could pour gin.

I will only take one museum director to make my point, first because I know him best of any, and like him, and second because he is one of the very finest in America, or anywhere today; Perry Rathbone.

Mary and I met him together when he came to be a juror at the annual exhibition—artists of Los Angeles and vicinity. I had known him slightly before, because he directed the City Art Museum in St. Louis and I had given him and St. Louis my Gauguin manuscript.

Mary and I had been "going together," as that lovely American expression goes when two people want to get married and don't quite know how to accomplish it for various reasons. It's also a period of great lightheartedness, and the addition of a person with mutual interests is more acceptable then than ever again in a marriage. So we took Perry on to show him the sights of California, including the fabulous San Diego Zoo.

One thing led to another, and Tijuana being across the border from San Diego, our thirst took us there. Perry adored it, and the wild kind of abandon that happens once you're out of your own land, happened sooner than usual this time. Before he knew what hit him, he was our best man!

Poor Perry left Los Angeles in a state of shock—and especially so, because he was not allowed to tell anyone our secret, both of us feeling slightly guilty to have done this without telling our families, who incidentally couldn't have cared less or more one way or the other. Perry kept our secret, and our friendship has endured over the years and my

187

admiration for him, as I learned more about his achievement in St. Louis, went out of bounds.

When he arrived in St. Louis, before World War II, he found himself in a typically artistically apathetic midwest city. There were a few collectors and patrons like Guy Blackmer, who had added much to my youth with his enthusiasm, and Joe and Lulu Pulitzer, who had already made the beginnings of their fine collection of French postimpressionists, but the museum, while way ahead of what it was when it and I first set up housekeeping, was still a museum and not an integral part of the cultural life and activity of the city as he was able to make it.

Perry, with vitality and charm, backed up by knowledge and nerve enough to paddle a power wheeler up the Mississippi, took St. Louis by storm. He brought the museum collection up to date by adding important modern sculpture and paintings and added to its already distinguished small group of old masters some immensely impressive pictures. For example, the "Portrait of a Young Man" by Rembrandt is one of the best in America.

But his two most important functions were to encourage local collectors and to bring life into the museum's social program. With a much needed flair for the dramatic, he jazzed up exhibitions with publicity potentials, like a man in a suit of armor to greet the capacity crowds who came to see the Berlin masterpieces when they toured America. He solicited my help on this venture, asking me to supply the suit of armor which, in turn, I asked of Al Nickel, the generous vice-president of Western Costume Company, who gladly loaned it for the entire run of the exhibition. It not only made *Life* magazine, but it gave the children of St. Louis a feeling of what the Middle Ages were like with a knight in shining armor to show them the pictures.

He put together a great and exciting show of paintings and everything else pertinent to life on the Mississippi, calling upon the resources of Washington University, and the Mercantile Library Association for their wonderful George Caleb Bingham paintings of Missouri.

He saw to it that Max Beckmann was brought from Germany to teach at Washington University, and with the help of one of St. Louis' most civic-minded young executives, "Buster" May, made that city almost the study center of German expressionist painting in America.

With his advice and taste he helped several new collectors get fine pictures, and started an art awareness in the press and in the public mind that has made the City Art Museum the center of cultural life. Great annual parties to which everyone contributes time and effort bring in new members and raise funds for all museum activities.

He made the arts not only chic but fun and, of course, built up his own reputation to such a degree of importance that the huge eastern museums began to cast longing eyes at St. Louis and Perry Rathbone. Sooner than anyone wished, Boston had made him a wonderful offer, and he was off to accept the challenge of a new post.

The majority of directors, whether in large or small museums, are just as excited and exciting as Perry. They work against public apathy and have, in the past few years, achieved unbelievable recognition for their particular museums . . . recognition to the point where a Hollywood wag was said to have remarked recently: "If the movies could learn to draw crowds like the museums, we'd be back in business."

Sometimes it would seem the best art in or around Hollywood is Art Linkletter! He is formidable, personable, enduring, and honest. As for the rest of art in this entertainment center, I believe Mr. Huxley, or someone equally witty, summed it up with this definition of the town: "Seven suburbs in search of a city." Cruel perhaps, but tempered by the fact that while perhaps Hollywood can't help it, the people could.

I don't suppose there has ever been a community upon which the attention of the world has been more acutely focused, and strangely enough it doesn't stand up in the light. Actors, as a group, are extraordinarily aware and civic-minded, but in Hollywood they have tended to become smug and perhaps justifiably a little frightened by the glaring eyes of the world upon them. If it were left up to them, the arts would starve! And they do, even the theatre. Great theatre people dread to play there, and the other arts are supported either by the society of the city, as in the case of music, or by a few earnest young newcomers who refuse to accept Hollywood, or for that matter, Los

Angeles, as a dead end of culture. The Sydney Brodys are a shining example of this new group.

But the "movie" people, who by the flick of a publicity agent could do limitless good for the arts, are listless. A few of them collect for varied reasons—love of it, fashion, investment, snobbery, conversation —but a very few lend real interest and support to the arts. Only a fistful go to exhibitions, buy contemporary local artists' works, lend pictures for public exhibition, or are interested in the basic purpose of the arts— education.

Perhaps the explanation of all this is the fact that my profession has decided to call itself "show business." Still even in this area when the arts prove themselves "commercial," somehow the moguls in charge of operations can't see them as potentially "good business." When Edward G. Robinson, Billy Pearson, and I were on "The $64,000 Challenge," our audience was estimated at thirty million per week. Museum attendance rose throughout the country, the sale of art books soared. The American people were at a pitch of art excitement. Six months later Charles Collingwood on "Odyssey" for CBS presented "The Revolution of the Eye," with David Ebin and I helping out on the script. The show, filmed in the Museum of Modern Art, was a sensation. It explained visually and simply what has happened to our eyes in the past fifty years, how we have come to accept new forms, new concepts of art. Thousands of letters poured in, demands were made to replay it, which they did. Everyone (even CBS) admitted it was exciting, and yet on presenting the idea to them as a possibility for a weekly or monthly show—no one would touch it. Someday some sponsor will get a chance at the audience of millions who want *educational* entertainment, and I have a feeling that out of sheer grati-tude the public will buy lots of soap!

Edward R. Murrow, who almost singlehandedly has kept America informed at a high level, recently visited my wife and me on "Person to Person." Out of the blue he threw me a question that I have a suspicion the whole country has asked and would like answered. His question to me was personal: "What kind of a TV program would you like to do?" And of course my answer was personal, too: "I'd like to do an entertaining educational show, not Sundays at three in the afternoon, but at the prime time at night." I added that I thought the first TV executive who sanctioned this innovation would become a national hero. I really think he would.

But back once again to Hollywood. Of course, it isn't just the actors, or "the business." It's the people of the city in general. Many of them don't feel they *live* in Los Angeles; they just seem to migrate there and squat. They build eastern or midwestern houses, they support the dear old alma mater of their elsewhere youth and neglect the schools and colleges their children attend in California. They run with the pack. Typical are the annual state picnics for Iowans, South Dakotans, Ohioans, etc., but I have yet to see mention of a Californians' picnic. Still it would take TNT or the worst drought in history to get them to move out of their new but not completely adopted state. I guess it's always the same in a new country, and California, for all its growth and potential, is brand spanking new, and needs a spanking.

After the close of The Little Gallery and the Modern Institute of Art I still felt the need for my chosen avocation and decided to make myself available to any and all art groups whose self-appointed job was the spreading of visual appreciation and delight. It led me into high adventure and some mighty hard work, for many of these groups seem to have been dedicated to the appreciation of dead art and violently opposed to anything which showed the slightest signs of life. For many years in California, these groups had held back modern art, or any other advance in art, and in inviting me as a speaker because I was a movie actor, they let themselves in for some rude shocks and, I hope, equally rude awakenings.

In one traditional city nearby, the art group had not only stemmed the tide of modern art, they even managed, through banality that amounted almost to genius, to destroy what little tolerable talent there was in the community. Under the guidance of some painters who should have been politicians—so cunning was their hoodwinking of those artistic, timorous ladies into looking upon them as saviors, masters, and minds—the art output was at an ebb lower than anything I have ever seen, but it was their smugness that made them intolerable. They were so sure in their lack of talent.

This group made the dreadful mistake not only of asking me to speak but of putting me through an hour-long tour of their annual exhibition where each exhibitor personally explained his picture to me in words of one syllable—two would have been too many.

After my gentlemanly castigation of them and their work, through which they sat in stony silence, I was bombed with some of the most inane questions ever asked—and they received equally inane answers. One little frizzle-top flower painter dared me to explain a man whose work she had recently seen, wherein the lovely trees and bouquets of flowers were inhabited with lovers and people and animals—Marc Chagall. There was obviously only one contemporary answer: the housing shortage.

Another lady queried Rico Lebeun's "Descent from the Cross," in which he hoped to "put across" the age-old message of "man's inhumanity to man," with the dainty complaint that she preferred her crucifixions "pretty." Even the plaster church art of today can hardly make this bitter act "pretty," try as they will with their make-up-kit complexions and rolling, mascaraed eyes.

I think my fellow actors have always been a little suspicious of me and my "art kick," as they called it. They could never quite figure out why, if I like it, I just didn't shut up about it. Why should I want to "sell" everyone on the ideas of collecting, working for the arts, buying American art, etc.? I must say they are right about one thing: I can't keep my big mouth closed about art. It has meant so much to me that I want to share it with everyone. In the case of Los Angeles, I see the great need for cultural activity, and this is one way to do something about it. Also, I've seen so many actors stagnate with boredom in Hollywood. They grow into themselves like toenails, and success being a pretty heavy crown, much of Hollywood's bad reputation is caused by boredom—doing nothing, in the misguided thought that there's nothing to do.

Quite a few people in my profession have been curious about seeing our collection, and occasionally some brave souls will make the mistake of asking to see it. Before they can change their minds, we invite them to dinner. For some reason, most of them come expecting to see the usual Renoirs and Utrillos, and I'm afraid that the unknown names and seldom-seen (in Hollywood) modernity of our pictures rocks them a little. Not being current with contemporary art, they have no basis for understanding. But I must give them credit for trying, even if the results have sometimes been hilarious.

Van Johnson, who couldn't be a nicer man, asked to see it one time, so we invited about ten other interested parties, as well. They were all close friends of each other, if not of ours, and the evening could have been called a success, had not Van, in a fit of laughter over someone's really comical but serious attempt to define an enormous abstraction by Richard Diebenkorn, thrown his huge frame on the couch, whereupon the seven-foot-by-seven-foot painting in question fell off the wall behind him—and on his head.

At a time like that I wonder a little about myself—about my "art kick"—for at that moment I hadn't a thought about Van's head. I just rushed to make sure nothing had happened to the canvas.

I don't for a moment suggest that Hollywood people are any less understanding about modern art and life than others, but they do have the chance to be more attuned to everything, more receptive, and they rarely take advantage of it. One thing I should say in their defense, however, is that while they may not make use of all their advantages to live life fully, they sure can live it up.

On my first trip to Hollywood I met Edward G. Robinson, whose collection was the greatest and actually the only serious one in the movie colony at that time. I found the town was a little suspicious of him, too. Why should he spend all his money on art? Recently, when Eddie had to sell his wonderful collection for personal reasons, they knew one answer at least—three million, two hundred thousand dollars. I doubt if many people, in or out of Hollywood, have made a better investment financially, to say nothing of the twenty years of joy and education those paintings gave him and all the others who saw them at his home, or in the many exhibitions where they were lent.

Eddie made an extraordinary selection of paintings, and while I'm sad he had to lose them, I wonder if it occurred to anyone in our government that we're the only country in the world today that would have let them leave its shores. There were many of them of such calibre as to be rated "national treasure," and England, France, or Italy would have never allowed them to be sold abroad. Obviously, this is a recent feeling on their part, since every country has acquired, one way or another, the masterpieces of every other country. But it is, most importantly, an indication of the contemporary evaluation of art, not only monetary but aesthetic. There is indeed more wealth in our museums than in Fort Knox—but it's of greater use, certainly, considering the vast attendance at those museums. I can't think of anything drearier than a visit to Fort Knox. Besides, it would be so frustrating . . . all that gold—in the ground.

I've let myself in for some pretty classy beatings in my art endeavors, too. I've stuck my neck way out and almost had it chopped off a couple of times.

My phone rang one day, and a lovely club-voiced lady purred at the other end: "Mr. Price, I'm the program chairman for the Women Painters of the West, and we would like to challenge you to a duel." It seems I had given out an interview in a movie magazine to the effect that painting was the one art in which women were still second best. They had dominated all the others for the last fifty years, but at painting they were still, as they always had been, second-rate—and worse.

My program chairman had read this while under the drier at the beauty parlor, and, still damp, she flew to the phone to track me down and challenge me to put up or shut up.

Naturally, I accepted, and the time and place were set. Wilshire Ebell. Luncheon, with debate afterward.

Now the Women Painters of the West are not just that. They're a lot more . . . a group of one hundred and fifty violently dedicated ladies who banded together to give strength, en masse, to their passion for painting. Most of the most-recognized lady painters belong, as well as the ones who are determined to make it but haven't quite. One thing sure about them is that they have painted the West. Exhibitions of their work abound in deserts in bloom, or out of bloom; eucalyptus trees fingering the western skies; and neat arrangements of western flowers set on, or against, Oriental brocades. Also, there would seem to be not a child born west of the Rockies who hadn't posed for one of these ladies . . . and many distinguished adults have sat, too.

I walked into the luncheon, a few minutes late, to find them all seated under a hundred and fifty multi-flowered hats. It looked like a giant still life. The program chairman led me to my seat, banged on a glass, and said: "Well, girls, here he is." No applause, no cessation of folding the peas into the creamed chicken. I sat down next to the president.

I had always thought that one of the reasons women weren't particularly good painters was their delicate femininity, but Madame President looked as though she could have whipped off the Sistine Chapel in two days. She had vigor, and she looked at me as though she wished I had posed for St. Bartholomew—after his martyrdom! He was flayed alive as they intended to flay me.

Luncheon over, almost without a word I was led to the auditorium, sat on the stage, and introduced thusly: "This is Vincent Price, who says ladies can't paint. And now, Mr. Price, defend yourself!"

I started out bravely with the assertion that women, being able to create physically, did not have the need to express themselves, artistically—that they were the real creative force. Besides which, they were the most practical of God's creatures and ran the world in which men could dream and, dreaming, could create the beauty they could not give birth to, except mentally.

I guess this left-handed compliment hit those ladies with a little less force than a good left hook, for after I'd finished my "defense"— brilliantly (I thought) bringing up examples from Sappho to Rosalba Carriera, Rosa Bonheur, Mary Cassatt, and Marie Laurencin—the storm broke loose, and I've never spent a more fascinating, stimulating, or quick-on-my-feet hour and a half . . . dodging those dogmatic dames.

The Women Painters of the West were completely equipped to take on anyone from me to Bernard Berensen. They knew their art history and threw it at me like shafts of hate. They quoted the few good women painters of the past and their trials to join the world of men. One eighty-year-old allowed as how in her next incarnation, if she was unfortunate enough to be a woman, she was going to get herself a wife to do all the dirty work.

We fenced Rosa Bonheur against Velázquez, as far as horse flesh goes, and they showed me a Vigée-Lebrun I never knew, who, according to them, was a better portrait painter than Hyacinthe Riguad or anyone else in the eighteenth century.

It was a heated argument throughout, but one with great fun in it, for they knew they were using the weapons of wish-fulfillment against my defense of historical facts. They also knew that the final emancipation of women was imminent and that when women did enter the world of painting, without the tinkling shackles of femininity, they would really be on an equal footing with men. And somehow I felt it would happen soon, which, indeed, it seems to have done. Women today are really painting—like men!

The loveliest comment of all came from a battered matron who had hurled many a witty and knowledgeable barb at me from the audience. Backstage she vised my hand and thanked me for saving her a thousand dollars. I asked her how, and she told me she had a husband and four sons . . . that her life was dominated by men and men's demands. Painting was her one way of withstanding this onslaught, her foot in the door to being an entity. But it just didn't work. She had grown to hate men and was thinking of going to a psychologist about it. I had saved her this fee. She had taken all her hate out on me!

My first job as a juror of a really big exhibition was the Los Angeles and vicinity show in 1948. The late Donald Bear and Earl Loran were my co-jurors. It was a time when the best of the local artists had stopped submitting to the local shows because of past policies of which they disapproved, and because any work in the modern direction had automatically been rejected by past jurors. The traditional California painters were in full power, though what tradition they were in, no one had ever bothered to define.

Of the fifteen hundred paintings, graphics, and sculptures submitted to us, a thousand were "traditional." Endless desert landscapes, flowers, and a procession of the most vulgar nudes ever not to grace a calendar.

Although I had no knowledge of either of my fellow juror's tastes and, being humble before their many years of teaching, painting, and museum efforts, I found we were swinging into the selection on the same trapeze. There seemed to be a determination to look into the traditional for a real tradition—not just one invented in California—and to discard it if it wasn't there.

As in all huge local shows, there was an enormous amount of amateur work and an equally huge quantity of just plain bad painting. In this instance, so few of the really serious artists had submitted anything, our big job turned out to be the difficult selection of even a small number of quality pictures. But we made it, and curiously, they were half and half, traditional and modern, fifty of each.

It was a handsome show, and my two friends left for their respective homes in Santa Barbara and Berkeley with the feeling of a tough job well done. I remained in Los Angeles, and two weeks later, when the show opened, I wished I, too, had left town. All hell broke loose. Letters, phone calls, and cat calls poured into the director, commenting on the communist infiltration into the arts. One rather primitive painting called "The Little Red Schoolhouse," which couldn't have been more charming and traditionally American (of the New England school, almost Grandma Moses), was singled out as "real Red." And the first-prize picture of "A Ruined Church with Figures" was termed anti-religious.

But the two culminating recriminations were really fun. Channing Peake, one of our best California moderns, showed a painting of a butcher block with a beef head lying on it. The composition and technique were much influenced by Picasso, but it was a forceful work, inspired by Peake's avocation as a rancher and cattleman. This was labeled as pure communist and was said to represent the decapitation of capitalism. I had never known before that capitalists saw themselves as cattle.

The first Sunday the show was open the whole mess came to a head and gave the museum national publicity. One of the "rejectees" was so incensed he decided to put on a real demonstration. I remember his painting well. In fact, I'll never forget it. It was a blond babe, lolling languidly on a settee. Everything was baby pink—the pillows, the rug, the chair, and the babe herself. It was a nude to remember, all right, painted with the same technique used on wedding cakes. So this particular Sunday saw our artist, ensconced on the stairs of the museum, an easel at his side holding the rejected painting. There the master and the masterpiece remained for all visitors to see, handing out literature to the effect that the museum, the exhibition, and the jurors were all degenerate, communistic, and disgusting; and to back up this propaganda, or maybe to be a front for it, was the babe herself in the flesh.

In Los Angeles when we're aroused artistically, we go the whole way! But in the words of one of our columnists, "Don't get me wrong—I love Hollywood."

In my eighteen years there I've seen some startling changes. Movie actors are now clamoring to get aboard the art wagon. There's not a home without *some* paintings, and one member of the colony has amassed an amazing collection of Bernard Buffet's work. I'm told he has fifty paintings. Unfortunately, I may never get to see them, since the New York *Times'* brilliant critic Aline Saarinen quoted me rightly as saying I was about to manufacture a "do-it-yourself Buffet-kit."

However, there is still that really dedicated little group of people, some in the picture business, who are working to bring art vitality to our community, and I've seen similar groups all over the country, whose unselfish concern is to try and give the American public a chance to see for themselves the enormous excitement of art—all art—from all times and places.

One heartwarming and encouraging affair happened a few years back when several artists got together and decided to get their fellow artists to each contribute a work to be auctioned off for the Bonds for Israel. Several hundred paintings and drawings came in, and suddenly they were hard put to find a place to show them and to hold the auction. The Beverly Wilshire, one of our big hotels, donated space; the United Jewish Appeal got behind them with publicity—and I mean publicity. Dirigibles flew over the city with banners behind them, proclaiming the "Art Affair." Planes wrote it in the sky, and the night of the event looked like an opening at Grauman's Chinese. Lights, cameras, action. I was the auctioneer, and the list of guest auctioneers looked like a De Mille cast. Sir Cedric Hardwick, Dore Schary, George Jessel, Pat O'Brien, Eddie Cantor, Fanny Brice, Richard Conte, Mark Stevens, Joan Bennett, Red Skelton, and Frank Sinatra.

We cleared $50,000 and had one of the memorable evenings of our lives. George Jessel got the bids up to $2500 for a three-by-four-inch painting of President Roosevelt, done by an eighty-two-year-old woman. As an auctioneer, he gave the greatest performance of his life. Fanny Brice contributed a $2000 painting to be auctioned off and got so carried away with the bidding she bought it back herself for $2500. Eddie Cantor, not to be topped by Jessel, harangued the crowd with songs and wit and drew a bid of $1000 for a clown painted by Frank Sinatra.

All this may sound a little theatrical. (Who am I kidding? It is!) But a lot of other cities could benefit by this technique, and they're beginning to. Great gala parties are being given in all the museums to raise funds, and the citizens are joining in the fun of art, realizing at the same time that the museum can be the center of the cultural life of their cities and that they do, indeed, inspire and educate young people to participate in the great visual feast that the creative act has prepared for all of us.

You can fill your life so full of interests and activities, if you aren't careful, you have no life at all. I had become so determined to see Los Angeles get some of the gravy, culturally, I was neglecting my eyes while gaining knowledge—not firsthand, but through friends and books. Earl Stendahl's gallery was my only contact with Mexican pre-Columbian art and, close as Mexico is to California, I had never been there except for some delightfully delirious excursions to Tijuana, that border town to end all border towns.

So one day I quietly decided to go deeper into Mexico and see for myself. Stendahl's storerooms had convinced me that Mexico must be one of the most provocative countries in the world, inhabited by the most versatile, art-producing people who ever lived. I routed myself directly to Guatemala, then to Yucatán, and home, via Mexico City.

The first stop was Mexico City—to change planes for Guatemala—and I really felt like a foreigner when I was tracked through disinfected sawdust so I wouldn't bring hoof-and-mouth disease to the Mexican cattle, and then was put into a magnetic box to be sure I had no firearms. But I really knew I was far away from home when we landed in Guatemala and my luggage was held for a day and a half while they fumigated it. I'd thought I was pretty disinfected.

On the way to Guatemala the pilot of our plane, having asked me the purpose of my trip and finding out it was to see the ruins, swooped down over the archaeological sights of Monte Albán and Mitla, outside Oaxaca. There were a few moments when I thought we were going to join those ruins in ruin. He flew so low we could practically see inside the tombs, and to see their plan from the air was very exciting.

I knew there were no ruins in Guatemala City, but I expected (or hoped) to be wrong. There were none, and the city itself, a replacement for the colonial capital of Antigua which was destroyed several hundred years ago, had little to offer in antiquity but much in charm. The museum is great, and much of the top Maya material from other parts of the country is there—marvelously wrought jade jewelry, intricate polychromed pottery, as well as great steles from Pedras Negras, one of the finest Maya sculptural sites.

Mayan art is very special. Its great appeal is the savage, complicated forms in low bas-relief, ornate and monumental. The marvel of it is that these highly cultured primitives could bring it off with the implements they had. They were not afraid to tackle huge, hard stone, brittle jade, bone obsidian, and crystal—stone against stone—from the most delicate ornaments to the largest stones and façades of great buildings.

The late George Brainard, in his little book about the Mayas, tells of their routine of life that allowed for the great amount of time they put in on their public buildings. The people of Mexico and Central America lived almost exclusively on one crop: corn. This staple was planted, harvested, and stored during one half of the year, and during the remainder the entire population worked on the monuments. They lived simply, in thatched huts, but upon their gods, and the priests of their gods, they lavished talent and time, unequaled in any land except perhaps Egypt. There is one difference. As far as we know, these comparatively small tribes of people, with few slaves, did it voluntarily.

In the museum there I had a chance once more to see the copies done from the fierce murals at Bonompak, which my friend, Giles Healey, had discovered some years before and for whom I did the narration of his film, *The Ancient Maya*. Tikal, the largest of the Maya cities, and Bonompak were impossible at that time to reach, except by a dangerous and long pack trip, and the only other important site, even vaguely accessible, was Quiriguá, a fourteen-hour trip by banana train into the heart of the jungle. I didn't have the time but I had the inclination, so I made arrangements through my taxi driver to charter a small plane and fly to Quiriguá. *The Ancient Maya* had been sponsored by the United Fruit Company, and as narrator I didn't think I had much claim to their hospitality. But I thought I'd mention it (whom I mentioned it to or how it worked, I can't remember), and it worked. An *autocarril* would meet me at the landing strip, near the site, and take me to the ruins.

The flight itself was wildly wonderful over the great jungle and along the turgid rivers. I asked my young pilot where we would land, in case of trouble. It was a mistake, for he told me that whatever landing fields there are may not be there next time you want to use them; the jungle grows that quickly. I was a little apprehensive, but a clearing did finally appear and we did land, and I knew what he meant. We came down on a cornfield that at that moment was being planted. A month from then there would be another field—you hoped.

The *autocarril* was there to meet me and my taxi driver, who, on the way to pick up the chartered plane, had said he had always wanted to see Quiriguá, so I asked him to come along. An *autocarril* is an old bus from which the tires have been removed and replaced by make-shift iron wheels that will run on the tracks. It's an interesting sensation, riding in one—a little like having the d.t.'s, but you're conscious you're having them.

We did reach the ruins by way of miles of banana trees that had been sprayed with some copper sulphate solution so that the whole landscape was blue-green against the dark green of the tropical forest. The ruins themselves are mysterious beyond all belief, set as they are now in a clearing, hacked out like a rectangular box, the walls of which are dense forest and vines. There, towering into the sky, are the amazing monoliths of stone, every inch of their twenty-odd feet carved with the most marvelous glyphs and symbols, topped by a beautiful serene face which again is topped by a headdress of stone plumes and beads. There are at least a dozen of them, varying in size and ornamentation, and since this was my first actual contact with Maya monuments *in situ*, none I have seen since has seemed more impressive.

I've never been to Egypt, but it will have to go a long way to top the land of the Mayas. Our American museums have some great examples of Egyptian art, but none I have seen can touch the Mayan for sheer excitement of design or, for that matter, in monumental conception. Egyptian sculpture seems cold and dictatorial by comparison.

On the way home from Quiriguá I asked the pilot to put down in some little village in the highlands where I could see native life and catch a commercial plane later that week. He let me out, after landing, of course, and I saw native life, frighteningly and firsthand. Finally, I connected with a plane back to Guatemala City—but that's another story and, looking back on it, an amusing one, but it wasn't then!

The trip from Guatemala to Yucatán is like flying over a green carpet, but the knowledge that that carpet covers some of the greatest ruins of ancient times, and treasures of inestimable value, made it a neck-stretcher par excellence for me. I never took my eyes off the terrain, hoping that some temple would show its head through the tangle of trees. But it didn't. At least not until we were approaching Mérida. Then suddenly the jungle was alive with ruins, like outcroppings of rock in an endless lawn. When and if the whole Maya civilization is brought to light, it will be a sight second to none in the world, for these were not as in Egypt and Greece—a conquered people whose defeaters destroyed and plundered. These are abandoned sites, deserted for a dozen conjectured reasons, but more often left intact for the greatest of all preservers—nature.

Yucatán is enchanting. The Spanish people (for they are more Spanish than Mexican) speak English with a soft, southern accent. This intrigued me, and I was told it was because most of them were educated in New Orleans. Until World War II, Yucatán had no airfield for commercial lines, and there still is no direct road to Mexico City because of the enormously high mountain range between this state of Mexico and the others. Because of this, Mérida has retained a lazy charm, and the tourist, when I was there only a few years ago, was still a rare and welcome attraction.

But Mérida is a colonial city, modernizing slowly, and far removed from the centers of Maya culture, Chichen Itzá and Uxmal. The former is a seventy-mile drive across the flat, heavily wooded landscape. Not too far out of the capital, you begin to feel the Mayas come to life. There will be groups of Maya-thatched huts, neat and white, and then a living face will confront you, right off the carvings and vases.

They are small, immaculate people with beautiful golden brown skin, slant eyes, and black, *black* hair. And the nose—large, arched, and wonderfully impressive—is somehow reminiscent of the people of ancient Crete. But they are Mayan, no question about that, and you feel nothing has touched them in two thousand years.

A little sign, the last of a fascinating series of unpronounceable names, announces that you have arrived at Chichen Itzá—the Well of the Itzas. A charming hotel with Mayan guest cottages awaits you, and your hosts are the progressive and interested Barbachannos. It was dark when I arrived, and electricity is still a rare commodity, so the ruins were swallowed in the dark. I had a fine dinner, served by Maya maidens in lovely native dress. I had prepared to stifle my curiosity with sleep, when over the trees the moon appeared . . . the maiden moon of Mexico.

The ruins are closed at night, but I begged one of the attendants to let me see them by the light of that moon. He agreed, and we trudged along the road, climbed a fence, and instantly I was a Mayan, too. The great pyramid, with its ninety steps, loomed ghostly white out of the night. Following my guide's instructions, I panted to the top and up the five more steps that, with the ninety on four sides, make intentionally the three hundred and sixty-five of our calendar. Breathless, I saw below me the great open plaza; to one side, the ball court; to the other, the Temple of the Warriors. It was not a view of details, for the moon cast silver shadows, and you could not see Chac-Mool atop the warrior temple, or the frieze of jaguars or skulls of plumed warriors on columns. None of this was visible. But if you looked through your romantic eye, the ancient people soon appeared and marched with solemn steps across the great expanse. A rattle and a flute made mystic music, and a quetzal feather turned peacock blue in the path of the moon. My guide said not a word, but he timed my reaction most dramatically. He somehow sensed that I was carried away to a point of sacrificing myself to Tlaloc (or some other night-walking deity) by throwing myself down the stairs—a bumpy offer, at best. Then he made the slightest of moves, and, slithering down the steps like a silent Pied Piper, my big feet hypnotically followed him clumping down each narrow rise to the bottom.

We walked in silence back to the lodge, and just before we got there he broke his silence by a stone-walled well. Once more the guide, he said this well was, by tradition, the home of Maya spirits but that he, being a modern Maya man, of course didn't believe that nonsense. I picked up a stone and dropped it over the edge. Dead silence, then a musical splash, and without warning a great rush of wind as hundreds of bats, their rest disturbed, took to the air around us. I was scared to say the least, but I recovered enough to take some money from my pocket for the guide. He was gone, vanished into the night, my Modern Maya Man.

Chichen Itzá is one of the wonders of the world. It is an entity not to be described in detail, though the details are wonderful and weird, strong and savage all at once. But one must go there, become a Maya for a minute, and come away with awe for the ancient peoples of America who created this equal of any other glorious monument to man's artistic genius that there is on earth.

Hollywood looks kind of new after Chichen Itzá, Uxmal, or Teotihuacan. Even the Prudential Building, that pride of nighttime Wilshire Boulevard, looks slightly prefabricated beside the hand-wrought stone-lace façade of Uxmal. Still, I suppose without these comparisons, you can never know the difference between a labor of love and labor. My wife, my son, and I take off for Mexico whenever we can. We have made incomplete surveys of the Toltecs, Aztecs, Mayas, and the exuberant baroque art and architecture of colonial Mexico. Of all the countries I've visited, I think Mexico still has more hidden charm than any place else and more in the open, too. It is a country not yet entirely modernized, where folk art is still the tradition and practice and delight of the people. Would to God it could survive commercialism, but of course, it can't. Each year we go there, something has disappeared. The Oaxacan pottery is thinner, less inventive; the Pueblo tiles become stenciled; the lovely old buildings are being patched with stainless steel and equipped with neon lights. Only the tourist towns, guarding their charm with hand on holsters, are able to hold back the advance of mass-produced taste and merchandise. But it's there, just around the corner, waiting to turn us all into identical nonentities.

Only through art can one retain individuality. Only the artist dares to see the same things differently. Art, indeed, is for the masses, but it cannot, or must not, be mass-produced. All of us who are, or want to be, an audience for the arts can help by our insistence that they be free from the dictates of commercial taste; by supporting them with our interest and incorporating them into our living. Make it a part of your life, and it will repay you in liveliness a thousandfold.

Actors may be the victims of some of the more terrifying publicity on record, and sometimes they may even deserve it, but there are nice moments when everything seems to be going your way, when the penalty you have to pay for being well known pays off. I have always left myself open for the pay-off, because in this avocation of mine it can mean the difference between an open and shut door to some world of art I've never seen.

Two big pay-offs have come to me and added enormously to this insatiable quest I seem to be on—to see everything ever done by man in the way of that old devil art. The first was an invitation by the Peruvian government to be one of the Hollywood personalities at their first world's fair. It turned out to be more of a Peruvian fair than one of the world, and the handful of actors brought from Hollywood had to make up for the rest of the world, along with ten of the most beautiful girls anyone has ever seen, who were "queens" from Latin, Central, and South America.

Marina Cisternas, the leading Spanish-language columnist in Hollywood, was our hostess and guide and, in sending off material to Peru, came to interview me. During the interview, which with the dynamic Señora Cisternas is always fun, we got onto my interests in Mexican and South American art. Marina was delighted, for all foreign countries love to have their visitors interested in them. Especially Americans, who are not supposed to be interested in anything but themselves and the rich and comfortable old U.S.A. The interview ended, and we all started to make ready to fly to Peru. I got some more books about that country and made my usual lists from the illustrations of what I wanted to see, and what's more—I read the books.

The flight to Peru is long and adventurous and beautiful. Mary sleeps well in the air, but I fly every inch of the way, so I was exhausted when we finally began our descent.

On arrival we were met by a group of the most distinguished Peruvian archaeologists and professors. They were extremely warm in welcoming us to Peru, and before we left the airport I had exchanged learned pleasantries with all of them about the Chimu, Nascan, Paracas, and Inca cultures. I was very thankful I had read those books, because the questions those gentlemen threw at me would have floored me, had I relied solely on the interest in Peruvian culture I had avowed to Señora Cisternas.

We stepped into the car to drive into town, but before we could leave, each of the great men shook my hand and kissed Mary's, and almost in unison said, "Good-by, Dr. and Mrs. Price. We look forward to your lecture on Peruvian art."

Thank God, we were alone on that drive with only our driver at the wheel, for the "Dr." Price and the news of my lecture turned my heart to ice. We rode in stunned silence and, had the manager of the Bolivar Hotel not sent up two wonderfully strong Pisco Sours, I might never have opened my mouth again.

What had happened, we found out, was that Marina, with expansive Spanish enthusiasm for my interest in Peruvian art, had embroidered it a bit until I had become not only a great expert on the subject to the Peruvian public, but they had decided since I knew so much to confer on me the title of doctor . . . NOT the degree, mind you, just the title.

My Spanish being non-existent, I quickly decided there was no possibility of explaining my way out of that doctorate, so Dr. Price, with the help of a genuine doctor—Dr. Walter Guiezieke, an American archaeologist of great note who lived in Peru—set about stuffing himself with knowledge of the fabulous cultures of ancient Peru.

It's amazing how much knowledge of a subject you can obtain if you're interested in it, how much more if you're challenged by someone to talk about it, and what an incredible amount if everyone around you thinks you know a lot to begin with. We really were given the A-one archaeological treatment, and what I didn't learn from the distinguished gentlemen who lavished their knowledge on me, I picked up from making some purchases in the shops of Lima. The dealers (as always, and everywhere) were extremely informative, and the first-hand feel of the material you get by owning something gave me a fairly keen insight into those many and brilliantly varied civilizations that populated Peru from before Christ until the conquest by Pizarro.

Aside from the architectural genius of the Incas, still so visible in Machu Pichu and Cuzco, and the superb polychromed pottery of the Nascan and Chimu peoples, the most impressive remains of ancient Peru are the textiles of Paracas. In the museum at Lima the finest of these weavings are displayed and beautifully modeled by male and female dummies, completely dressed in the most brilliant designs and colors, and accompanied by stuffed llamas, who are also covered from head to hoof with wonderfully woven goods.

The variety and invention of these designs stagger you, and as you look at them in amazement, it hits you all of a sudden that you are looking at paintings by Paul Klee or Joan Miró. Once again that sensation so prevalent in the arts: that time has no stop, that yesterday, today, and tomorrow are all fresh and new and strangely alike in feeling where the peak artists and artisans are concerned.

Another pay-off came on tour with *Don Juan in Hell*, Shaw's excerpt from *Man and Superman*. The three men in this piece were Charles Boyer, Cedric Hardwicke, and myself, and what a treat it was to be involved with these master actors and meaningful men—Cedric, whose wit is as refreshing as English rain and just as plentiful, and Charles, whose Gallic in-person charm surpasses even the classic personification of it which is synonymous with his name on a billboard. We spent the days of our one-night stands in the local museums. Actually, we lost Cedric after about two weeks. He'd had his fill of museums. But Charles is as avid a museum-goer as I am and has a fine collection of French paintings, the authors of many of which were his confreres as a young actor in France, for the arts are inseparable there. So despite the loss of our British friend, we continued, separately or together, to see what each town had to offer. Charles was amazed at the wealth of material in American museums, and while I knew more of them to begin with, I was mighty impressed, too. Kansas City, with its unparalleled Oriental collection; Cleveland, since then even richer in rare and wondrous gifts from the late Leonard Hanna; Toledo and the glass collection plus one of the finest Velázquezes; Portland and the Northwest Indian pieces—everywhere fine examples of world art.

We never confessed it to each other, but the whole tour was leading up to a grand climax neither of us expected to achieve, the Barnes Foundation in Merion, Pennsylvania. We had both heard of the difficulties of getting into the Barnes collection from museum directors (who had been banished as a race by the irascible doctor) and from just plain John Q. Public, who had tried to no avail. The doctor had died a couple of years before our proposed visit, but things hadn't eased up. Ted Thomas, my ex-Yale roommate had lived in Philadelphia for fifteen years and tried desperately to get into it, but hadn't made it. Only one friend of his had ever been there, and he had pulled a trick that had become legendary. He had heard at his garden supply depot that a load of manure was being delivered to the Barnes estate, so he bribed the driver to let him deliver it. Dressed in dirty overalls, he made his delivery, unloaded it, and then rang the bell, saying he'd heard there were some "pitchers" in this house. The doctor welcomed him with open arms, and he spent a tenuous two hours, keeping his elegant Harvard accent from showing—but he saw the "pitchers."

I told Charles about this ruse, but the thought of Charles Boyer in overalls, and with the world's most famous French accent, sent us into hysterics. We both resigned ourselves to making inquiry, but we hadn't the slightest idea we would get in. We asked everyone we knew, and they all shook their heads sadly and promised they'd try.

Simultaneously, one night we were summoned to be in Merion at noon the next day, and you can believe me, we were there waiting at eleven forty-five, finger poised over the bell which was sounded on the stroke of noon, and for the next two hours we reveled in the opulence of the doctor's hundred and fifty Renoirs, ninety Cézannes, dozens of Matisses, Soutines, etc., etc., besides extraordinary African pieces and his exemplar collection of hardware, locks, hinges, etc., which are mounted between every painting. Miss del Mazo, the present curator and long-time friend of the doctor, personally escorted us and couldn't have been more gracious or informative. Subtly, at two o'clock, we found ourselves where we had come in, and that being the length of time visitors are allowed to stay, we were let out.

There's no question about it. It is one of the things to see in this country and worth every effort to get to see it. One day I'm sure the bans will be lifted, and all who desire to may see it. For Charles and me it was a treat we talked about for the rest of the tour, gloating in our success to all we met who had not been able to get at it. We came to some conclusions about the pictures there that rather amazed us. First, that Renoir, en masse, is pretty hard to take. One hundred and fifty candy-box covers of pink and white ladies and children make you want to go on a sugar-free diet. And our second summing up was that Cézanne is one of the big masters of all time. Until you've seen those gem-like Cézannes in the Barnes Foundation, you haven't seen Cézanne. I know I've worked the word to death, but they are GREAT.

Meanwhile, back in Hollywood, the industry was trying its hand at making movies about artists. *Moulin Rouge*, glamorously lit by Eliot Elisofon, was the life story of Toulouse-Lautrec, and for the first time in my life I wanted to ask for my money back. How they could reduce to absurdity the story of a genius, I'll never know, but they did. The sound track that kept repeating over and over "Poor little Toulouse-Lautrec" should have ended up with "Poor little audience." They turned the life of one of the most beguiling nineteenth-century artists (and a man of innate dignity and unconquerable will) into a sentimental soap opera. They only equaled this with the life of Frédéric Chopin, which should have been titled *Kiss the Blood Off My Piano Keys* but wasn't.

However, occasionally the industry does tackle an artist's life and come up with a work of art. *Lust for Life,* from Irving Stone's sentimental and sensationally successful novel by the same name, was translated into the most moving moving picture I ever saw. Imaginatively produced by John Houseman, vehemently directed by Vincente Minnelli, and heroically played by Kirk Douglas, it was relentless in its canvassing of Van Gogh's life, good and bad, rough and smooth, colorful and drab. It treated him like a creator and made his tragic self-death a triumphant testimony to the true artist's purpose—to report life as he sees it. You, or at least I, felt no tears at his death. Only a sense that if a man can achieve what he did, then, to quote Van Gogh himself, "In an artist's life, death perhaps is not the hardest thing there is to bear."

I F I COME FROM A LONG LINE OF ANYTHING, IT'S A LONG LINE
of collectors. I've told of my mother's penchant for collecting, my father's hoards of fuses, light bulbs and essential knickknackeries like
corkscrews, knives, bottle openers, and luggage. My youngest sister is a
pack rat whose husband used to send her off on a trip every other year
so that he could get rid of the tons of paper, string, old toys, candle
ends, and huge balls of tin foil which she never stopped collecting from
World War I. In fact, she never threw anything away. The rainy day is
a constant threat to this dear sister of mine. She had something saved
for every one, and since we are known for our floods in Missouri, she
felt she should be well equipped.

My older sister doesn't collect material things, with the exception
of family mementos, but she could never stop collecting people, and
she is the rightfully proud possessor of the world's largest collection
of friends. It may have started when she won the "Kindness Cup"
at finishing school. She may or may not still have that cup, but she
still has every friend she ever made.

My brother really specialized in *not* collecting, with one exception
—clothes. As untidy and unmade-bed-looking as I am, he is neat, slick,
and immaculate . . . in a word, well dressed.

A great many members of our family collected debts. At one point in the depression of the early thirties, my staunch, self-effacing father was known to be supporting thirty-five real relatives and sundry friend-relatives.

I should mention my one grandmother, whom I never met but who, according to legend, was forever collecting her wits and herself.

I was a collector from the day I was born, and I was born curious. I was also born with a warped sense of where to save and where to spend. I'm penurious in odd ways, like electricity saving and using everything to the last drop or bite, but have always gone hog-wild for any art object. This is my cross, and until the greatest auction sale in history cuts me down to the bare essentials, I'm doomed to carry that cross—and by the way, I collect crosses.

I must say my beginning instincts were right. The first thing I had the sense to collect was money, without which—— Well, need I go further? Penny banks grew heavy, and an early love of secret hiding places—books made into boxes, secret panels and loose bricks and bathroom tiles—gave me the thrill of buried treasure as I secreted hard-earned dollar bills or shiny silver coins behind or under them. I begged my family to forego toys and nonsensical children's books and give me money or, later on, with patriotic pride, War Savings Stamps. These lovely stamps had everything for the budding collector: pictures, patriotism, and prosperity. One way and another, I collected enough money to start buying bits and pieces by the time I was twelve, and to put at least a down payment on my trip to Europe when I was sixteen. I still have hang-overs of all these traits; I still hide money and have pathetically small "picture" accounts in several assorted banks, east and west. I sneak little money into them, and out just as quickly, much to the disgruntlement of the bankers. But by this time my eccentricities are becoming widely known, if no less begrudgingly accepted . . . and I still turn off lights, causing many a guest to have to grope his or her way down the front stairs.

Money is the root of all evil, and collecting derives from the same root. Perhaps it's evil, too, but as Shakespeare's tomb bears witness,

"The evil that men do lives after them." So, without finishing the quotation, I'll just say thank you to the great collectors who have left the world infinitely richer, and hope that perhaps one day I can write a book about them, not only the famous ones, but the ones who went broke, who literally pawned their souls to gather unto themselves peculiar riches.

If I have a credo, a philosophy of life, it's connected intimately with collecting. The things I have collected are my bulwark against boredom, and gratitude is not left out in my accounting of the fortune of wonder I have found in the world of art.

But, before I get too far into this bug of collecting, it might be well to define the word as I have learned to interpret its several meanings. All collectors I've ever known will agree that it is a disease, one from which there is no cure, and the only serum known that can prevent it is poverty. It can also *cause* poverty. Secondly, it is what is loosely known as an instinct. You are always hearing about people who have an instinct for it or, more vulgarly, a nose for it. Come to think of it, it is an animal sort of instinct at that. Collectors are daddy bears protecting their new acquisitions, bull walruses fighting competitively to be married to some object, pack rats picking up and putting down beauty, or hoarding squirrels storing away goodies. And the nose has a great deal to do with it, in story, if not in fact, though I've never smelled a painting and I can remember only one incident where my nose actually caused me to (in this case) uncollect something; a Northwest Coast wooden Indian bowl, whose generations of blubber storage could not be coaxed to leave it. So, it left me.

If you can define collecting, or what it does to you, it does this above all: inevitably, if you fall in love with something you want to possess it, or at least sample it. I know there are many varieties of collectors, but the ones I trust most and who interest me most are the ones who just can't help it. They are the "unfortunates" (and I say that lightly) to whom a casual glance in a museum or at an exhibition is not enough; they want to handle it, X-ray it with their mind's eye, feel it, if it is touchable. They have to go to bed near it and wake next to it, and in the end, "marry it" by purchase, since borrowing does no good. You can even play all sorts of tricks on yourself—like hiding it or walking down a different street—but eventually, it will burn its way through steel doors or drawers onto your walls and tables.

The other kinds of collectors are those who do it for investment, for snobbery (some even for hate, it would seem); those who take art off the market and put it in seclusion; the collectors who must have everything of one kind—who only look for the rarest or the cheapest or the most expensive—even though they may begin to collect for love, they mostly seem unloving, and without the real motive for collecting, which is a longing to be at one with an object.

There's one question that must be answered: why collect at all? Well, one way to answer this is to affirm that almost everyone is a collector of something. Daily you read about people dying on skid row, only to have their mattresses ripped open or a safety-deposit box discovered, stuffed with cash and securities. Housewives collect everything: spices, string, paper, pots, pans, silverware, glasses, china. Tourists collect everything everywhere. There are serious collectors of rocks, gems, buttons, fabrics, books, stamps, firearms, arrowheads, ceramics, copperware (how well I know), toy banks, mechanical toys, dolls, post cards, match covers, knives, forks, woods, spoons—in fact, there is hardly anything that isn't collected by someone. People press flowers, butterflies, bugs; they risk their lives to get specimens of fossils, rare insects, fish, stones, pearls. Just name it, someone will seek it out and carefully put it away from harm, and that's another important aspect of the disease—preservation.

Children start immediately to collect. They ruthlessly destroy what is commonplace to them, like toys, and deftly guide a tin soldier, a doll, a blanket through the desolation of their childhood years to safety at the other side. When a Tarzan book takes their fancy, they want more. They build collections, they save their allowances to buy stamps, flip cards, cigar bands, samples, and because of their natural destructiveness these childhood objects become among the rarest collectors' items, their chance of survival being so slight.

I remember when I first became conscious of the value of rare books. Searching through my family's bookshelves for anything rare, in the seat of our music bench I came across a first edition of *The Adventures of Tom Sawyer*. Trembling, I opened the cover, and the contents revealed two generations of youthful crayola colorings of the illustrations, with my sisters' and brother's names dashed boldly in green wax across the ends, and my own first marks neatly cut with a knife on the inside of the back cover. Value, nothing—not even sentimental—since my pot of gold had been emptied by loving hands at home.

One of my first serious experiences with other collectors came about in 1931 through an assignment given me by my two nieces, aged six and eight. I was embarking on a trip abroad with the Yale Glee Club. They had been collecting everything as little girls will, in a dilatory fashion—samples, wedding cake, wishbones for a rainy day, and toward the end of spring that year they started in on book-match covers. They had done amazingly well with traveling uncles, grandparents, and parents' friends, and had many a neat cigar box stocked with covers from all parts of the U.S.A. and Canada. As I was leaving for an extensive tour of Europe, city-wise at least, they extracted a promise to keep my eyes open and not to pass up an opportunity to acquire (or steal) any and all match covers. I, of course, agreed and started at once in New York in bars, hotels, restaurants, etc., to steal, pick up, and as occasionally as possible buy these rare and geographically informative objects. At least two dozen went up the gangplank with me to be used and then carefully flattened out, rubber-banded, and saved. Several choice items were acquired in transit from glamorous and semi-glamorous fellow passengers, and one serious altercation came about as I dove for a discarded match cover, tossed irreverently in the gunwales by a non-collector no doubt, only to be staggered to the deck by head-on contact with an elderly gentleman who was also a collector. We half-laughed over the incident, but he, being elderly, got the item, which came from a remote hotel in a remote town in the state of Washington. He had never heard of the town, hence its rarity. But the adventure turned out well, as he liked my collector's instinct. Because he was elderly and traveling first class, every time we met, when I snuck up to first class, he bought me a beer, and he even turned out to be a distant friend of a more distant cousin, which seems to happen to me wherever I go.

Collecting brings people together. He showed me his haul, since coming aboard, and it was prodigious. Obviously, I was in the wrong class, or else being so close to the boilers my classmates and fellow cabinmates were snitching lights from the stokers. Match covers were rare down below, and, come to think of it now, my elderly upper-class friend may have sneakily descended to glean my fields while I was practicing glee with the Yale club. But he was fun and the beer was free.

France was our first point of contact, and I drooled at the prospect of risqué covers from the Folies-Bergère. But the Swedish match king still had a firm grip on Paris, and wooden matches in boxes (which were *outré* to my nieces) were the order of the day. My main sources in Paris were careless or thoughtless Americans who, wary of wooden matches and frightened of the wax ones, would finally use up folders and throw them under passing taxis, under which I almost found myself several times. Anyway, the sweet music of their horns became familiar, and I rejoiced in their warnings.

The outcome of that promise was twelve hundred covers, or thereabouts, picked up everywhere from the sewers of Paris to the Grand Canal. Each had a little history, a little romance, and I enjoyed collecting them immensely, even if, on presenting them (all ten pounds of them) proudly to my nieces on my return, I was informed curtly that they were no longer interested in match covers and would I please give them my collection of cigar bands which my father and brother had picked up for me some years back.

Reluctantly, I threw them away, as the vogue had stopped, but I still treasure one match cover. On being entertained at the White House by F.D.R. on the occasion of playing *Outward Bound* for his polio benefit, I stole a book of matches. Back at the hotel I snuck the memento out, only to find not the presidential seal but a motto reading "Stolen from the desk of the President of the United States."

To end this episode, may I say I still find my pockets full of matches whenever I return from a trip, and some special ones are carefully put beyond the reach of myself and my seventeen-year-old son, who (he thinks) nobody knows smokes.

The junk store is, I would imagine, the first quarry of the young would-be collector. It was mine, and a temple of covetousness it was. My favorite one was damned difficult to get at, being miles away from home; still I had a million excuses ready to take long bike rides to see friends about homework, etc.

Early treasures have a way of disappearing, and all I have left of that junk shop's yield are the disassembled parts of a Chinese junk, carved out of ivory. It was disassembled when I bought it at the age of twelve, but I put it together only to have it wrecked by dusting hands at home, a dozen times, at least. That and a piece of bone from the catacombs in Rome, which, being very tall, I stole from an upper tomb on my first trip to Europe and which for years I kept neatly and tenderly entombed in a tuft of cotton, cradled in a German-silver matchbox my mother had thrown away. When I found it, it was badly dented but, I felt, a fitting home for my lost saint's bone, which I still revere —when I can find it.

The junk store still holds a ghastly fascination for me. There are very few of them anywhere in the United States that I haven't been in. There is always a chance something is there that everyone has overlooked, or, as I prefer to think, they just weren't smart enough to know what it was.

When I first came to Hollywood and things were very tough (my first picture being a flop), I took up my slack time by prowling around the wonderful junk shops that existed then, all over the town. Now they are "antique shops" and grand to commeasure with the growth of this metropolis. But at that time they had the uninterior decorated jungle atmosphere that really made them dens of possibility. My son was about to be born, and I was saving my money, but one day, wandering amongst the junk, I hit it big. I came upon the most beautiful piece of African sculpture I had ever seen. It was a hundred dollars, which I knew was too much, but I had to have it. Also, I knew my poor wife would hate it (and me for having bought it); so I also bought an amethyst bracelet to put around its neck to ease the blow when I showed it to her. The blow was struck, and I had guessed right. She hated it, but she loved the bracelet; so all was not lost, and I was allowed to keep the statue in the closet.

In those lean days I made no pretense of trying to buy anything good, and all I was adding to my small collection was, in truth, junk, but come to think of it, I've always been a collector of everything. There was even a desperate period in which I collected butterflies firsthand, at the source, in fields of goldenrod, and being the most allergic of men to whatever it is that goldenrod has, it's no wonder that collection was short-lived. I can still hardly see a butterfly anywhere without sneezing.

I've pressed flowers, strung shells, polished rocks, stuck stamps, mounted post cards, blown eggs, pinned insects, skinned snakes, refinished furniture, clipped clippings, hoarded Christmas ornaments along with the best of Americans. I've never paid out a penny without looking to see if it has an Indian head. I automatically peer inside every book everywhere to see if it's a first edition, and I'm probably the rudest guest any collector can ask into his house. I've just learned, at my ripe age, to say hello to my host and hostess first, before gluing my eyes to the walls or shelves or wherever their treasures are displayed. My wife tried to break me of this nasty habit by pointing out my resemblance to a newly met art friend who came to a party at our house—his first visit. He walked in, vaguely said hello to us, cased the joint, and then proceeded to take five of our other guests on a guided tour of the collection.

I recently had an overwhelming urge to collect spoons. They seem so fundamental, and they really are very beautiful, especially primitive spoons, which must have been invented just after hands, if not before.

Mary broke me of that, however, and I gave up without a whimper, but drawings, which are my passion, she can't break me of, deride them as she will, comment on their lack of color, their sketchiness. I still manage to sneak them into the house, hide them in drawers, save old frames, save money to have them matted and put in the old frames. I'm sure she's not fooled for an instant, but the pleasure of sneaking a drawing into the house and looking at it surreptitiously is too great to admit she's been on to me all the time.

She has her own absurd collecting passions, too. She collects everything I don't: cookbooks, copper molds, appliances, and above all, junk. Recently the Carl Laemmle estate was destroyed to make room for a subdivision. Mary made it a point to be there with the wrecking estimator. Hardly a worn wooden turning or a piece of tile left that enormous estate that wasn't taken directly to our garage. Even a lonely clump of lethal cactus was rescued by her from the path of a bulldozer. It was only when she took me into the basement where, with lustful eyes, she showed me a whole fake Mayan temple that I drew the line. But I had to eat my words when a half-ton, out-of-date, and out-of-use fireless cooker weighed down our station wagon and was, eventually, turned by her capable and imaginative hands into the greatest double ice bucket of all times. It doesn't even leak, and two strong men can lift the lid . . . if they've had only one drink.

Her cactus-collecting period was the most difficult and dangerous for all of us. It culminated in a breathless escape from the state troopers when we fetched fifteen barrel cacti, ranging from cracker-barrel size to beer barrel, from the washes of southern California. It came to light they frown on the removal of native cacti from their natural habitat (so, I might add, do I), but we were safe. She saw to it that we stole them from private property.

Coming from Arizona once, she hid a particularly vicious one in the glove compartment. Her smuggling triumph was somewhat flattened by the fact that, once across the border, she found she could have brought it into California legally. Crestfallen, she forgot all about her prize. Weeks later a giant-sized stigmata was received by me when she asked me to look for her gloves in that compartment.

On a recent trip to Mexico she discovered tile, as a medium. Now, where expensive wooden floors met our feet in our old Spanish house, glorious patterns of multi-colored tile meet the eye, and she has become an expert on glazes, grouting, and ceramics in general. We have our own kiln, and what we can't buy or gouge out of some condemned building we, God help us, make ourselves.

In 1950, Mary and I set off on a European trip. I was to do a picture with Errol Flynn, whose looks and vigor were being tested for the last time before he decided to become the character everyone had always thought him to be. Mary designed the costumes for the delightful French actress Micheline Presle. That was the reason we went to Europe, but the result, because the picture was doomed from the start, was a return to the U.S.A. three months later, with a pretty exciting collection of stuff.

We didn't know it, but it was a last gasp for the middle-income collector. Five years later the prices of everything began to soar, and all kinds of art and art objects were vacuumed from European shops by the collectors of the world at large.

That summer, there still were treasures to be found, and we got our share. Mary was interested in the art of the kitchen, and, having mastered French to the extent of "Avez-vous des moules à gâteau en cuivre?" she did indeed triumph over many a reluctant storekeeper who was forced to retreat into the kitchen and bring back a copper cake mold or else receive the full turn on the heel and out, by the Prices.

Their variety was really impressive, and I do think she gleaned some of the best cake molds that were left in France and Italy. Hitler and Mussolini had melted most of them down during the war years, so they really have become scarce, and the modern machine-stamped molds have little character or inventiveness of shape. Hers run from the lively lobster to the stately lion; from Victoria Regina to the austere symbols of the Church. No ladies have ever visited our home without jealousy oozing out of every pore when they see her collection. I particularly love the ones who depreciatingly toss them off by, "Who has the time to polish those things?" Bitches!

Errol Flynn was disengaging a princess at that point, and she was apparently hard to break off with. Her royal blood, I suppose. But if that match was not made in heaven, the results for us were heaven-sent. Errol arrived a month late, and since he was co-producer and co-writer, plus star number one, we could hardly start the picture. So there we were, poor things, stranded in Paris with all expenses paid and a tidy salary coming in. Nothing like this had ever happened to us before (or since), so we really had a chance to case Paris, art-wise and pleasure-wise. We bought a little secondhand English Standard so that the environs, as well, would not escape our scrutiny for drawings and copper molds.

We cruised up and down and around France in our little British bug, a car so relentlessly Protestant that it would balk every time we hit a cathedral town. This pleased the French, not because it stalled, but because Mary refused to learn to drive it and consequently had to push it through Rheims and Chartres and all other cathedral towns, with lines of robust Frenchmen happily looking on but offering not a shove to help her.

We came back with some lovely loot—about twenty drawings, fifty copper molds, enough white faïence china for a sit-down dinner for thirty, and two of the most precarious objects ever brought to these shores—a delicate little Greek angel of the fifth century and a monstrously heavy sixteenth-century bronze king from Benin.

The angel we found our last day in Nice, after the picture was completed, and we carried it everywhere we went, packed in a little wicker basket with yards of cotton around it—by plane, train, car, and foot, until it landed on our mantelpiece at home.

The Benin bronze we acquired our last day in Paris, too late to ship. We were crazy about it and, not having had it long, wanted to see it the minute we got home. I was afraid of getting it through the French customs, as it could have been considered national treasure, in which case they could have paid me what I paid for it and kept it.

I needn't have worried, for Benin is in the British part of Africa, not the French, and they couldn't have cared less. But I always look on the gloomy side of every customs transaction, so I rolled it up in the trousers of my best suit and put it in the overnight airplane bag. I got it through the French customs by pretending it was my quota of brandy, then I paid one hundred and twenty-five dollars excess weight to take it on the plane. (It weighed forty-five pounds.) Everything was under control until we started for the plane, whereupon it dropped through the bottom of the overnight case and spread my pants before it like a carpet as it rolled down the ramp. Everything was retrieved, no one was nabbed by the police, but in New York, some fifteen hours later, the customs man, questioning my right to bring it in duty-free, declared it was neither old nor a work of art and that I would have to leave it there, rolled up in my best pants, until an expert could examine it.

We might just as well have sent it around the Horn by canoe. It, and my pants, arrived four weeks later, and even then I had to take my friend, Ralph Altman, to expertize it and get it released and into my custody.

But as crazy as I am about ancient artifacts, the most satisfying aspect of collecting is buying contemporary art, and that's what you have to do to really enjoy it—buy it. It satisfies, all around. It does the double duty of satisfying the collector because, through it, he is involving himself in his own era, along with the artist, who's earning a living in his own lifetime. As a by-product, and a very important one, it satisfies the dealer, too—at least, those few dealers who put their faith in the future of art and not in its past; those few who forego immediate reward, perhaps only to end up with the satisfaction that what they have gained is the knowledge that their taste was theirs and not the dictates of traditional taste, or momentary taste, or the taste of those collectors who will only buy what is critically assured or publicly approved.

I try to see everything I can that is being done today. I go to student shows, club shows, big galleries, little galleries. I can't possibly see them all, for America is brimful of art, bursting with the art energy that always follows industrial energy. But I manage to see enough to assure me that as long as the visual arts don't allow themselves to become a "trust"—monopolized by one city, one section of the country, one income bracket of the people—they will remain healthy.

The theatre has been destroyed for the American people at large by the New York "trust," critically and financially, and music has only kept its toehold as a national entity through the vigorous application of a few dedicated people who are willing to work for its acceptance, not only by those who can afford to (and should) support it, but by those who live it and feel the need for it as a fulfillment of the all too often emptiness of life.

The West Coast and Middle West have suffered terribly from the old-fashioned idea that New York is the center of everything artistic. And the New Yorkers aren't solely responsible for this. It is a very human weakness to want to go away from your own back yard to picnic in someone else's. People want to wait until they get to New York to see the shows and buy their paintings.

I'm not as advanced as the following might make me sound, but I get around more, lecturing, etc., and see more because of that. Friends have been bewildered by some of the paintings we buy. Afro, the great Italian contemporary, is an example. Because we were in New York several years ago we had the opportunity and bought an Afro. He had not been shown on the West Coast. When we got it and showed it to California friends, they thought we were a little wacky, but several of them would gladly pay for their mistake to get one now. We've bought some duds, too, and we've paid for those mistakes, but they still hang on our walls and serve to make up a whole picture of our changing taste.

I would like to own a fine Paul Klee, for example, but when I had the chance to buy them reasonably enough for my pocketbook, I didn't particularly like him, and, commensurate with the selling price, I still think he's vastly overrated. He is a charming "little master," but

I have yet to be sold on him as the messiah of the twentieth-century art, as most of my friends see him. My blind spot perhaps.

I'll admit I'm as stubborn about some artists as my friends are about the ones I like, and if that doesn't make horse racing, as the saying goes, it sure makes collecting. Certainly, I'd love to have some of the masters, but I honestly believe I'd rather have someone completely unknown, whose accent I have to pick up, interpret, and understand before I can look him in the eye as an accepted friend.

Since my major collecting passion is the work of young or contemporary artists, and since my budget is usually whittled down by having bought everything I've fallen in love with within the last six months, I force myself to weigh and consider contemporary pictures, monetarily as well as artistically. With the work of a new artist—new, that is, to me—I find myself going through something like the following procedure—sometimes I even talk like this, out loud:

"O.K., Vincent, what do you do when you look at a painter's work for the first time? How do you look and what do you see?" Obviously, what I have to say is no dogmatic standard, but let me analyze my reactions to a specific painter. Spring, 1958; Santa Barbara; the painter, William Dole; I have never seen him before.

I walk into the gallery and am immediately charmed. The water colors are clear and bright, the lines of the drawings delicate but strong. He obviously is saying what he has to say the way he wants to say it. There is no hesitation in these reports of a trip to Italy. He is in a true American tradition without being eclectic (he stems from Demuth, Marin, Feininger); there is a desire to record beauty here and a true way of seeing it. One picture called "Narrow Street, Florence" I would like to own. It doesn't matter what it costs—I'd make any sacrifice if I decide I can't live without it—but can I live without it? Aye, there's the rub—and the escape. To be this critical, in my case, is to be economical. If I can argue my way out of owning it, I save money. So let's go. It fits into my pattern of collection—it's original, new, well done, and it has a tradition. And it's beautiful, serene, and those are qualities that sometimes worry me. Would it inquire enough of me—

would it ask me lots of questions over the years, or would I just accept it on a wall and forget it? That I don't want. Now, it's possible it's so beautiful it will always make demands on me—like an Ingres drawing and certain Feiningers. They have the mystery that can belong to perfection—mystery of how it is done, not technically, but spiritually.

In the same museum is a show of John Paul Jones' work. I own one of his. Let's compare feelings. I bought my Jones five years ago and I love it. It hasn't let me down or anywhere near answered all that I ask of it—like . . . is the miracle of its technical beauty a trick or superficial? Does it wear thin and end up just beautiful? No, it does not. Now, would this water color by Dole?

When you buy a contemporary painting, you have to look ahead to your future with it. If you're buying the "Mona Lisa" or a Cézanne or any of the already decided on masters, true, it may end up boring you, but neither you nor anyone else is going to complain. Time has set its approval. But not so with the new.

So, here in Dole, because of the tradition behind it, one question is answered; time has approved the style, and the fact that it's a recognizable picture of something—that helps too. It will always be a narrow street in Florence, but as a report, is it valid? I don't know yet, but all this conjecture assures me one day I'll own one of his pictures, and then I'll know for sure.

Asking yourself questions like these is part of the fun of collecting, especially of collecting contemporary art, and especially, *especially* contemporary American art. I don't think there's a question in anyone's mind, except perhaps, the French and some Americans, that America today is the art center of the world, creatively and collectorally. We are producing, and slowly the public is being weaned from the breast of Europe and buying American art. I have a passion for it, because I find it more stimulating than the art of any other country. It has verve, zip, go, pep, and it still has the magnificence of experiment. It also has the bewitching tentativeness of a young boy, trying his voice after it's stopped cracking. It hasn't reached the dull baritone monotony of the slick young Europeans.

There are so many American painters who are better than good, and a few who are great, that I could make a list a chapter long. Gottlieb, Pollock, Rothko, Motherwell, Kline, Brook, Reginald Pollack, Okada, Reinhardt, Glasco, d'Arista, Cohen, Lebrun, Woelffer, Kienbusch, Broderson, Parks, Villierme, Strombotne, Wyeth, Perlin, de Koening, Hoffman, Kriesberg, Warshaw, Graves, Anderson, Tobey, Callahan, Diebenkorn, Morris, Amato, Brice, Sheeler, Watkins, and dozens more. There is every kind of painter, every form of vitality. To be current with what's going on in the United States, you really have to keep your eyes open. It's a tough job to keep up with it, and it isn't made any easier by the art magazines, who get carried away by one group or another, almost as though their bottom dollar was bet on certain ones to win.

Not arbitrarily, but for many reasons, I'd like to take three of them I particularly admire and whose work I know very well and in each instance own at least two of their pieces. In other words, while it's not my bottom dollar I'm betting on them, I've been willing to put up or shut up, and since I've put up, I'm not going to shut up.

Rather than say I think they are great artists or even that they have a chance at greatness, I'm going to say why I like them and what I know about them that makes me like them.

In 1958, Mark Tobey of Seattle, Washington, won first prize at the Biennale in Venice. That exhibition, along with the Carnegie in Pittsburgh, is the largest and most comprehensive art show in the world. The prizes awarded mean something. I hasten to add, this is not why I like him. Mark Tobey is quite an elderly man. He has been painting for a long time; he has had many exhibitions and one brilliant retrospective. Europe knows his work well, and he is considered by many to be one of our foremost artists, in fact, one of *the* best living artists. He is comparatively unknown in America. There are many collections, the calibre of which demand a representative work by Tobey, but they don't have one. There are dozens of art-minded people I know who, though they may know his name, are unaware of his talent. I don't know why this is true, but perhaps he just hasn't the flair for publicity so necessary in our day for recognition.

Yet I can think of no one who reflects more brilliantly the movement, the animated hieroglyphics of our trafficked city life. He paints the luminosity of a city at night as only one can see it in our electrified land. He writes on his canvases the language we all know so well, of hurry, speed, the ever changing glamour of the streets. This he imbues with the nervous serenity of the Orient. His art has an insistence the commercial advertising world should envy, for commercial art, being dictated by the so-called practicalities of the business of selling, loses the mystery of communication by being blatantly communicative. Nothing is left there to the imagination, as it is in Tobey's work, and yet Tobey can "sell" you the poetry of modern life, even in its confusion. He helps you decide in its favor by showing the essential beauty of action.

I know Mark Tobey slightly. But the second of my three is a long-time friend William Brice.

He is the son of the famous comedienne, Fanny Brice, and that fact has much to do with his early development. Through her, he was thrown into early contact with the arts and at a precocious age began to draw and paint under the tutelage of Harry Botkin, a painter of great skill. By the age of eighteen Brice could draw beautifully and paint slickly in the style of Botkin, but with more innate taste in subject matter. This was to be expected, for to this day the great trend in America is to follow the master. Whether the master encourages it or the student submits to it, I don't know, but each good teacher has turned out ten imitators to every one original talent. Almost invariably, the imitators remain in teaching, or disappear from the art scene altogether, while the original talent, in revolt or acceptance of the good points of his master, plus a desire to embellish and outlive him, has a tremendous struggle to arrive at originality.

In Brice's case he was also plagued by the acceptance and admiration of the group of highly artistic people of his mother's acquaintance. They knew he had talent and probably would have been content to see it stop right there. His early work presented no challenge to them, nor did they want to be challenged. He was included in group shows, came off well, and without a doubt, because of his position and security, could have gone on to academic perfection and further security as a "little master." Instead, he chose a road of development—hard, up and down, searching—which led him many places but ultimately to *his* place, which, in essence, is a continual starting point for new adventure.

At that early point of security he met the painter Howard Warshaw, a man from a basically deeper artistic background, in that his parents were devoted audiences rather than performers, but with no security, financial or otherwise. At the same age he had already undergone many influences without a definite master, aside from his own definite admirations of such men as Eugene Berman and the neoromanticists and surrealists in general. From them, Warshaw had learned the magic of line and invention. But for Brice, he was a new experience, and for Warshaw, Brice was a desirable, stable friend—the respect and prospects of learning were mutual.

Voluntarily, Brice stopped painting for well over a year—to learn to see, to study drawing, and, most important, to leave himself open to the whole world of art, past and present. He took in and digested art history from classic to modern; he broke the image and put it together; he made pictures from everything—burlesque shows to meticulous, almost invisible still lifes. He dug deep into the mystery of the flower, selecting the rose as an image, at once beautiful and savage, the thorn being an equal form to the flower. From the garden he examined the sea, and he saw the shore as a discarded garden, alive with the tortured shapes of water things without water. And from the sea itself, he extracted what was blue in depth and what from sky was reflection, where white was foam of after-fury, and where a white is nothingness in contrast to the elements within, above, around.

These "absolute abstractions," as the sea itself, gave form to images and to the human figure, too. Now, from the rocks, monumental members of the human race break out, try to detach themselves, still wet and wondering if they will make it to be beheld as men and women. Where does he go from here and why the constant change of vision? Let me explain it this way, for myself, at least. The audience today is bigger, more awake, more eager for new vision, more receptive for a change. Brice's technique is there. His eye sees everything; he teaches art as a visual experience. He cannot be expected in America today to play to any one audience. He will not, I think, grow stale in sight, to see a single world when all the world is his to look at and, through him, for everyone to look at, too—and love. If he owes anyone a debt it is to the same master most young painters owe—Picasso, who continues to be amazing as he continues to be amazed by life, its change, and his to catch, change, and produce the greatest world of vision ever conceived by one man. Brice owes this debt without eclecticism, but by acceptance of the fact that if one man could see and do it, all men have the chance.

The third painter, Richard Diebenkorn, I have known only a short time and his work a little longer, but I use him as another example of the American painter, because he, too, has fought his way to originality and is not afraid to tackle the American art audience in its many moods. In his early work he has a sense of space and color and pattern which seems to have intrigued our mid-century painters more than anything else. When I first saw his work, I had the wit to ask myself (and no one else), "What is it? Why does he see like this? Why is there no identifiable form, why no virtuosity, dash, or amble in the brush stroke?" And I didn't have an answer. But I liked it—in fact, I was terribly excited by it—so I bought one and had the hysterical experience of trying to take it home in my Hillman Minx, the canvas being five feet by six feet, and the Hillman very little bigger. I drove one-handed with the top down and held onto the crossbar of the stretcher with the other. A sudden gust of wind caught the canvas and took me out of the seat as the car sped along a few hundred feet with me standing straight up, my foot down on the accelerator and no hands on the wheel.

Modern painters, feeling the lack of public demand for their work, paint big, and Diebenkorn paints bigger than most. Brice for his largest canvases—some seven by nine feet—invented the name "wall paint-ings," which my wife, trying to fit one between two windows, terms "wall-to-wall paintings." But, "wall paintings" they are indeed, for ex-cept for something to hang them on, the wall becomes obsolete and extinct.

Anyway, safely home with the Diebenkorn and having obliterated a wall by hanging it, we fell deeply in love with the painting and for the five years we've owned it now, that love has grown. I'll tell you why. This painting demands nothing from you but enjoyment of it. It doesn't say I'm a landscape, portrait, or even an abstraction of reality —it just hangs there to be looked at like an ever present and ever chang-ing sunset. In different moods and light, the lights and moods change— you can discover it. My wife, when once asked the title of it by a group of visiting ladies, summed it up. She said, "It's called 'We Like It!' "

In his latest work Diebenkorn has gone back to the figure, the human figure, and to the landscape he once saw abstractly he has added an identification with the figures. The object is the person, and the landscape and roomscape are symbols surrounding it—symbols at once of the art language and containers of the object. The reincorpora-tion of the human figure in this work seems to fill a need to get back to reality as much as the complete non-objective subject matter of a few years ago was the need to get away from reality, as such, and to see the natural intent of things in nature, the intent of color against earth, above it, on it, and beneath it, so that now the figure is the color against the earth, the furniture, the architecture—and the palette, being the same, the change becomes a natural growth out of a double idea.

When I use these three painters as an illustration of the determina-tion of the American artist to have claim to an original approach, I use them because of this possibility of change in their work . . . not change for its own sake, but change for the sake of growth. The clarification of all the ideas that have come to our artists through the most intimate knowledge of world art, has been through reproduction and the vast report that goes on in our day of the art of the world.

I like buying contemporary artists because it makes me feel I'm in on something big that's being done now. Of course, I'd like a fine Matisse, a great Cézanne, a Titian, Tintoretto, and a hundred others. I love to live with works of art. But I have learned to look myself right in the wallet. I could never own a great painting by any of those famous names, so why not own something I think is great or good or even that I just happen to like? I really don't think, in my case, it's just the sour grapes of financial inability. I really prefer making up my own mind about my time than having time tell me what I should like or own.

That's one facet of collecting I adore, but as I've said, the greatest thrill the collector can have is the "discovery." By discovery, I mean many things: (1) something someone thought was something else, but you know to be different; (2) something someone overlooked who was in the shop just before you were, but your eyes are brighter and you didn't overlook it, although sometime later you understand why they did, and wish you had; (3) something extraordinary which you "sense" is better or rarer than other people think, and it turns out to be so; (4) and lastly, something which you never heard of but which, after you've "discovered" it, turns out to have been "discovered" importantly many times before, but anyway was a discovery to you like a well-known little resort where everybody goes—or Paris.

These are complicated sentences, but with a seeing-eye dog you can follow them. So let me lead you.

A dear friend of mine who runs the only remaining bona fide junk store in California with real treasures—and I won't tell his name or address for all the tea in Boston—and who is indeed a dear friend of mine, since he knows me better than I do myself and can always outsmart me money-wise and always tell if I'm in a buying mood or not—well, this friend knows a great deal about most of his merchandise—his guns and clocks and even objects and paintings of a certain age. But about modern art, he *don't know nothing*, and I'm not about to educate him. One day on my weekly visit to his shop (and one must visit him weekly to obtain any kind of a score of success) he let me wander as usual, and as I was sidling down the second aisle, preparatory to my final farewell chat, he couldn't stand it any longer, and, rushing past me through a tight clench of second-hands, he exited into his secret cubbyhole (where hangs, in my mind, the original "Mona Lisa") and came out with a little unframed canvas about six by eight inches. Thrusting it into my ever eager hands, he said, "I think this is a genuine Dugassie."

Not to show my ignorance of this master, having just won $64,000 for my knowledge of art, I said, "Oh yes, yes, the great Fauve painter." For indeed it was a fine Fauve painting, and damn good, whoever did it.

"Fauve?" said my friend. "Who knows from Fauve? It's Dugassie, the one who did dancing girls."

Well, Degas—Dugassie—it's not too long a jump, and my heart would have moved over to the other side, had it had a chance of being a Degas—but alas, it was a Fauve, and who's to be choosy for $40 with Fauve paintings almost as rare as Degas?

I turned it over, and there on the back, in his neat handwriting of 1906–09, was the signature of André Derain. My friend was talking away, telling me how he got it. A nice elderly couple had been parted by the death of one of them, and the other couldn't stand to have their honeymoon memorabilia left in the house. Fifty years before, in Paris, they had bought this little treasure on their wedding trip and had kept it because it reminded them of their crazy Bohemian taste at that time when no one was buying the works of the Wild Beasts, let alone bringing them back to America for derision. Their tastes had changed when they settled down back home, into good U.S.A. conventionality, but this "mistake" they loved, and, anyway, they only paid $15 for it then. Their marriage certainly hadn't been a mistake, but now that was over, so why not get rid of memories? And so the "Dugassie" came to me. A lovely story. True? I don't know, but I love my Fauve Derain, and I love having discovered it. All concerned had profited, except perhaps, my dealer friend, but I can't really worry about him—he'll get even with me a hundred times before either of us is through with each other, or much older.

Probably the most impressive "discovery" I ever made was made secondhand, but it could not have been sent to me through more capable hands than the fabulous book dealer, Jake Zeitlin, in Los Angeles. Jake had known about this item for many years but had had to wait out the whims and vagaries of the owner before he finally was able to get it and sell it to me.

The background is intriguing and, I think, gives a clear picture of why I wanted it and why it ended up where it finally did.

Paul Gauguin, that most romantic figure of French painting who did what every man on earth wishes in the secret places of his heart he could do—escape—was, besides being a wonderful painter, a very vociferous writer. He never came close in this art to the genius of his friend Vincent van Gogh, but he did have something to say on many subjects and a lot to say on the things he wanted to escape from. Gauguin wrote four books, among them the idyllic *Noa Noa*, the revealing and humorously lecherous *Intimate Journals*, and a treatise called *The Modern Spirit and Catholicism*.

The longer he stayed in the South Seas and the more he degenerated from the pattern of the man he was meant to be, the more the Church was determined to land him, at last, and save his soul—which he had no desire to save or to have saved. His private war with the Church was never ended, but he felt it put him in the position of firsthand critic on the evils of church government in the islands and of the whole, to him, ridiculous idea of trying to turn these beautiful godlike people into un-God-loving Christians.

He set his hand to this treatise with fervor and lent his pen the venom of his revolutionary nature. He wrote ninety meticulous pages in longhand and bound it in a hand-made cover, beautifully designed and lavished with drawings, front and back, of the birth of Christ, in which he portrayed himself as an angel. On the insides of the covers he pasted two unique woodcuts, across one of which he wrote, in exquisite print, "Paradise Lost."

At his death this book was sold to a sea captain who in turn sold it to a doctor in Honolulu. The doctor had it translated and found to his horror that it was, in his opinion, violently anti-Catholic—and he belonged to that faith. Actually, the manuscript is not anti-Catholic, but anti church and church misgovernment, which was indeed prevalent in the islands at that time. But the good doctor didn't examine the difference, and, first carefully encasing it in an expensive protective box, he then locked it in his vault, out of harm and criticism's way—for twenty years!

When Jake finally persuaded him to sell it, it was in better condition probably than if someone had cherished it, without the fear of excommunication.

I bought it, not because I shared my mother's worrisome apprehension about the Pope wanting to rule the world, but because it was a rare statement by a rare and controversial artist. And another reason was that typed into the front of it was a magnificent letter to his friend Charles Maurice, in which he quoted Shakespeare (in English) and made comments on his greatest painting, "Where do we come from, why are we here, and where are we going." This letter seemed to me the entire spirit of the book—this and that tragic "Paradise Lost" written on the end wood block.

When my mother and father died several years later, I wanted to give a memorial to them to the City Art Museum in St. Louis. I knew this would tickle Mother, while it might have upset Dad—for he and I shared many a snicker over her worries about Catholicism and had many a serious discussion about tolerance of religious belief, which both of us held to be absolutely imperative, not only to the Christian, but to the American way of life.

I feel proud of that gift in many ways. Not only is it important in the understanding of Gauguin's personality, and beautiful to look at, but it adds another uniqueness to my home town, where the Catholic population is culturally very aware and could not look upon it as anything other than one man's opinion. Recently these people have pledged themselves to sustain (and have already built) a monument to Catholicism, a library which contains microfilm of every volume in the unequaled Vatican Library in Rome. St. Louis and Rome are the only two places on earth where that priceless material is available to students. It's another proof of the need felt by Americans to back up their material success with cultural endowment.

Our greatest "find" happened only last year in, of all places, Laguna Beach, California. Laguna is noted for many things, such as a mile of quaint shops containing every known shape of modern ceramics from square eggcups to ten-foot-long sectional dachshunds. It has a couple of excellent antique shops and a wide variety of artists, good and bad but never startling. It's a mecca for artistic tourists because of its annual Art Festival, in which the citizens "bring to life" the great masterpieces with living people who, by the end of its three-week duration, are half dead with tourist fatigue. They have tackled everything from the "Last Supper" to "The Blue Boy," but they'll have to wait for my admission money until they take on the "Quernica" of Picasso. Anyway, it is not exactly a town in which you would think you could find a major art work.

My wife is British-born, and she has one quality in common with another British product, the English setter, in that once she's on the scent of something, the chances of her coming back from the hunt with it are very high. We would never have this treasure, had it not been for this admirable trait. The story goes back several years to when Leonard Kaplan, an artist friend of ours in Laguna, told us an eye-glistening story about a lady there who had some enormous stone sculptures from Mexico. Questioned further, Leonard waxed very vague, and we could never pin him down as to her whereabouts. But Mary never stopped thinking about it or trying to get it out of him. One lovely day in Los Angeles she suddenly announced that we were going to Laguna and were going to find that lady if it took us the whole week.

I have no idea from what cubbyhole in her filing-cabinet mind she drew this decision. It had been at least a year since we'd talked of it, and I had honestly thought the whole story a myth. Needless to say, we went to Laguna and tracked this poor unsuspecting lady to her lair, only to find the sculpture had been put in storage. With a certain amount of unsubtle assistance, we got her to take us to the storehouse,

236

where everyone was out to lunch. By this time I was convinced the whole thing was a fraud and that the most this so far fruitless search could uncover would be a third-rate fake. But Mary persisted, and after the attendants returned from lunch we were reluctantly led through the usual labyrinth of the storage warehouse and ended up in a dead-end corner where the gloom was barely penetrated by a single low-watt bulb, some twenty feet away, which hung down into a baby's abandoned crib, casting prison-like bars of even denser gloom on everything.

Through this we could indeed make out some large rocks, piled in a corner, even if the only way we could tell they were rocks was by contrast to the mountains of other materials like wood and old mattress ticking. Getting to see these tempting objects was almost as difficult as the preparations for kissing the Blarney Stone. You had to squeeze past old lamps, cribs, and rocking chairs and finally press yourself flat against a huge wooden crate, and there you were, at last face to face with what, in that cavernous gloom, looked like the most exciting five-and-a-half-foot stone deity of the Huastecan culture of Veracruz we had ever seen.

We tried to adjust our eyes to the light (or lack of it) and to see some semblance of the figure's features. You didn't dare strike a match, since all the other clutter around us had been put there not to be burned up. Suddenly a shaft of light hit the figure. One of the attendants had climbed a mountain of junk behind us and held a flashlight. The drama of that moment we'll never forget. The light revealed not only what we had suspected was true—it was indeed Haustecan, one of the great pre-Columbian cultures—but with the exception of two clean breaks in the headdress, the figure was in mint condition.

There it was, the great squat cube of the body, the heavy feet slightly relieved from the native stone which remained its base; the arms held to the belly and the breast; each hand hollowed to hold a banner pole; and then the head, magnificent with earrings and a high conical hat, behind which a nimbus of stone sunrays shot out. The face itself, in low relief, was delicate and, in this startling light, utterly spiritual.

It was all the stories of hidden treasure come true. It was like breaking into an untouched tomb in Egypt or discovering the hidden staircase inside the great pyramid at Chichen Itzá, and climbing it to find that altar room atop with its stone jaguar, inlaid with jade and cinnabar.

Behind us a soft narration by the owner was taking place, unfolding a story equally adventurous. An oil company years ago had sent her husband to Veracruz to begin the first exploration of that valuable oil site. One day a mechanical "clam shell," dredging into the soft sand, brought up the head of our idol. The crew was more excited than if they had struck oil, and all oil work ceased until they had recovered the rest of it. The centuries had been kind. It had fallen face down, preserving the features, and the tremendous weight had worked it into the sandy soil almost six feet deep.

When it came time to return to the United States, all concerned determined the idol should come, too. That was thirty years ago. Today the Mexican government would rightfully never allow this treasure of their past to leave. But it had, and here it stood in a Laguna warehouse, waiting for us.

We had saved some money for a trip abroad, but this we had to have. Europe could wait, but how could we leave this wonderful thing in the darkness when it had waited there so long, so patiently, just for us?

I have just read Aline Saarinen's fascinating book about the great American collectors of the past, *The Proud Possessors*. It tells the story of those millionaires who vied, in the century just past, to glean the world of its greatest art to bring it home to America. All these treasures are now the property of the American public. That time is past. The great millionaires are few and far between in these days of high taxes. The treasures are almost all gone, too, but the desire to collect can never die, and there will always be something to find, for the horizons of art are broadening every day. Twenty years ago we knew so little of the art of Mexico, but today we recognize in it the greatness of our own

238

heritage, or if not strictly our own, at least of the lands we have adopted and made our own.

Although for some collectors there is as much excitement in finding the most trivial object as there is in the discovery of a lost masterpiece, the high points are the experiences that justify the whole mad pursuit. For one reason or another, I'm sure most collectors periodically have grave misgivings about their passion. There are times when I look myself squarely in the eye, and then I look around at the walls and shelves loaded with everything I could lay my hands on and afford (even at some on which I still owe a payment or two), and I have a quickly suppressed wish that a fire would break out—so that I could collect the insurance and start all over again—or that I'd never get another job (that wish is really short-lived) and could never buy another pot, painting, or pre-Columbian booboo. But even as these dreamy thoughts are floating in my mind, I'm thinking of something I saw on my last trip to New York, or I'm subconsciously off in my car to Jake Zeitlin's Red Barn to see if he has come across any more drawings. I realize, with horrible certainty, that I'm a pushover, my heels are completely round where art is concerned, and I'm certain that even if I end up in the actors' home, I'll be collecting stamps or paper dolls or anything I can lay my hands on—although I hope it won't be my old "notices." I want to remember my future and not my past.

But back to the high points!

My father ended his days pathetically alone in a marvelous hospital-home for arthritics in Tucson, Arizona. He wouldn't come live with any of us, and since he had enough money to be taken care of beautifully, he wanted to be in the sun, and he wanted to be taken care of—beautifully. He was, but it depressed me to think of him there, and every chance I got I'd fly over to see him. He took a dim view of these visits (though deep down he was very pleased) because they interrupted his routine. I had a lot of time on my hands as a result and prowled the streets of Tucson for *anything* to do.

A year before, Ralph Altman, the best dealer in primitive art in Los Angeles, had fired me with enthusiasm for the little-known but wonderfully expressive work of the Indians of the prehistoric south-western United States. Their geometric black and white or red and black pottery is unique in the history of ceramics in its combination of naïveté and sophisticated design. I had bought a cup from Ralph, dating from the twelfth century and coming from the Mesa Verde culture.

Shades of my archaeological youth. I remembered my discovery of the burial ground that summer in camp, and indeed one of the bowls I had dug up had traces of black and white design. I had not, however, been allowed to keep this one. It was put into the camp "museum." But this cup from Mesa Verde rang a lovely bell, and Ralph and I decided to keep our eyes open for more where that came from.

A hot, dead day in Tucson was to be the eye opener. There in the window of an "Indian Trading Post" (one of those places where they traded Indians out of everything) I saw a black and white pot. It was rather undistinguished, but I thought there might be more inside. Upon inquiring I was told that they were very rare and any Trading Post that had one was lucky. I bought the one in question for very little. Just why it was so cheap, considering their knowledge of its rarity, I don't know, but I tucked the prize under my arm and was half-way out when a booming voice caught me from the back of the shop with a lusty, "Hey, come back here!" My heart sank. The saleslady had sold me the pot for too little, and I might have to give it back or pay much more.

I was tempted to play dumb and complete the exit, when the voice boomed closer. "You like them old Indian things?"

"Well, yes." I wasn't going to tip my mitt if there were more or if the voice decided to charge me more for the one I had.

"I got hundreds of them back of the shop. Want to see them?"

The story ends with a crack the actor Hans Conreid made on seeing my two hundred black and white pots.

Said Hans, "You're one actor no one will ever be able to say he hasn't got a pot to . . ." End quote.

I have never lost my interest in the American Indian, and today as a commissioner of the Indian Arts and Crafts Board of the Department of the Interior I'm trying to help preserve and stimulate the native arts of our country.

Then once again Mary was responsible for a great find and again through Ralph Altman. Ralph had heard there were a few things of interest, if questionable quality, left in the old John Barrymore mansion high up above Hollywood. The great actor had been gone for many years, but the people who had bought his home had also saved some of the furnishings from the debacle of the sentimental auction of his effects after his death. Most of the good things had been snapped up by fans or friends, but there was a chance that what was included in the sale of the house could contain a surprise or two.

Any good dealer worth his nose will follow it to all conclusions, so Ralph was on his way. Unfortunately, Mary was in his shop when Ralph decided to go, and Ralph couldn't get out of taking her. Besides, she claimed she was only interested in seeing the house. She has a passion for old houses, the more peculiar, the better, and this one with its history and its legends of subterranean passages was supposed to be *really* peculiar.

I said "unfortunately" a moment ago. The misfortune was Ralph's, for when they got there, before they ever got in the house the two of them, and Ralph's wife Pat (all of whom are equipped with 20–20 vision where treasures are concerned) spotted, simultaneously, a magnificent object, towering above the now abandoned swimming pool. Twenty-five feet high, it stood glaring down at them, those three speechless people—one of the most glorious examples of Haida sculpture in existence. A totem pole from the classic period of 1870 with its lovely warm browns and reds still glowing on the three great figures which compose its height. At the bottom a great bear-like creature, paws pleading; and on his head, a pale lean man who holds before him a gigantic fish which reaches from his shoulders to his toes; and on his head, hawk-nosed and savage, crouches a great bird, his tail behind him abristle with red feathers made of shingling.

Most totem poles look to me like carved telephone poles. Figures of animals and fish and people statically surmount one another and only bring to mind the H. Allen Smith book, *Low Man on a Totem Pole*. But not this one! This was sculptural and dignified and beautiful. Being a burial post, it was sculpted in the round so that the three creatures retain their separate identity as completely realized forms.

Once the three treasure hunters got over the shock and joy of seeing it there, they knew without a word spoken that there was as little chance for Ralph to buy it and sell it to anyone but Mary as there probably was of moving it from its cement foundation. Shoulder to shoulder the trio walked to the house to start playing that exasperating yet thrilling game of waiting till just the "right time" to broach the subject of its availability.

So far they had no idea who owned it even, and of course no idea if he or she would think of selling it. Had I been there, I could have saved them this anxiety, for I know of no three people more relentless or more thoroughly determined to get what they set their caps for than my wife, Ralph's wife, and Ralph.

They got it—and guess what—we have it.

The thrill of the hunt, the gamesmanship in the competition for the quarry—these are some of the symptoms most commonly associated with that incurable disease—collecting.

Somewhere before we end these notes about collecting, I must try once again to say straight out what I hinted in the beginning. Everyone collects, but a lot of people believe that collecting art is beyond their comprehension or their means. That they should think it is beyond their comprehension they can ascribe to the educational inertia of our American system, which refuses, even in this most productive period of American art, to believe that seeing is a large part of believing and that belief in our way of life is what they all are striving for—and what we damn well better be striving for in a time when it is pitted against the rest of the world to survive or fail, as we SEE fit to let it.

The other misunderstanding is that it is beyond their means. Yet the people of the United States live beyond their means, gladly and disastrously. They have let themselves be sold the biggest bill of goods in history by a Frankenstein—industrial advertising—of their own making. We all are perfectly content to make down payments on any luxury we're told we can't live without, but we can't quite bring ourselves to chance investing in ourselves through education, art, or any of those splendors we lyrically call "the best things in life" and which we expect, because Tin Pan Alley tells us so, to be *free*.

I 'VE JUST REREAD EVERYTHING I'VE WRITTEN SO FAR, AND IT almost makes me blush. Such a blatant declaration of love I've never seen . . . and in public, too! Well, I can't help it, and secretly I'm very pleased to find I'm just as much in love as I ever was, after all these years. In my case it's really the old story of, "We met in grammar school, went steady through high school and college, and we're still happily married."

There's one thing about a long-time love affair. It keeps you on your toes. You never know what mood tomorrow will bring for either of you, so you always have to be ready to accept whatever comes.

One thing is certain: the arts keep you alive. They stimulate, encourage, challenge, and, most of all, guarantee a future free from boredom. They allow growth and even demand it in that time of life we call maturity but too often enter with a childish faith that what we learned in youth is sustenance enough for the years when most men are mentally famished but won't admit it—or when they are apt to curb their hunger with the sops of complacency, security, and the assurance of death.

Today America offers us a delectable feast of creativity. It is growing, and Americans must grow with it. Education needs the adult mind to carry on its purpose . . . that learning never stops. Curiosity, the child of education, must be vitaminized by further learning. To put it bluntly, while the child is father to the man, the man, in turn, must be a father to the child and guide this child with adult hands to true maturity.

In this story my love affair has been with the visual arts. They have been the ideal, all-purpose mother, mistress, wife kind of love, and if I have slighted the other arts, it isn't because I particularly believe in artistic "monogamy," but rather that love is a single purposed thing . . . one affair at a time.

All these years of action and reaction in the visual arts add up to some definite conclusions. True, I've had the good fortune to see a great deal, and I'm eternally grateful that I've squandered that non-monetary good fortune in pursuit of vision. However, I'm constantly going out and coming in again. . . . The older I get, the more I'm convinced that I'm only *beginning to see.*

Just as nature and man are never static, art is constantly changing and growing . . . sometimes even diminishing. Not all great periods in history are great periods in all the arts. Painting may flourish at a time when the drama or music is stagnant. One country may produce great poetry, great prose, while at the same time its architects are creating monstrosities. Yet somehow the arts are a complement to a man, a nation, or an epoch. They fulfill a need in one direction or another . . . they fill in the gaps in civilization. But they are all ever present right beneath the surface, waiting to be needed and used.

For the past few years I've been lecturing to schools, colleges, and civic groups around the country. I've been amazed at the vital interest almost everywhere in the arts at large, and particularly the visual arts. The American people really want to learn to see. They have hoped from the medium of television to have the same chance to see that they were given by radio to hear. Radio gave us the diploma for appreciation of every kind of music, but so far television has let us down. It has not taken up the challenge to educate at this crucial time when education is so greatly in demand. That will come, I hope, but in the meantime, if I have had any success as an inciter to seeing, it has been because I have been able to break down, by my personal enthusiasm, some of the nonsense written about art which, to one degree or another, makes all of us feel shut off from it.

The history of art has become so separated from the history of man that the former no longer seems what it actually is . . . a by-product of the latter. It has become rarefied and special, where it should be commonplace and everyday. The very recent and fantastic upswing of the art market has given yet another tug to separate the creative act from the continent of man's behavior and usefulness. . . . Who can afford it?

I have hoped, in this very personal diary of my own love affair with art, to persuade the readers to share with me the questions that have, and will, come up for them as they have for me. I want them to question themselves as I have questioned myself, for instance, in my desire to know the art of the past and, at the same time, accept and get to know the art of today and be ready for the art of tomorrow.

If at times I've been demanding—that you like this or that because I do—it's because I believe this is a way to start seeing something you perhaps have missed. But it is always personal. In other words, I hope that my life's devotion to seeing may open a few eyes that have been shut by fear of seeing something new, and will open a little wider the eyes that squint at art when it is the one thing in the world we can really afford to be wide-eyed about. It's there for us to enjoy, given to us by our fellow creatures, not by any miraculous or mystical power. Art is only another person's way of seeing, and seeing more or less greatly—according to his talent. For the majority of us who do not have the talent, it is, or can be, a way of seeing through another's eyes the wonderful worlds of reality or imagination . . . of truth or fiction . . . of actuality or abstraction. The human mind and the human spirit are not, and never have been, one-sided, and we cannot expect that one aspect—the sense of sight—to be other than many-faceted, too.

Over the years I've made some notes for myself, since the professional art writers only succeed in losing me with their directional generalities. This is not their fault . . . it's mine. I'm sure you've deduced, through the pages of this book, that I am inordinately curious and must always explain and clarify to *myself*, reasons why *I* see as I do. Hence, these notes:

Art is the conscious effort of man to reproduce himself and his surroundings for his own oral, tactile, or (and) visual pleasure and the pleasure of his fellow man. It is the spiritual expression of his most physical desires. It is, at once, the first love of the higher man and the greatest need of those less high, intellectually.

The art of painting is liquid involvement with the rigidity of natural forms. . . . It is the breakdown of these forms into plastic experience.

There is equal pleasure, both inward and outward, in the creation of a work of art and in the struggle by the audience to be at one with it . . . that is, to attempt to comprehend the artist's meaning, and yet to retain one's own emotional identity with it.

A work of art is the most valuable material commodity there is, because it involves two spiritual enterprises: the creation and the appreciation. It is the complement of life itself, being equally spiritual in its origin and in its fulfillment.

Art is a "constant." A civilization will achieve a certain art summit which a succeeding civilization will achieve to the same degree of stylistic perfection (or imperfection) without any direct influence from one to the other.

Art is the product of the Creative Act, as much as a child is the product of the Act of Love. The instinct for both is in each of us. The most fortunate of us love and are loved, and, even more fortunately, some of us have the power to create thoughts, philosophies, music, poetry, painting, the arts—all of them—as well as children.

The Creative Act is very much a part of children. They create, imitate, criticize, make comment on everything. They observe and translate freely, both verbally and pictorially. They are truly free, and as they lose that freedom—or it is taught out of them —they lose the will to create. Yet the power to create is ever present, and often comes back in later life as a hobby or, sometimes, as a serious profession.

The first works of art do not really differ thematically from the most recent . . . acts of impulse, memory, and love. The fertility symbol, the Mother Goddess, the phallic shape, all share importance in the identity of the first art works. Why? Simply that they are instinctive in all men, and in early man were of the utmost importance. Early man, desirous of a family to help him hunt, to stave off his enemy, gave thanks for his manhood to its source, the fertile Mother. He fashioned her full of himself, pregnant with help, milk-breasted and swollen with promise. As leisure, the god-parent of art, gave him time to think and to be grateful, he looked for other copy. He saw, in the beasts that fed him . . . that fulfilled his desire to hunt and to conquer, new images to remember, and he decorated his primitive shelter with marvelous pictures of beast-behavior and, occasionally, with his own image, behaving as a man among beasts.

To his dead child, he gave a toy to play with when the long sleep was over; to his chief, mementos of his prowess and symbols of his strength; to his love, the tokens of his respect. He adorned her in death as he liked to see her in her life—the idol and reflection of his opulence.

Life is short and art is long, but death and art are eternal. A man's art, a civilization's art, are its immortality.

All praise of God, all gratitude, is art. Bach, Raphael, the architects of Chartres, the Psalmist, Shakespeare and the glorification of man, the impressionists and the deification of nature . . . all arise from the same instinct that made the first Mother Goddess.

Many people are blinded by fear of seeing something different, or of seeing anything differently, or by the inability to differentiate between what they know how to see and what they *could* see if they knew how.

Look at a work of art as directly as you would look at a different natural scene . . . a sunset, sunrise, or the changing abstract patterns of the earth from an airplane or railroad window. We are constantly surprised that what we see from one point of view is entirely different from another, and, similarly, we are shocked that one painter's work is so different from another's. Yet with those we admit to being great, we accept the difference, calling it simply a signature. Ingres and Michelangelo are as separate in their vision of the human figure as the Marilyn Monroe calendar photo and Duchamp's "Nude Descending a Staircase." Which is the more vulgar, I leave for you to decide.

I wouldn't dare presume to tell anyone how, or why, to look at paintings if literally hundreds of people hadn't asked me to. I've shot off my big mouth so publicly and for so long about art, I guess I've left myself wide open to all questions.

Everyone wants to be able to enjoy the visual world, but lots of people have mental blocks about it. Sometimes it goes right back to the old cliché; often it is a kind of timidity, almost fright, at seeing something different. The world of women's fashions is much the same. We joke about the new ones, and we ridicule the old ones, but the norm—or what we accept—moves around in the middle. A startling change this year will bring what was new last year into focus. In other words, we get used to it and accept it.

Vincent van Gogh is probably the greatest example of the non-acceptance-rejection-acceptance- (and finally) adoration pattern in modern art. He sold but a single painting during his lifetime. Other artists admired him, but the public and critics thought he was crazy. Slowly after his death people began to see in this "madman's" work

something exciting that no one else ever achieved, and into these tor-
turous visions, they began to read the meaning of modern life. Nature
itself began to look like Van Gogh saw it to the point where, today,
his vision is public vision and exhibitions of his work draw the greatest
crowds. It is almost impossible to buy a Van Gogh today, and if you
can, you will have to pay the highest prices.

There are so many areas where the title of this book applies . . .
"to like what you *know*." Take Amedeo Modigliani. His audience is
also enormous today, and yet twenty-five years ago, if one had fore-
seen how very definite and sure his place was going to be in the future
hierarchy of modern art, one could not have failed to appreciate him.
And there was a reason for his position. The rebirth of interest in the
background of man, in primitive man, hit Modigliani with full force,
as it did Picasso and others. They saw in the severity and discipline
of African and archaic art something they needed in their vocabulary
to enable them to say what they needed to say. Modigliani took the
masks, the elongated form, the static sculptural pose, the sightless eyes
and interpreted his sitters in that elegant language. He did it so su-
perbly that we see it the other way around, and I often hear people
comment on how a piece of African sculpture resembles a Modigliani.
This discovery in primitive art of a valid source of modern inspiration
is what gives him his established place in our visual catalogue. Knowing this twenty-five years ago, it would have been easy to have understood Modigliani and, if you'd been smart, to have acquired one. They
are so rare today, his slightest pencil sketch can fetch a large sum.

But believe me, looking at art or buying it for the sake of investment is the quickest way to cheat yourself of its real enjoyment. In
learning about art the mistake can often be more profitable than the
"good buy." Taste is meant to change visually, just as much as our
palates like change—and a raw persimmon is the best lesson you can
have for the appreciation of a ripe one.

I made a booboo a few years ago that really left me in a state of
shock but at the same time taught me a lesson of caution I'm not
apt to forget. I bought a drawing by Vincent van Gogh from a reputa-

ble dealer. I'd always wanted one and this was a beauty. I really had to put out for it, and it was tough at that moment, for jobs were scarce. "Never let an opportunity to get something good slip by, if you can afford it"—an old motto of mine that has cost me plenty. It was a brush drawing of cypress trees. What could be more Van Gogh? It came from Holland from a private collection—a good pedigree, but above all, I loved it, so home it came to take an honored spot on the wall. Everyone agreed with me that I had a fine thing; that is, everyone but one of the few people in the world whose taste and eye I trust completely.

Estrella Katzenellenbogen lives in California now, but once ruled the Berlin art world with her extraordinary perception and infallible instinct for contemporary art. She had a magnificent collection of old masters, moderns, and was one of the first to buy Paul Klee and the German expressionists. She knew everyone art-wise before Herr Hitler took over her home and her collection, and she had to exit Germany, leaving behind most of her finest possessions. But what she was able to bring with her was her awareness of talent and her impeccable taste, and these attributes have kept her more alive than money or treasures ever could have.

But Mrs. Kellen, as we call her, took one look at my Van Gogh and in her tactful way said it "bothered" her. That was enough for me. Though I still loved the drawing, I started to get other opinions, ending up with one of the great experts, Carl Schniewind of the Chicago Art Institute. Mr. Schniewind wrote me his reaction to the drawing, and as I read it I shrank two feet. According to him, it was a most obvious fake, definitely one of the famous Van Gogh fakes that had inundated the market in the late twenties. My only consolation was that dozens of good collectors before me had been fooled, but all I felt like was a fool.

I had to return it to the dealer, because it represented too big an outlay of hard-earned cash to be able to take my lesson and pay for it. Occasionally, I still sneak a look at the photo I have of it . . . and damn it, I still like it—but to be true to the title of this book, not after what I know.

To the eternal comment that art is something above the grasp of the average man, let me say that from my own experience in it I've never met anyone who didn't like something in the arts. The only trouble is that something you like you are apt to take for granted and no longer think of it as art—it's just something you like.

There is nothing less formidable than a work of art. It is there for you to enjoy and sometimes *not* understanding it is a joy, too, because it gives you somewhere to go—to understand it. The real trouble, the real misunderstanding of art is largely due to you yourself, either in your refusal to enjoy it or your timidity in thinking that it's above you—yet how can we say we understand Rembrandt, Leonardo da Vinci, or Vincent van Gogh (and most people say they do simply because they recognize the subject and the artist's name), or any of the other profound masters, and in the same breath say we can't understand Picasso, for instance? Believe me, it's no more of a compliment to the former than it is an insult to the latter. Picasso's abstractions are simple compared to the depth of Rembrandt's psychological examination of his subjects. The abstractions are the work of a young experimenter who learned all he could from cubism (or the breaking down of form into its essential natural shapes—the sphere, the cube, and the cone) and who then went on in growth to other forms, other ideas. His genius, like Rembrandt's, is that he always remains himself, a seer who looks until he sees in nature what he wants to see. None of us see the same things the same way—two versions of the same story are always different, each side of the same face has a look of its own. What you didn't understand yesterday, you will learn to understand the day after tomorrow, if you try. But to understand the relationship of the mature Rembrandt to his sitter (or to himself as he paints his majestic self-portraits) would take a volume of the most sentient analysis, whereas cubism can almost be dismissed as an experiment, exciting and wonderful as it is, that led to bigger things, just as Rembrandt's early superficial portraits led to his last troubled masterpieces.

252

One other damper on the everyday enjoyment of art is that often people feel the right to criticize or misunderstand someone else's work. Artists themselves are particularly guilty of this. Filled with their own theories, their own visions, they often cannot see someone else's as valid or genuine. The fact being that all of us are frustrated creatively in some way, it irks us to see someone else successfully making a statement of being. This is one reason why so many people identify themselves with past masters and refuse the present ones. There is no danger involved in liking something established, but look out if you express yourself as in favor of "today," for then you have to justify your stand and that takes a lot of guts.

Possibly the best way to enjoy fully the creative act is to like what you like but leave yourself open to learn. Let's take a problem I had with Rubens.

Peter Paul Rubens is generally thought to be one of the greatest painters of all time. He was a man of enormous influence, not only in his own time, but today as well. He had a rich, full life as a painter and a personal life which included two beautiful wives and recognition by his king. He was Ambassador to the Court of Spain, and the world sought him out to sit for him, to own his works. But Rubens, to my taste as a young art student, was "too much." Way too much. He held the mirror up to nature so close the breath showed, for certainly nothing in Rubens is dead. Even his *nature morte*, his still life, is squirming and alive. The fish flop, the flowers bristle with vitality and dew, the table cloth is crisp, freshly woven. His painting is all noise, the noise of daytime life. His women? Well, so much has been said about his fleshy women, the only expletive in our time that sums it up is, WOW! They heave and groan and belch and blow and writhe and squirm, their bosoms pop the tops of their dresses like champagne corks, and his men look lusty enough to take care of these moorless blimps. So I suppose, to someone brought up on a Constance Bennett as an ideal, it was overpowering and I rejected it. We reject religion for the same reason. It gets in the way of little living until you get lost enough to be forced to live big or be lost forever. I should explain about Constance Bennett. Built like a slat, her hipbones protruding, she fostered a whole generation of dietetic women. She wore dresses which managed to look like they were still on the hanger. But enough of that. I knew about soft, bosomy, comfortable women, but that wasn't the fashion then, so perhaps I was normal in not liking Rubens' women.

Anyway, in spite of Miss Bennett, I was determined to know why Rubens was a great painter. No one seriously interested in being greatly alive can afford to reject greatness in the dead. Even if we can't or haven't time fully to understand Darwin, Nietzsche, Plato, Bosch, the fact that they are great in time's eye makes it imperative we know at least why, if not how. So I set out to know Rubens. I looked at every painting I could find in every gallery or museum, and I read (or looked at) every book, and finally I came across his family tree—that is, the family he left in influence . . . not his seed, but his seed's seed, as it were, the flower of his art and his way to make me, living now, see him, living then.

Rubens begat Fragonard, Fragonard begat Delacroix, Delacroix begat Renoir, and though Renoir didn't begat me, he is vaguely my contemporary. So, if I could understand Renoir, which I could, I could understand backward to Rubens. He is the father of romantic art, and the romantic art of Renoir and especially of Delacroix has always made music for me . . . the music of romance. It was this genealogy that made me understand his vitality, his acceptance of life as something to enjoy, rather than suffer through. The knowledge that sleep is good for you because it makes you more awake; that food is more pleasurable than sleep because it is beautiful and good for you; that sex is more than a sensation, that it is the satisfaction of nature enjoying herself, flowers and fish and animals, ferocious and tame; that breasts and buttocks and clothes and armor and fields and trees were all put here or made here for us to pick and eat, be scared of, love, caress, pat or wear, protect ourselves with, run across barefoot or lie beneath to make love—and then I understood Rubens because this was what he understood and set down and handed down through

Fragonard to Delacroix to Renoir who understood it, too, and left it reinterpreted for me to live with. He understood that life is to live with and that it is worth living.

The more you learn about something the more you love it, but many people are afraid of learning about art. To them it's a foreign product, dangerously controversial, and only for the select few. Yet more and more young Americans are beginning to be *un*fooled by the time-payment advertisements of manufacture and are turning to the arts and crafts, to hand-made things, for their decoration and enjoyment. They know that an original by some young artist can be had as inexpensively as a machine-made copy, and that it's so much more personal. Reproductions of famous paintings in this technical age are superb, but two things are lost by buying them: the realization, thrill, and satisfaction of having made up your own mind about something original in art, and the fact that through your purchase you have helped no one, neither yourself nor an artist. I have come more and more to the belief that we owe our arts a thousand times what we are paying them. We support our cigarette factories, soap manufacturers, beauticians, all the luxury and pleasure businesses of our over-indulged civilization, but we pay our painters an average wage of a little under a thousand dollars a year, and yet when the future digs us from the past they won't care how we smell, what we smoke, or if we bathed. All they'll know of us will be our architecture, our paintings, sculpture, poems, laws, philosophy, drama, our pottery and fabrics, the things which our hands made and our minds thought up—oh, the machines they'll dig up too, but perhaps they'll point to them as our destruction, the wheels that drove us down to death.

Art is love-times-love; the creator loves it and his audience adores it. To miss the sensation of loving art is to miss a kind of parenthood —false pregnancy perhaps—but as Van Gogh said, "If, defrauded of the power to create physically, a man tries to create thoughts in place of children, he is still part of humanity" . . . a big part.

To put oneself in tune with the creative art of others is to be more human than when out of tune with it, for the part of the audience is as great as that of the performer, and in many cases it requires as much sensitive receptivity as was required from the artist in sensitive productivity.

To prove my point, let's take the most controversial as well as the most productive artist of our time, Pablo Picasso.

If I had Aladdin's lamp and could make any wish, I'd be Picasso, even if it meant I had to trade my comparative youth for his few remaining years. He is not only the man most alive to his time, but he has been largely responsible for creating what is stimulatingly acceptable visually in that time. He alone of all twentieth-century artists has made the transition from taste to taste ahead of *public* transition. He has been prophetic as to how we should see and has set the stage for how we *can* see.

So much nonsense has been written about this giant that it has almost diminished him to a trickster, a clown of art . . . volumes of expletives and volumes of explanation and somewhere in the middle of all this, pressed like a flower, is the man and his work.

I like Picasso for his vitality, the same reason I like Rubens, but I like him more for his modernity, for his inventiveness. I often hate Alexander Graham Bell for inventing the telephone. It intrudes on my life, but I couldn't live without him. I often hate Picasso because he sneaks up behind me, disturbs me, makes me laugh just when I want to be serious. I concur with one of his wives when she said she had to leave him because she was "tired of living with a monument." But a monument he is, and somehow, just when you've had too much frivolity from him, he will stab you with a triumphant series of paintings or drawings or those magnificent lithographs in which he reproduces earlier men like Cranach, then reduces them and deduces from them his own puissant analytical observation.

When you think of his paintings in their respective periods, they are always ahead of their time. The "Demoiselles d'Avignon" is still the most mature eclecticism, the most knowledgeable borrowing from primitive art ever concocted, and it was almost the first. It actually is a primitive painting with all the savage sophistication of primitive art.

Truly, I wonder if consciously Picasso has painted for every kind of art audience. Your Aunt Minnie, who will claim he can't draw, is in love with his clowns; your Uncle Joe, who thinks he's crazy, can understand those meticulously licentious drawings of peasant lovers in the hay; your young niece delights in the "Girl with a Rooster" because Picasso has painted it as both she and the sitter would have done it, with arrested tenderness and humor.

He is as profound as life and just as ridiculous. He borrows tricks from life to play on everyone alive, but I think many a self-styled art critic takes him too seriously when he himself is not about to. To enjoy Picasso is to enjoy the grand joke—life. He is Till Eulenspiegel with a paint brush up his behind.

And that remark brings us to the reverence for art—the museum whisperers, the pussyfooters, or the snobs who don't know what they like but THEY LIKE ART, by cracky!

For me, half of the fun of museum- and gallery-going is watching people. The student who is setting down in a notebook every clue he can pick up from the actual work before him that will unravel the mystery of what his art teacher is talking about in class; the lady who comes to enjoy her favorite, and only her favorite, and who swings happily through the rest of the gallery which could be hung with the world's greatest paintings, but she's not going to see them; the child who, having been dragged there by his parent, escapes for a moment and discovers something for himself. He stands before it, open-mouthed at the revelation of this new identification; the professional art lover who quotes Malraux, Elie Faure, and Roger Fry before every object until you suspect he has no opinion of his own; and then that delightful soul whom you occasionally overhear saying to himself in a loud voice, "My God, isn't that beautiful."

I'm extremely profane, unconsciously so, when I see something great for the first time; I don't know why, but beauty and profanity are related to me in the same way. It may be that I want to think of art in the vernacular, but I have no control over what comes out of my mouth when my eyes take in great beauty . . . it might just be the reason I avoid going to museums with elderly ladies.

I would like to be able to explain the thrill I got when I walked into the Art Institute in Chicago one summer day and saw six young working men eating their lunch in front of *"La Grande Jatte."* I thought of Gertrude Stein—picnics on the grass alas, picnics on the grass. A picnic within a picnic.

I trust people who are violent about art, as long as they aren't closed-minded. But, unfortunately, most art blowhards are also art bigots.

Fifteen people sent me that impudent book called *Captions Courageous* for Christmas in the hope that I'd be shocked at anyone who would dare be so irreverent about some of the greatest master-pieces. The shoe was on the other foot. I thought it hysterical, while the one *nouveau* art lover I gave it to didn't crack a smile. That may sound pretty smug, but I think I like Van Eyck's "Arnolfini Wedding" well enough to think the caption "Tell the press we're just good friends" very funny.

I have seen as many paintings that made me happy as ones that made me sad, and therein lies the biggest trap into which the average picture viewer falls. Art should only be serious, profound, emotional —my foot. Shakespeare's comedies are just as brilliant as his tragedies. *Petrouchka* proves Stravinsky's genius as much as his most serious symphony.

In my profession the comedian has always been underrated, and yet every actor will tell you that playing comedy is twice as hard as tragedy. Cary Grant gets my vote every year for the Academy Award, and Jack Benny makes any method actor look like an amateur, and I love that mad, wonderful last-of-the-clowns, Red Skelton.

If I could prescribe a single rule for looking at a work of art it would be to enjoy it. If we're honest with ourselves, we have to admit we enjoy our tears just as much as we enjoy our laughter. The only moments of life that are a bore are when we don't care one way or another.

I don't believe art can, or should, be shoved down people's throats. An art background can be just as revolting as no art background. The lack of it in my parents' home spurred me into a gallop to get at it, but in my own home, which is full of it, my problem is to make it a home and not a museum. Fortunately, my wife Mary has made it a home, and the five hundred objects don't have signs on them, DO NOT TOUCH. That's what they're there for.

When he was a little boy, my son Barrett and I made a pact about going to museums. He would look at the Indian relics, the guns, and natural history, and I could look at the pictures. I knew he was just as apt to revolt against art as I had been to revolt against the lack of it. So five years of museum-going was spent in separate sections.

Then one day a "crossing over" happened for both of us. I found myself again becoming violently interested in the art of the American Indian, and he was becoming curious about what I saw in those pictures. He grew to like my side, and I liked his.

In art, religion, and politics the respect must be mutual, no matter how violent the disagreement.

There's a lot to be learned about how to see a painting by learning how painters see themselves. The self-portrait is a fascinating study. From the beginning of time man has looked to himself as one of his most interesting sources of inspiration and information. A painter is an ever ready sitter for himself. Looking at Rembrandt through Rembrandt's eyes, in any of his dozens of self-portraits in oil, in ink, or in the etchings, you can see the very meaning of the first precept of all philosophy, "Know thyself." Or in Tintoretto's many visions of himself throughout his life, there's the earnest young painter and the brooding wide-eyed mature master of those mighty miracles of paint, looking at himself, an old man who has seen into the miracle of miracles, man! There's Michelangelo, who could not resist signing the "Last Judgment" with his face dripping in the flayed skin of St. Bartholomew. All through the history of art the painter and sculptor looks into himself to see the one person he struggles his whole life to know best, to know at all. If they can solve the riddle of themselves, surely we can trust them to help us solve the mystery of sight. To them, we entrust our vision and see more profoundly through their know-how.

One of the deepest revelations I ever had concerning the insight of an artist into himself, and one which moved me almost to tears, was a nude self-portrait drawing by Albrecht Dürer. It is an unfinished sketch, obviously done for himself alone. The expression on his face is so humble as he stands there studying himself, wondering at the marvel of his manhood and humanity. It is an expression, wonderfully different from the curious arrogance of that early and elegant self-portrait in Madrid. In this drawing it is an aging man, lost in the awareness of himself, like a small boy before a mirror in those first moments of physical self-discovery. It is a landscape of anatomy, a man not separate from plants and trees and birds, but part of nature, like a natural holiday in celebration of itself.

What you learn most from these self-portraits is the depth of real artists' observations. If we can see little or nothing in the vapid society portraits of today and yesterday, other than a flat lifeless likeness, it could be because the artist saw nothing in the sitter and could contribute nothing of himself; or perhaps he had nothing to contribute to the nothing that sat before him. A bad portrait is a double negative.

It's always exciting to deal with the masters and masterworks. It's a safe ground to tread, the path of the past and the famous, but what must concern me most, as an artist of sorts, too, is the art of my time. I don't think I would ever have been as concerned with it if I didn't love and know a lot about the past. It was only when I realized that my senses belong to me, a man of my time, right now, that I learned to fully enjoy all sensual experiences. Whatever the opinion of the future, it is being created today. All ideas are dated from when they are created; from the beginning of the world, B.C., A.D., down to today. I have learned impatience with the believers in "past perfect, future imperfect." Whatever we now do is valid. The present is indicative of us, and you don't have to scan any more than the past fifty years with their incredible changes in all ways of life—art, living, travel, everything—to be aware of the validity of this. If you cannot understand a valid expression of contemporary art, perhaps it is because you are an invalid in your own time. You may be using the crutch of the past to see, to read, to think, and even to move. I'm six foot four, and the airplane is a rapid-transit torture for me—but I use it and I admire it. Horses are too slow and even more uncomfortable.

To be a part of your own day, you have to keep in tune with tomorrow through those who will make it whatever it is—young people.

After one of my lectures (I think it was in Kansas) I was sitting around with a couple of hundred students, swapping ideas. The young men and women of America have such vitality and curiosity, I can't begin to answer their questions, and often I question them and come up with marvelous answers that become part of my vocabulary of ideas. One question really hit me, and though I couldn't answer it then, about three weeks later what happened that night came to me, awkwardly at first, but perhaps by now I've refined it enough to make it intelligible.

QUESTION: I feel cheated, living where and when I do, by the stress being put on scientific studies. I don't feel I'm getting anything out of college to be lived with later on. What should I do?

It was obviously not the question of a malcontent or a slob, for I asked him what he meant by "living where and when he did," to which he explained that he felt his home town had all he wanted opportunity-wise, so he wanted to live there. He also realized that the time in which he was living was full of excitement, but that added something which would make his life exciting was missing. We fenced around a bit, because I wanted to find out if he had any idea what was missing. Other kids got into it, and it came to light that he was an excellent student, majoring in the sciences, and that he was very popular. He had no ambition to be President, or a movie actor, but he was ambitious to have a good life. Finally, it came out . . . he felt he had no talent.

We threw that word around, all two hundred of us, examining what it meant for one to have talent. To him, it meant the ability to communicate with all kinds of people on all kinds of subjects. His father, by his son's account, was a man who never talked about anything at home but sports and business. Nothing entertained him, and every attempt on the part of his children to do anything away from the average was derided, if not forbidden. College and an art appreciation course, taken as a "gut" course, had opened his eyes. This, he explained, was why he felt cheated. He had never looked at anything in his entire life. He had never been made to read anything good at home or in high school, and the only thing his father considered praiseworthy was his ability in mathematics. Consequently, math was his major in college, and with Sputnik in the air his advisers frowned on the frivolity of literature or art courses. America needs scientists, of course we do, but anyone with any sense of civilization will agree that a one-track mind gets you nowhere, not even into orbit. Our greatest scientists know this to be a fact and report it constantly.

The answer actually came from all of us that night. Others in the group felt it, too, and the air was electric with the exchange of ideas. One young girl confessed the same feeling in reverse; her education was all art, and she'd been lost when thrust into a curriculum that demanded the three R's. The answer was balance, but the concensus was that the arts were being neglected, and while it is true we need more scientists, science has become a necessary implement of modern life, but perhaps the educators as well as the students are being caught up in it without looking to either side for those delightful detours that make us tick, as individuals, all the way around the clock of a life span.

To be involved in the momentary necessity completely is a dangerous mood. It is easy to get along in because everyone is in it. But it can be a prison impossible to break out of, even for adults, and sophisticated ones at that. Public information media, such as movies, TV, and the theatre, get caught in fads all the time. At this writing they are trapped in reflections of the downbeat; everything is gloom and despair and no box office. Modern painting could be in the same danger, and we could end up in a world of congoleum and coat hangers.

We all have to see our age through to the end, even if we don't like it, but my point is that it's much more fun to see it through than to close your eyes and mind and stumble along life, angry at the whole thing.

No one knows what the final evaluation of contemporary art will be. People who are just starting as collectors and appreciators are always asking me who I consider to be the best young painters, the ones most apt to succeed. To try to forecast that information would be as fruitless as a high school yearbook "historian's" predictions of "the boy most likely. . . ." In my experience "the boy most likely" is rarely the one who shoots his bolt publicly in high school or college. It is more often than not the one who is quietly conscious that what he is out after throughout his education is the acquisition of knowledge which will be applicable to everyday experience.

"The artist most likely" has the same problem. He must not get caught in the web of fashion. He must report himself and his day with full knowledge of both. He must make some comment, some honest and very personal statement in whatever way he wants, technically and/or spiritually. What I get out of it must be the same excitement I get from a thoughtful friend of long standing. For me, a work of art must have the security I feel in those rare persons who never take me for granted and whose contribution to me is reciprocally stimulating.

Epilogue

I N THE WHIRL OF 1959, AND FOR MANY HECTIC YEARS PRE-
ceding it, the price one has had to pay for a modicum of success is more
success. No time to fool around with that delightful toy called "life."
Don't get any fool ideas into your fat head that you can live on past
success. If you've made it to sixth vice-president, there are five more to
make it to first. Then there's the presidency, board member, chairman
of the board, and . . . death! Don't think because last year was a good
one, you can coast along in this one. . . . Don't imagine for a moment
that if your house is paid for, and the last installments on the car,
refrigerator, stove, washing machine, and hi-fi set are just about due,
that that lets you out. Keep on going. . . . You owe it to the
government.

Well, what do you owe yourself? Do you dare take time out to
listen to the grass grow, or can you even afford the expense of getting
far enough away from life's daily cacophony to *hear* it grow if you
took the time?

Do you ever wake up with the feeling that during the night a
thief has been in your life, robbing you of time?

Do you ever rub your eyes and suddenly find you're awake and
not asleep, as you'd grown to suspect you were?

264

About three quarters of the way through the writing of this book I found myself knowing, firsthand, the classic sensation of drowning that I mentioned in the beginning. I was seeing great empty bubbles that looked suspiciously like the future, mixed in with the bubbles of the past that were so full of iridescent memories. Nature's eyeglasses, which I'd been fitted for in my youth and through which everything looked so beautiful, no longer served to keep my vision focused on the signs along the road . . . the signs that warn one when the danger of boredom is near.

I was telling myself (and you) the glories of the visual arts . . . how rich they can make your life . . . and all the while, I was dying of poverty. I was doing something I've always tried to talk others out of . . . looking at reproductions. I wasn't even curious to see the real, the original thing.

True, I was keeping up with the art of my time, but so violently and with such determination to be contemporary that I could only remember, through these pages of my own book, that I was ever a child—seeing things for the first time, new things, old things. I was forgetting how to see for myself what was directly in my line of vision: beauty.

I reread a passage I'd written about "always feeling at home in Greek art, though I'd never been to Greece." I discussed Tintoretto and said I thought him to be one of the greatest painters who ever lived, though I'd never seen the Scuola di San Rocco in Venice. Without having seen it, you can only half know Tintoretto, and a poor half, at that.

In short, while not intentionally trying to kid anyone else, I was kidding myself. Of course, I have seen all the Goyas, but where? In books. What I've written about is for real. The experience of seeing has been the highest experience of my life, and I've seen a lot of actual Goyas and a lot of actual Velázquezes, but I'd never been to the Prado in Madrid.

What do you do when you find yourself out in a lie—even a white one? Well, one thing for sure, you don't put on black, you don't mourn and beat out a staccato *mea culpa* on your breast. You go! Get the hell out! Take a chance! Forget you're an American, living in the suburbs of success, hoping to move into the big city. . . . You *go!*

November 16, 1958 . . . Gordon Washburn, director of the Carnegie Institute, has invited you to be on the jury of the great Pittsburgh International Exhibition, the largest exhibition of contemporary world art. Your fellow jurors? Distinguished, alive, alert art minds of all types: Marcel Duchamp, who painted one of the greatest masterpieces of modern art, "Nude Descending a Staircase"; Leonello Venturi, brilliant critic, author, and teacher of art, aged in the arts but more modern than a second-year art student; James Johnson Sweeney, one of the leaders of art judgment in our day, director of the Guggenheim Museum, unbelievably knowledgeable in the art of this century; Mary Callery, one of the few great women artists and a sculptor, at that . . . cosmopolitan friend of many great artists, owner of a superb collection, and as we say in the theatre, a real "pro," in the art world; Raoul Ubac, considered in France to be one of the few artists working in today's language but in the great tradition of French art; and *you!*—actor, lecturer, collector, *amateur!* Let's not kid ourselves, Vincent. You may have seen a lot, but Professor Venturi has seen a lot more. All of your fellow jurors are in the arts. You're in the theatre —an art, for sure—but . . . You have only one thing to recommend you . . . maybe two: passion for the visual arts and the fact that you have the good fortune to be able to communicate that passion to others, and for the past few years have had the chance to do it successfully (thanks to W. Colston Leigh, who persuaded you to be a professional lecturer). Maybe one more recommendation. You have exchanged ideas with thousands of young people all over the United States on art. Go ahead. Judge the whole world of art in Pittsburgh, but be damn sure you're aware of the company you're in! Listen, and be honest with yourself; look, and be honest with the painters; vote, and remember—the winners will more than likely outlive you, in more ways than one.

Results? You discover that, after looking at five hundred paintings and sculptures, you're still in love with the creative act . . . that you may not be as erudite, as brilliant, as creative as your fellow jurors, but (pat on the back) you still can see and you still *want* to.

Now . . . get the hell away from today, from making a living, from being modern, and look the past you love so much right in the face. Resee what you've seen, and see for the first time what you've seen only in books and dreams. Get on a jet—that's modern—and go to Greece—that's old!

The jet is a great invention. Besides being a world shrinker, par excellence, it has much of the quality and charm of a roller coaster. And it's big. Once, years ago, on a ten-stop, cross-country air trip, I turned to the man next to me and said, quite genuinely: "What keeps these big goddam things up in the air?" He was a nice man, whose face I never bothered to look at as I sat enthralled with a brilliant explanation he was giving me of the theories and principles of flight. When he had finished, I understood at least that, chances were, airplanes were here to stay and that nothing could be more logical than that they should fly. When we finally made Los Angeles and I finally introduced myself and honestly thanked him, he said, very calmly: "Not at all, Mr. Price, I enjoyed it. My name's Rickenbacker."

The point of this vignette is that he gave me the inside information then, but as to what keeps these jet things up, or what makes them go—— Well, I'd better meet up with Mr. Rickenbacker again.

So Mary and I took a jet to Paris and on to Rome. In Paris, where almost nothing ruffles the French indifference, the flight was so new they almost ran out to watch us land. They didn't run, actually, but two mechanics did shake their heads . . . slightly.

The whole trip was so magical we didn't even look for the Eiffel Tower on the way in or out, and we made Rome so quickly from Paris we were still exclaiming over the beauties of Switzerland when we landed at the Rome airport, just in time to make our plane for Greece.

(Mary and I couldn't get over the fact that we'd left New York the day after my Carnegie jury job, and the next night we were in Athens!)

I don't know exactly what I expected to have happen to me when I first set foot on Greek soil, but of one thing I was fairly sure—I wouldn't be given the gift of tongues, and, indeed, I wasn't. I couldn't understand a syllable. It was 8 P.M. when we landed, so I didn't really think I was going to be Superman and see the Acropolis in the dark. But I did expect *something*, and nothing happened at all. An airport is an airport anywhere, I guess, and a foreign one is a clambake.

But at first glance a glimmer of an impression struck me. Greece was a very modern country, efficient and polite, the people beautiful and confident. I say a "glimmer" because any crystal-clear picture was, for the moment, shoved aside by the heavy-lidded anticipation of sleep. After a jet trip, a transfer in Rome, and a bumpy ride to Athens, Morpheus was the only Greek we were anxious to meet.

But on the way to the hotel in a taxi, we were shaken awake (literally and figuratively), both of us now open-eyed and open-mouthed at the amazing activity of the city. Every Greek in Athens (and there were very few tourists at that time of year) seemed to be out for a walk, a talk, a cup of coffee. The town was jumping, an exercise the Greek auto drivers make absolutely necessary to avoid being hit by them.

The hotel was wonderfully comfortable, but we'd been so completely revived by the city's buzz of activity, en route, that the arms of Morpheus would have to wait.

We freshened up as fast as we could and went out to see if war had been declared, or what. We found that everyone was simply out to make love to Athens. The people of Athens were reveling in Athens. The Acropolis was dark for the night, but I swear, even if it had been flood-lit, I don't think we could have taken our eyes off these beautiful people, enjoying their city.

I had whimsically asked for a room overlooking the Acropolis, and I *got* it! By stretching your neck out the bathroom window (if you could open the window), and bracing your feet against the bidet for the final thrust, you could see one and a half columns of the Parthenon. But that was enough to do the trick. The next morning, though it took all my strength, I managed the view, and as soon as we could coffee and croissant ourselves, we were on our way to *the* place.

The Acropolis was literally swarming with people. For a second we were annoyed, having come purposely out of season to avoid tourists. And then we realized that ninety-eight per cent of that crowd were not tourists but Greeks. It was Sunday, and the Athenians were out bright and early to make love, once again, to their city—even after the debauch of the night before.

And then when we could shift our sight from the beauty of those buildings we turned to see the cause of all this adoration of Athens.

From the Acropolis, whichever way you look is a gleaming city of white houses, buildings, apartments . . . a city built from almost nothing, in a little over a hundred years, to a metropolis of over a million people. One of the most ancient of cities, which centuries of misfortune had almost reduced to nothing, is once again one of the wonders of the world. . . . Modern Athens.

Anyone who has a word about artists not being appreciated during their lifetime must question this cliché in Athens. The name of Phidias is still in the thoughts of everyone, and though there are only glimpses of his work and his design, the wonderful little Acropolis Museum reminds you of his greatness, which you have to see—and I had, full force, in the British Museum. The ancient argument will never be settled. Lord Elgin undoubtedly did practically steal the sculptures from the Greek people, but when he did it, they weren't Greek but under the heel of Turkey, and much of the Parthenon had already disappeared. Many of the buildings, on the rock above the city, had indeed gone altogether. Would the Turks have taken the marbles? Would the Greeks, stumbling out of their long war for freedom, have had the strength to resist firing the marble for lime, or using it to build much-needed homes and buildings? Who knows? Anyway, now you can see, between London and Athens, much of that superb sculpture, and the effort, time, trouble, or money that it takes to see it is worth it.

But the greatest thrill of ancient Athenian art is, as in so many other periods of art, not the work of known artists but that of the anonymous ones. Anyone I've ever known who went to Greece has felt impelled to send me a post card of the archaic sculpture of the young priest, carrying a calf on his shoulders, and for whatever reason they felt the need to do this, it worked on me. That was one of the "must sees" on my list. I knew it to be in the Acropolis Museum, but my first visit there didn't reveal it. I asked a guard by pointing to a photo of it and translated from his signs and gesticulations the catastrophic news that it was behind a padlocked section which would not be opened to the public for a month or more.

There are ways to get everything in this world—everything, that is, except enough time to get everything you want out of it. Padlocks were made to be picked, and a kind word, a tear, jumping up and down and screaming, even a dollar bill can be some of the methods of "picking." But the simplest way is to ask and ask and ask, until people get bored and so does the "padlock" . . . and it springs open.

I asked and asked and asked and asked, and suddenly I asked the right person, and there we were—standing in an unfinished wing of the Acropolis Museum, before a score of figures all carefully wrapped in plastic, like wares in an American supermarket. A huge workman who appeared to be delighted that someone had "picked" the lock hastened to snatch off these covers, one by one, and there, before our startled eyes, were all the masterpieces of archaic Greek art.

Lord Elgin hadn't known about these, nor had the Turks, nor even the Greeks, for they had been dumped under the earth two thousand years before, to act as fill for the new buildings of the Acropolis in the sixth century before Christ. The earth, which makes its choice to destroy or preserve when treasures are buried in it, had chosen wisely this time. These beautiful, smiling girls and handsome men and graceful horses survived, almost complete, their color decoration often unimpaired. They certainly make up one of the most moving collections of sculpture in the world. And then, at last, we came on the young priest and his calf. There is no portrayal of sacrifice that can compare to it. It is not bloody, savage, wanton, or obscene. Merely a young man, carrying with utter tenderness his prize possession for the pleasure of his god. Even the calf, enchanted with his voyage and the chance to be close to his master, seems aware of the privilege awaiting him in death.

Who knows whether this was considered a major work of art when it was done, or if it was the work of a master or some new young talent—trying to impress by giving all he knew to make his reputation. It will always be one of the major fascinations of art history that so many of the greatest things have come to us without labels of any kind. It proves to me, each time it happens, that the name means nothing. It is the spirit of the act. . . . Who wrote the Bible?

The Greeks, in their few years as a nation, have taken great pride in their past, and the museums, great and small, are wonderful working tributes to this pride. They are beautifully installed and marvelously informative. The National Museum, a fine example of architecture (naturally, Greek), is flooded with the best material found in the last hundred years and contains really great examples of all periods, which have escaped the acquisitive hands of generations of Roman, Venetian, Turkish, British, and German archaeologists, collectors, and plunderers.

The government sees to it that at each historical site a museum is set up and kept up to house the finds of that location. But aside from the treasures, the places themselves carry enormous magic. Corinth, for example, is such a site, naturally and geographically, that you understand at once its importance as a trade center. There is always something terribly dramatic about standing where a great man stood and imagining his problem and his time. If you reread St. Paul's letter to the Corinthians, you know how important he considered it on his crusade for Christianity. He knew that success had gone to its head, but he felt Corinth worth saving.

There are so many names of famous places in Greece where all but their names have disappeared. You drive through Eleusis and Thebes, and they scarcely exist. But one place does exist which strikes you as a miracle that it ever existed at all . . . Delphi. Very holy places have a mystery all their own, and one of the mysteries of Delphi is how and why they ever chose this inaccessible spot on which to erect such a forest of shrines. You really had to believe to be able to make that trip in ancient times, and the clue to the strength of their belief is seen in the few great statues and buildings which have survived the disaster of change of faith in that inspiring place.

There is a terrible frustration when you try to imagine Delphi in its heyday. None of those meticulous, caricature restorations give you any feeling at all. Only when you gaze into the enameled eyes of the Charioteer of Delphi can you sense some of the magic that once existed. Or when you lift your eyes from the ruins and see Mount Parnassus, which time can never change, you do believe that this indeed could have been the birthplace of a god.

The two most understandably important sites we saw were Knossos and Mycenae. Crete is an island that seems, on the map, to navel the whole Mediterranean, so it is absolutely believable that a great civilization must have flourished here. Even though the Palace of Minos is much reconstructed and much restored, it does indeed give you a picture of the wealth of this extremely early culture. Once again, the museum is a progressive delight in which to follow the achievements of the earliest Cretans down to those who fell, at the height of their power, to the greater power of the Greek mainland.

But for me, it was at Mycenae that I was able to recapture completely the drama of an age helped, of course, by the fact that the stage was set by one of the greatest dramatists, Aeschylus, and the site once occupied by some of the most dramatic characters ever to be dramatized—Agamemnon and Clytemnestra. Then when you return to Athens and see the golden treasure of Mycenae in the museum there, this bleak site, overlooking the lush Argolis plains, takes on real significance. What a fortress it must have been to warrant those noble lions to guard it forever.

Greece, even in the short time we were there, withheld none of its beauty. The light is unlike the light of any other land, as has been said a thousand times, and, bracing yourself against the lashing winds in the temple at Sunium, you feel a part of that tough, ancient world which gave more to the mind of man than any other era—to make his life graceful and to justify his existence.

I came away with a new understanding of Homer. He had seen his time so thoroughly that he became the first to reach the summit of an artist's true calling: to report what he had seen. If we speak of the blind Homer, it is of the old artist who simply shut his eyes forever so that men might see through his memory's eyes and be assured that they indeed are gods on earth—if they will accept the chance to live greatly.

Our travel agent, Ruth Batchelor, has the genius of selling tickets to everywhere as though she can hardly wait to go there, too (and many's the place she's been), so that when our plans for Greece were made, she simply included two tickets to Istanbul, with the curt advice that we'd be near it—so *see* it.

I'm continually staggered by the fact that today everything is so close to everything else. Istanbul! . . . My God, I'd thought it bordered on India. But a quick hour and a half from Athens, and we were flung into the most extraordinary airport I've ever seen. It's a modern version of the Tower of Babel. I, who can hardly make it for breakfast in French and German, and can only say "how much" in Spanish, was completely bewildered by the rush of languages that came pouring out of everyone at the Istanbul airport. Unfortunately, my Mary was at an equal linguistic loss.

After the customs had succeeded in making us feel not only dishonest, but unclean, we were purloined into what is called a taxi. It ran all right, or, rather, the third one we were thrown into and dragged out of ran—but we had the feeling that once those rubber bands (which obviously powered the motor) were unwound, it would stop forever in front of the Istanbul Hilton.

I'll say one thing for Mr. Hilton. He sure knows how to pick a site. His Istanbul hotel sits a commandingly discreet distance from the Bosporus and looks out on just enough mosques to give you a feeling of being in another world . . . one that promises to be exciting, and is.

I know that really seasoned tourists are loath to put themselves in the hands of a private guide. However, even though we had had such fun in Greece on the wonderfully conducted "Chat" tours—huge, modern buses filled with people from everywhere and staffed with two of the most enlightened Greek ladies as guides—we decided to take the advice of Mildred Combs, our dearest friend, and hire her private Turkish guide for our three short days in Istanbul. It was not without a sense of appreciation that we did it, for a movie actor can get into a lot of embarrassing situations with a guide who decides to play it grand with his public charge, to say nothing of adding on a lot of expenses. But the moment we met Kahan Pekmener, we knew the city would unfold for us as completely as our time allowed, and it did. We are always quick to inform a guide that we are there to see, and not to socialize or *be* seen . . . that we are much more interested in being impressed than impressive . . . so get on with it, and except for food (of which we want the most typical and the best), we want to *go!* . . . and *see!*

He got the message and we went. I had never thought about Istanbul at all, but Mary was carried away with the dream of it as the entrance to the East, as the bazaar of bazaars; and since I didn't have anything but a few mosques on my sight-seeing menu, we played it her way. But we soon found out that there was nothing to buy in Istanbul, and that prices were extremely high and the merchandise very inferior. So we both gave up and let Kahan show us his city, in his way, and what an enchanting city it is.

The whole city landscape is dominated by those crazy mosques, one bigger and more minareted than the next, and all glistening and shimmering in the brilliant sun which, when it wearies of bathing the mosques, fingers its brilliance in and out of the Bosporus and the Golden Horn. The narrow streets, a few still lined with the soon to be demolished bric-a-brac wooden houses of the last century, wind up and down the gentle hills that all slope down to that historically important (and now, even more important) waterway between Russia and the rest of the world.

Ships, cars, people, pigeons, and cats all seem to have equal importance on the streets. The ships practically dock on the streets, where the cars and people are swarming to get wherever it is they're going . . . through the clouds of pigeons and fields of cats. Then suddenly you turn off a street just wide enough for two cars, and into another not wide enough for one car—and there, by miraculous maneuver, you meet and pass a horse, wearing blue beads and tassels, and a wagon, wearing everything. You park and shuffle down through a labyrinth of little footways, take off your shoes, and you're in a mosque walled bright with tiles and carpeted with wonderful old rugs and people.

The mosques in use are very impressive, and while few of them are triumphs of interior decoration, they have the appeal of a cofferful of unset, precious gems in the hodgepodge of tiles and colored windows and elaborately carved stone. And the minarets from which those disturbingly demanding calls to prayer pierce the clear air, are truly inspiring to see. To try to figure out how they were made and how anyone ever gets up inside them only adds to their charm and mystery.

The people of the world at large may dislike Americans for our success, and for putting them in debt to us, but in both Athens and Istanbul we have left them remembrances of their own past—restored by us—that must touch a spot of gratitude in some, at least.

The Kaaryie Mosque, an ancient Byzantine church before it became a mosque, could easily have been destroyed by just a little more time, had not the American Institute of Byzantine Research gone to work to restore and preserve some of the most beautiful mosaics that exist. This is something to behold, this story of Christ in bright, colored mosaic on gold mosaic. The whole conception of the work, the composition, the draftsmanship are unexcelled anywhere and make up a wonderful picture of that excitingly rich period of Christian art.

In Athens, the American Institute of Classical Research has excavated the Agora, or market place, below the Acropolis and restored the great building at the end of it so that while you are seeing what is left of this very ancient site, you can see what it was like when it functioned as the center of that city's life.

Mary's disappointment over the bazaars and their goods had to be assuaged, so our delightful and informative guide took us just outside one of them where they make the copper and brass "antiques" they sell inside. Here she purchased, over my dead body (it's been dead so many times and stepped over by her, I wonder how I've survived), an enormous copper brazier, brand-new, but dated 1874. This we had to take with us on the plane to Rome, then ship it from there, as the Turkish government, for some unexplained reason, frowns on exports and imports of anything . . . including coffee.

All of our lives we've been drinking Turkish coffee—but never in Turkey—and except at the Hilton, where they concocted Nescafé into a pseudo-espresso, we didn't have it once on this trip, in Turkey. They don't import coffee and they don't grow it. There's no such thing as Turkish coffee . . . in Turkey.

But there are cats, and some of the nicest, best cared for cats in the world live in Istanbul. There's one little park where discarded cats live, at the expense of a doting populace. Here, if you're tired of your cat, you can bring him to live with hundreds of other cats until someone else has a feeling for him and takes him home. It may sound a bit peculiar, but it works in Istanbul, and the cats approve of it . . . and I've heard of a lot less humane ways of disposing of cats, in America and elsewhere.

There are two places in that city that have little or nothing to do with art, though the Turks think them artistic and they do, in a funny way, go in and around art and come out startlingly wonderful: the sultans' old palace, the Topkapi, and the new one, the Dolmabahçe.

The old palace defies architectural description, since no sultan ever lived there who didn't feel impelled to add a building of his own, or redecorate an existing one in his favorite style, according to the vogue of his moment. The only word to describe it is—wild!

There seem to be a million rooms, large and small, bare or decorated within an inch of their lives as the saying goes. And that's the saying for the sultans, themselves. They were decorated within a half inch of their lives.

Five beautiful, white, plastered rooms now comprise the treasury in which are displayed the "treasure" (and it must be in quotes) of the sultans. It seems no sultan would use or wear anything any other sultan wore, nor would they throw it away, so every stitch, every pearl, diamond, ruby, emerald each of them owned is there. It is said to be the most valuable collection of jewels in the world, and I'm not going to be the one to dispute it. There are, for example, a dozen diamond eggcups—to start the day off right; there are emeralds and rubies the size of silver dollars, and one emerald, said to be the largest in the world was held to be of such value by its sultan that he ordered it to be sold if anything should happen to him, and the Blue Mosque built with the proceeds. I have never priced a mosque, but this emerald looks like an even exchange to me. It hangs on a golden rope from the roof of a golden throne, and is the size of a pack of king-sized cigarettes.

The palace rooms themselves make Hollywood completely believable. I never would have dreamed that so much assorted junk could be gotten into one small room, except by a set dresser, and one with very little taste at that. But the kitchens are beautiful, inside and out. The exterior looks like a quarter mile of perfectly constructed kilns, fitted one against the other, and inside, they are like great brick caves, subtly arched up to the roof where the smoke escapes through the tall brick chimneys.

Today they are the display rooms of the sultan's chinaware, and if the signs are to be believed, the collection of Sung Celadon must be the most extensive anywhere. No one told us what they ate, but whatever they ate, they ate off the best there is. Literally thousands of dishes, services of all centuries and makes, many of them gifts from visiting royalty, comprise this collection.

The new palace was completed well into the nineteenth century and makes all other palaces look niggardly by its lush décor. Every extravagance was lavished on the huge edifice, and again, it all comes off like an old MGM movie. There were obviously millions of dollars spent on the crystals, the rugs, furniture, drapes, and ornaments, and they were worth it, if only for the total effect of opulence. But other millions must have gone into the hundreds of paintings on the walls, and without exception they are worthless. I've never seen such a collection of dreary art under one roof—proof, I suppose, that money can't buy everything.

This may all sound like the quickest trip on record, and it was, but with the exception of Istanbul, where we went for fun, the whole plan was to refresh our eyes—to see again, anew, the marvels of antiquity without knowledge and appreciation of which the new can become very stale. Besides, we've found that if you don't do things when you have the chance to do them, you never get another chance.

For six years we had been hiding money in a "travel account." We never looked at it, in the hope that it would grow, unaccountably, and so when we took a peek one day, to our joy the savings would just cover the travel expense. But why try to justify such a glorious experience?

We left Istanbul for Rome, looking more like refugees than usual with Mary's copper brazier wrapped in Turkish newspaper and string that wouldn't have held a bunch of beans together, let alone thirty-five pounds of new antique copper. The flight over the Aegean Sea, with its thousands of islands, made me want to jump out and swim to each one of them. I mentally put down a cruise of that sea and a visit to those fabled islands as a goal for the next cookie-jar bank account.

One of those exciting moments in the air happened as we came into Rome. The weather was uncertain and planes were piled up over the airport, so our pilot circled the city about five times before coming in. Usually it's an exasperating experience, but Captain Whoever-he-was did the most spectacular job of touring a city by air that I've ever known. Of course, it's some city to tour, but he approached it from a different angle each time, and you could really feel the reason for Rome being where it is. The Tiber, winding through the green hills to the sea, and then the city following it and, in some places, hiding it with bridges to swallow it altogether where it lined its banks with enormous buildings. Old Rome, new Rome, the parks, the palaces, St. Peter's centering everything, the Forum, and just before we landed, looking back you could count the seven hills and trail the aqueducts out to the airport where we finally came down.

I had never been to Rome in the winter, and we didn't plan to stay there long, as not too many years before we'd shared a lovely summer fortnight seeing it. Where Rome is rather languid in the heat, it bustles and bursts with activity in the winter. All European cities, feeling they belong to themselves once more after the onslaught of summer tourists, are so much more alive in the winter, and Rome is one of the most alive. Even in the late December afternoon there was great activity and much good spirit everywhere. Even through the taxi window you could sense the Christmas time coming up.

I had chosen a hotel at the top of the Spanish Steps, because I love the Spanish Steps and I especially like going down them. From the foot of those steps Rome spreads out in all directions, and as soon as we had pulled ourselves together and, by this time, we were beginning to fall apart, physically and otherwise, we intended to make the descent. Our wardrobe was getting that lived-in look, because there comes a time when even the best wash-and-wear shirt, or lady's blouse, begins to look like it's been slept in. And flying, get-you-there-fast, as it does, is a wearing way to travel. (Very few birds could stay up that long, fly that distance with such short stops, and not be wing-weary.) So the pulling together took a little longer, and besides, the view from our little balcony was beautiful. Anyway, we finally made it, though we felt as complicatedly exhausted as the above description may have made you.

We both decided the one place to go in Rome that night was the

Piazza Navona, where Bernini's fountains would sing us a song and the good Italian cooking would make up for the tons of lamb we had eaten in Greece and Turkey. The taxi pulled into the Piazza, and to our horror, the whole oblong was shut out by dozens of little wooden and canvas stalls. Our hearts sank, but we got out anyway, and, entering the enclosure, we came upon one of the most happy sights imaginable. Each stall was filled with thousands of little figurines for the Nativities of Christmas. They ranged in quality and price from the cheapest and most banal little Christ Child and Madonna to exquisite sets of thirty figures, vividly colored and with genuine eighteenth-century faces, made today in Lucca. It was all I could do to try and convince Mary that if the good ones came from Lucca, they would be cheaper and better in Florence, which is close to Lucca. I knew I had a losing battle on my hands, whichever way she took my argument. But for the moment, I won, and we left the Piazza Navona, Mary secure in the knowledge that one of those sets would make it to California, and I firm in the hope that she'd forget about it.

From our balcony at the top of the Spanish Steps we could see most of that part of Rome that still has a Renaissance flavor, plus the dome of St. Peter's, and, straight ahead, the great squat dome of the Pantheon. The weather was cold and clear, and the whole city sparkled from the rain of the night before. With the short time we had to stay in Rome it would almost have been worth it to sit on that balcony and see what the sun had to say to Rome, then watch the night come down with those timid European electric bulbs turning the gray-brown buildings yellow. But you can't do that in Rome. You have to be on the streets . . . in the galleries and shops to become alive to it. Besides, we had Christmas shopping to do for what, at that time, always seems like a list of thousands.

Living where we did, it was as though the Steps were the exit from the hotel. There was a street, of course, but we couldn't bring ourselves to use it.

That morning we decided to take one of the side stairs that lead off in both directions from the main descent, and fate directed us—as it always does—to one of the best contemporary galleries, halfway down. The Gallerie Schneider is very progressive, run by two nice Americans, and shows one of our favorite modern Italian masters, Afro. I was overjoyed to see his name on the roster of the Gallerie and went inside to leave a message for him—that he had won second prize at the Carnegie International. It just happened that this was the day the news was to come out. The secret had been in me long enough, and Afro was a friend, so everything was timed perfectly. Mr. Schneider was very gracious, said he would call Afro, and to please look around—a fatal request. Mary and I both knew that we were trapped, even before we saw the exciting painting by a new young man named Buggiani. We asked to see more, saw them all, and bought two. Afro wasn't at home, but just as we were about to leave, having become the owners of two Buggianis, the door burst open and in came two old friends . . . Earl Stendahl, the pre-Columbian art dealer from Los Angeles, and Eugene Berman, the great stage designer and romantic painter.

The rest of the day was a Roman holiday we could never have planned. Earl, Berman, the Schneiders, and anyone else we could find ate, drank, went shopping, reminisced, and generally had the best possible time. Earl was full of his great pre-Columbian show in Munich, for which he had made a cast of our huge Huastecan figure, and Berman was equally full of the wonders of living in Rome and of his collection of Etruscan vases. We were full of Greece, Turkey, and, most recently, our new painter, Buggiani.

That night Rome, our friends, the Spanish Steps (which we had to ascend three times, following our enthusiastic dealers and painter) had us licked. We rolled into bed with the glow of gratitude that only comes from a rich and stimulating experience in the world of art.

We may all be a peculiar lot . . . often broke, often dissatisfied because we're not doing more and better work . . . but we know how to have a ball that makes the rest of the world seem square.

One day left in Rome! What to see? . . . The Vatican? . . . Yes! Having listened to Berman go on about Etruscan art, the Villa Giulia?

. . . Yes! Not all of Rome, but a lot, we'd seen. And there was the shopping. So the Forum? . . . No. . . . Churches? . . . No.

Mary went shopping, and I went to the Villa Giulia, one of the best Etruscan museums there is and an enchanting old palace housing it. I'd read a lot about the Etruscans, beginning with *Etruscan Places* by D. H. Lawrence, and had long been in awe of the giant terra-cotta warriors in the Met in New York—and that beauty, the "Diana," in St. Louis. But there's no museum in America that gives a clear picture of that mysterious civilization through its art and artifacts. Then there was a story told us in the ancient civilizations course at Yale by the humorous Professor Rostovtzeff that made Etruscan archaeology particularly fascinating.

It seems a young English archaeologist, on an Etruscan dig, was more than eager to be the first to crack the language that had so long withstood translation. He was fond of examining every fragment of writing long after the older men had passed them by and given up any hope. In particular, there was a low, round pot in perfect condition, even to its one graceful handle. On it was written, in the strange script: "ITIS APIS POTITIS." It intrigued him. It sounded like Latin, yet it didn't mean a damn thing.

At two o'clock one morning he broke in on the senior member of the dig, wild with excitement, screaming: "I've got it! . . . I've got it, Professor! . . . 'Itis Apis Potitis' . . . rearrange it and you have, 'It is a pis pot, it is.'"

The Villa Giulia has a great many inscriptions and pots that look vaguely familiar, but I really couldn't take the time to rearrange all the letters. (However, from what I'd read of the Etruscans, there might be some pretty spicy passages to be found if I did do some rearranging.)

They were very great artists. Their pottery is graceful or bold, their paintings among the most beautiful ever done, and their bronze and terra-cotta sculpture mysterious and strong. I came away with another note for our next trip: a jaunt to Tarquinia, on the coast just north of Rome, to visit the famous tombs.

Mary and I met at the entrance to the Vatican Museum, as prearranged. I didn't know that her important shopping was to buy for me, for Christmas, a marvelous Etruscan pot.

She had had a wonderful, comic adventure which came to light when I opened the present Christmas morning. One of the little shops we had visited with Eugene Berman had four or five fine examples of the famous black Etruscan pottery, but they were all being held for a customer who would decide the next day what pieces he wanted. Mary was determined to have what he didn't want and I'm sure was there the next morning when the antiquarian raised his forbidding iron shutter. She had carefully measured her hatbox, for there whatever she bought would have to be hidden from my prying eyes.

The antiquarian had told her two pots remained: one small one of no great interest and the other the most spectacular one of all, left behind by the collector for some unknown reason. It is a great cup, measuring in height nearly twenty inches (with the handle), and the bowl about ten inches in diameter. This was way too big to fit in the hatbox, but a phone conversation with friend Berman resulted in the suggestion to rebreak it where it had originally been repaired. Mary agreed, as she knew how I love to repair things, but the antiquarian balked on the grounds that what he mended stayed mended, and it couldn't be done.

I don't know what Mary had to say, but the next two hours were spent laboriously dissolving the glue he was so proud of and ended with Mary victoriously putting the pieces in a brown paper bag and rushing to the hotel to hide her purchase . . . my Christmas present . . . in her hatbox. The most remarkable point of this story is that she met me at the Vatican Museum right on the nose of the appointed hour.

Whoever designed that circular stairway that gives entrance to the Vatican (and I *should* know) certainly succeeded in two things: it's a delightful way to go to heaven and an impressive road from today to yesterday. Whether or not it's pretty, good design, or whatever you may be looking for in stairways, it certainly serves its purpose. It gets you there with your dignity intact, feeling grand enough to take on the task of seeing some of the world's most beautiful creations.

I'd been to the Vatican many times over the years, but the experience in any great museum is always new. Pictures or statues that impressed you the first time take their proper place in your memory, and some become an immediate remembrance for their beauty while others trail off, either to second place or sometimes to oblivion. There's no reason in the world why you should rave over even the best each time you see it. Vision is always new. It is memory that is old . . . or that makes things seem old. So when we came upon the Raphael "Transfiguration," which had moved me almost to tears eight years before, I was staggered to find myself critical of it. It all seemed posed, an advertisement of religion rather than an act of faith. But on leaving that room, which has become more a memorial to Raphael than a gallery of his paintings and tapestries, I was completely swamped by the beauty of a Bellini "Entombment," from the Pesaro Altarpiece. There is no sentimental staging here. This is the act, itself. The dead Christ, on Whose face is still the resignation of His last words, is supported strongly by a bald old saint whose only concern is to see to it that the young saint anointing Christ for burial is doing a proper job. Holding the jar of ointment, behind the two saints, is the massive severity of Peter. He contemplates his dead Master with a look of stern wonder at the act of ingratitude that caused this suffering, while, at the same time, there is a resigned, prophetic calmness about him, for he seems to know this is to be the fate of all of His followers.

It is so inevitable—the death of all men—but there's the wonderful hope of mankind redeemed throughout the whole conception. Giovanni Bellini had now given me three of my greatest art experiences: the "Agony" in London, the "Saint Francis" in the Frick, and this "Entombment" in the Vatican.

For some odd reason I had never before been in one particular room of the Vatican Museum where those marvelous fragments of Melozzo da Forlì's frescoes are preserved . . . those angels and saints, so famous for all of us in reproduction. What charm the angels have,

and what strength the saints! . . . They are from the apse of a cathedral, according to a drawing which shows the original location of the
fragments, but why the "whole" was destroyed, I haven't been able to
find out. I will. There is no end to discovery in art.

We revisited the sculpture galleries and marveled more at the
original Roman sculpture than at the hundreds of Roman copies of
the Greek. Most of all, we longed to jump into that gigantic, red,
porphyritic bowl from which only the gods could have quenched
their thirst.

The little door is still there, through which you enter the giant
world of Michelangelo—the beginnings of the world and man which
he so passionately re-created. We entered it, hot on the heels of the
new Pope's election, and were intrigued by that comical little stove
through which the news of the Pope's ascent to the throne of Peter is
made public.

Each time I see the Sistine Chapel, I am in hopes that they may
have lit those other wonderful paintings below the great ceiling, but
I haven't got my wish. It still belongs solely to Michelangelo. And
Perugino, Botticelli, and the others who worked there first are still
doomed to the gloom of his shadow.

But there is one tiny chapel where he throws no weight and where
a gentler spirit than his is equally majestic and just as virile. Many
experienced sight-seers miss it, and it shouldn't be missed . . . for
many reasons. It is a jewel, and like all good jewelry, more than an
ornament. It is the little chapel where Fra Angelico tells the stories of
St. Martin and St. Stephen with such narrative tranquillity you can
almost recite them by heart when you leave.

It was this little glimpse of the blessed Angelico's genius that
made us stop in Orvieto the next day, on our way to Arezzo. We had
hired a car and driver on the theory that economy on a quick trip was
foolish, and besides, the memory of that countryside between Rome
and Florence had haunted us for seven years. Our guide-driver on this
trip turned out to be neither. His efficiency as a guide is best summed
up by his remark, as we entered Florence. He looked around at us and

said, with the light of new information shining from his eyes, "Florence is a very old and interesting city." As a driver, he was even less informed, since he managed to lose his way three times before we left the city limits of Rome! Finally, as our nerves began to stand out like television antennae, he tossed the map of Italy into the back seat and said, "Well, I suppose you know where you want to go and how to get there." Only through Mary's ability to keep a kilometer or two ahead of him on the map were we able to get to Orvieto and finally to Arezzo, that night.

You needn't go much farther than Orvieto to get the feeling, complete and unchanged, of what Italy was like in the fourteenth, fifteenth, sixteenth, seventeenth, eighteenth, nineteenth, and twentieth centuries. It hasn't been altered one bit, and the view—as you come over the hills from Rome and look down into that valley, then make out the rock on which the city nestles—is one of the breath-takers of the world. There's no question as to why Orvieto was built where it was. It's a perfect fortress. The rock and the city are one . . . in fact, the rock even controls the design of the city, the streets being like the crevices in which they were built. As you wind around them, you feel the rock itself is still showing, though centuries of habitation have covered it forever.

I don't know how much the great cathedrals were used in their heyday, but almost without exception they seem deserted today. Great empty caverns of carved stone, they seem to be the lonely home of an aloof deity. Not the little churches, which still have life, but the cathedrals. They are like summer houses, closed for the winter, and when you visit them in winter as we did, they are cold and bleak and forbidding. How the murals and frescoes have survived the extremes of Italy's winter cold and summer heat, no one will ever know, but it is a tribute to the technical genius of the Renaissance painters.

From the outside, the cathedral at Orvieto, with its bright nineteenth-century mosaics and the rosy marble, promises a possible warm interior. But once you step out of the sun, you're in the perfect deep freeze. There is more natural light inside than in most, but it does nothing to warm either the effect or the temperature. There is no furniture whatsoever, and the general feeling is that God has moved out, lock, stock, and pulpit. Then when you're about to give it up as another cold testimonial to the power of the church, you look off into a little chapel to the right, and the "heater" goes on. You are warm all at once beneath the clinical torments of Signorelli's "End of the World" . . . damned humanity, writhing to make it out of the grave into heaven. This chapel, unlike most others where great frescoes live, is wonderfully lit by the sun. The colors are crisp, and Signorelli's mastery of the walls—his incisive drawing, his talent to make you believe in the story—are all visible, for a change.

Then in the semi-shadow of the ceiling a new light is noticeable, and you become aware of those glorious blues, pinks, yellows, and off-whites of Angelico. As I said, you are warmed by these works, but your bones begin to rattle, and the surest cure is a quick dash across the square to a bottle of that pungent Orvieto wine. Life looks good . . . it matches the memory of the better-than-good paintings you have just seen, and with Mary back at the road map, we uncircled down from the rock and on to Arezzo.

The topography of the Italian landscape, with its valleys and quick-rising mountains, makes every city or village a post card to send home, and, as with Orvieto, you can never question the situations of these cities. They try to be, and succeed in being, almost inaccessible. Of course, modern life has made some changes, but it's amazing how, once you've passed the factory or the railroad station, you drive straight back across the centuries to what was.

Arezzo is a train stop, and it does have industry. Housing developments do circle the bottom of its rock, but inside the old city—bustling with shoppers and gay, young people walking arm in arm down the old streets—you are completely fooled into the past, except for the costumes, the clothes. Everyone is wearing the latest fashion, simple, elegant clothes of international design.

Everyone was happy—except us. Our idiot driver had made a

wrong turn, so we arrived in Arezzo an hour later than we'd planned, and in winter that means the difference between light and dark.

Before we could look for a place to stay, I insisted that we try to see the Piero della Francesca "Story of the Cross" by what little light was left. So we urged our guide to find the Church of St. Francis—maybe on the *first* try. We stopped in a small square to ask our way, and it turned out that our stopping place was the Piazza of St. Francis. We were parked squarely in front of the church itself!

I'm sure that in all the world, this is the strangest exterior behind which to house such glory. It reminded me of a broken down adobe wall, somewhere in New Mexico. It is one of those Italian churches for which someone sometime must have had great plans, but the money ran out. The most battered façade, completely shapeless, with loose brick fragments, threatens to tumble on anyone who dares to enter, menacingly greeting the pilgrim, come to see one of the most important works by any painter of the early Renaissance. The inside is equally neglected, and though there are some very early paintings that promise to be interesting, only an owl could have that promise fulfilled in the tomb-toned nave of St. Francesco.

The Pieros are not visible at all when you enter the church, and we had come in on an afternoon mass which packed the front half of the church. Any attempt to get near the altar (behind and above which the Pieros exist) was next to impossible.

There was a small, well-lit room in which candles were sold, as well as every known reproduction of the great frescoes in black and white and color. I bought some just to make sure that the originals were on the premises. Then by pointing at the cards, then at my eyes, then at the church, I managed to convey my desire to see them, where-upon a roly-poly priest came from nowhere and, running interference for us through the praying devout, led us, red-eared with embarrassment, right up to the altar, then quickly behind it.

There above us, faintly visible, were the frescoes . . . but we were better off looking at the post cards. I must have had a classic look of disappointment on my face, for all of a sudden another priest came

288

running over, flicked a switch, then ran away again. From the ceiling some fifty feet above us hung a bare electric wire and twenty feet down it an inverted tin shade with a low-watt bulb. Then another twenty feet and the same. Altogether not more than the light of a good one-hundred-twenty-watt American bulb illumined this illustrious work above us, but in the gloom of that church, it seemed like a Hollywood première. We could see the lifework of Piero della Francesca.

Art critics have written for years just why art lovers should love this and be critical of that. I've always resented it, especially since most of them write in a language that is completely foreign to me. I either like it or I don't, and if I don't, I try to get to like it—to know about it so I will know why I either do or don't like it. I realize that I've said this before, but for me, a picture is an emotional experience . . . through my eyes . . . and I believe emotions are simply passionate thoughts. You can't think with your heart.

Much has been written about Piero della Francesca, especially in recent years when modern critics have been busy discounting the taste of yesteryear as they inoculate today's readers with their own taste. Raphael has suffered, as have others, from this reshuffling, but Piero has only grown with each new appraisal of the great works.

However, you cannot see this man's work without going to Arezzo and farther on to Borgo San Sepolcro. A few exist elsewhere, but his major contributions are there. I daresay that fewer people, who profess love or knowledge of art, have seen his masterpieces than those of any other great painters. In this dismal little church, with everything possible against proper viewing, are creations comparable to the Sistine Chapel, the Elgin Marbles, the Scuola di San Rocco of Tintoretto. Above all, they must be compared to Masaccio's frescoes in Florence as the greatest existing achievements of artistic dignity. Others are more exciting, more real, more emotional, but nothing I have ever seen cuts through all the frills of man, all his affectations, to his essential dignity and oneness with divinity as does Piero della Francesca's works.

We had no time to see the city after we left the church of San Francesco, but we did want to see the people who, as everywhere we'd been, were out in droves, having a wonderful time. We swung along the main street and found much to our delight that many shops were still open. I wouldn't say Arezzo is Paris, as far as shopping goes, but my Mary doesn't need Paris to get us caught up in a sea of bundles and bags. In one of the windows were the Lucca Christmas figures, better and cheaper than in Rome. I tried to give her the old business— that Florence was closer to Lucca—but Mary's not one to be fooled twice, if she's actually ever been fooled once, at least not by me. We bought the thirty immensely perishable little figures, which came conveniently packed in a supposedly portable package . . . the size of a storage van. For the next hour I knocked people in the head, shins, and back with my clumsy package (which Mary promised to condense into a small wicker basket she planned to buy in Florence). I knew there was trouble ahead, as we had been through three countries already, and, being us, our thirty-five-pounds underweight with which we started from home was so far cut in half and heading for the excessively expensive excess excise of the airlines.

At the little hotel in which we chose to rest overnight, we saw the Pieros for the last time—this time in reproduction, each and every one nicely framed. They lined the stairway, the halls, and the bedroom. The Queen of Sheba, herself, was in the bathroom.

Before we went to bed, Mary created a little crèche on the nightstand, and I had nightmares of those thirty plaster figures, cast in lead, and my life savings being signed over to TWA to get them home!

The little town of Borgo San Sepolcro, thirty miles from Arezzo, contains the other great Piero. We drove there with our no-sense-of-direction driver and made it, but once there, he threw us into a turmoil bordering on despair. He'd never heard of Piero della Francesca. We finally got through to him that he was a painter whose work we liked, and would he please inquire as to the whereabouts of his great "Resurrection"? He inquired, all right, and with his usual accuracy came back with directions which took us directly to a large memorial statue to Piero, this being the town of his birth.

Only by endless gestures to everyone in San Sepolcro did we finally find the home of that painting, and then learned the horrible fact that the place was closed!

I have one special idiosyncrasy in a case like this: I suddenly throw myself on the mercy of the police. Even with no Italian, I got my message across, and one of the strong arms of the law was induced into reaching out for the keeper of that little city hall.

After freezing for half an hour, the man arrived and we were allowed to see a painting worth waiting a lifetime to see . . . hot or cold. . . . Man humiliated and dignity reborn!

When you drive on a United States freeway, you are always conscious of population expansion. Housing developments are everywhere, and the gas station is never out of sight. What is amazing in Italy is that all those centuries of civilization could have gone by . . . the automobile introduced . . . good roads constructed—and still from one city to another there is not a trace of any of this progress, if it can be called that. White oxen still plow the fields; grapevines take the place of telephone wires, draped in a continuous line from anywhere to everywhere.

More amazing than this landscape status quo is the fact that the same landscape exists in all the paintings of the Renaissance, so that when you drive along, in actuality you are weaving in and out of pictures by Piero, Castiglione, Raphael, and all the others. Sometimes the towns they painted bear their names, or vice versa: Pietro da Cortona, Leonardo da Vinci, Zorgo of Zorgi da Castelfranco . . . the artist forever in communion with his native land.

One of my favorite sculptors has always been Jacopo della Quercia. I had seen some few originals of his, but I knew that Siena was his home town artistically and that the fountain there was his chief work. Also, I knew a lot about Siena from photos and books, but I was completely unprepared for the beauty of the city itself, its crystal-clear light, and the cathedral.

It seems to have had an organizing mind behind the architecture and décor, which of course it couldn't have had, since it was built over several centuries. But none of the others I've seen are so completely realized; none come off with such elegance. The rich ornamentation which invades floors, ceiling, walls—inside and out—is never too much. It is beautifully controlled, and you come out of it feeling that you've partaken of a perfectly planned banquet . . . full but not stuffed.

Jacopo della Quercia's fountain is no longer there. I think the pigeons must have picked it to destruction. A copy stands in its place— perfect, they say, in every detail, except that no genius went into it— and what's left of the original genius is pitifully covered with dust and neglect . . . on the back balcony of the town hall.

Still, for all that's missing, there are a few figures left that give you a clue to the vanished grace it must have had. "Charity," I believe she's called, who survived most intact, is there, but she's like a stone which time has worn away to a pebble of her former beauty.

When I knew we were going to be able to take this trip, I reread what I'd written about my reaction to Florence when I was sixteen— about the feeling of anticipation in going there, the wonders I saw when I got there—and now, thirty-one years later, leaving Siena and seeing the sign pointing to "Firenze," I felt the same way.

During those thirty-one years I'd never stopped reading about Florence, and I doubt if a week had gone by in all that time when I had not had some contact with something in that city. The history of art takes its center there, to draw the circle of the past and present. Nowhere was the spirit of ancient Greece more keenly felt, and from no other place have modern men taken more inspiration. It is the navel of art today, if not the womb it was yesterday.

As we drew nearer the city, I could feel my heart going a little faster, and when we passed under the old city tower gate and our chauffeur made his final banality about its age and interest, I was at home . . . quite at home.

Miraculously, he found his way to the hotel on the Arno, where we made an immediate decision to send him back to Rome and continue our trip in the care of someone who knew where he was going. The thought of what he might get us into on our next stop, Venice, was dampening to the spirit, and anyway, we wanted to *walk* Florence, stem to stern.

The drive had been a long one and cold, so Mary took to the tub while I took to the streets and for two hours resembled a madman, trying to remember where he'd lost something, rather than a man coming "home." Every church was open, for it was a holy day, and the streets were throbbing with people whom I'm afraid I scattered in my frenzy to see as much as I could remember of all I'd seen before. I went to the Duomo, ran through it, dashed over to the Signoria, saw the copy of "David" and the original of "Perseus," did a fast double-take at the Giambologna fountain with those exquisite, elongated nudes (something I'd overlooked at sixteen), then started up the Arno past the Ponte Vecchio, and cut off a little side street and into a little church where people were streaming in and out. I got as far to the side as I could, so as not to intrude in the services, and found myself staring at an odd little sign, in English: "Donation for the Lights." I put a donation in the basket and noticed a switch above it which I clicked and which quickly dispelled the darkness of that corner chapel, revealing one of the most charming of Ghirlandaio's many murals, "The Miracle of the Child of the Spini Family". Now I knew I was in Florence, where every corner reveals some treasure and where you can never fail to be surprised by beauty.

Back in the hotel I lay in the tub, literally trembling with anticipation and the absolute knowledge that we, or rather, I, had bitten off more than I could chew in the three days we could afford to stay there and still make our other stops.

I took the guidebook and made a plan of attack . . . to try to see as much as possible without wearing ourselves out, and without spoiling Mary's thrill at being there for the first time.

We saw everything that I particularly wanted to see, missed much I want to see another time . . . and I'm afraid I made Florence a nightmare for Mary, after all. We saw the Uffizi, the Pitti, the Bargello, the

Brancacci Chapel, Santa Croce, Santa Maria Novella, the Riccardi Palace, the Convent of San Marco, the Accademia, the Palazzo Vecchio, the Duomo, the Baptistery, Santo Spirito, the Boboli Garden, Santa Trinita, the Medici Chapel, the Piazzale Michelangelo, the Badia Church, Sant' Annunziata, the Ognissanti, and much more . . . and even though I'm the most avid sight-seer alive, I must admit it was too much, too fast—but divine.

My God! They never stopped, those Florentines. What achievement! It would be foolish to try to describe any one thing or any dozen, but as well as I thought I knew the art of Florence, my eyes were opened to two experiences, at least, that have changed my mind once again, just when I thought it was made up.

In art, as in life, it isn't always the wallopalooser experience that stays with you. The big boys are so big they can sometimes become a bore. But along will come something—either small in size or from a lesser artist or in my case something I just had failed to put down in its proper place in my memory—that does the eternal trick of great art— make you feel insignificant.

The Uffizi is such a vast hoarding place of masterpieces, most of them obviously so—the Botticellis, the Bronzinos, Titians, da Vincis, all Italian—that you are apt to overlook the very few foreign paintings they have. So, completely off guard, I came upon the Portinari Altarpiece of Hugo van der Goes. Right now, and in my right mind, I would have to say it is the greatest work of art in the whole Uffizi collection. (I may change back to some of the others, but when I remember it's been thirty-one years since I saw them, and consider all the looking I've been through, I think maybe this conclusion will stick.)

This is one of those rare, large, story pictures, the "Adoration of the Shepherds," that never is a bore, in toto or in part. You really can wander from detail to detail, from face to face, from corner to corner and never lose interest or lose your profound admiration for Van der Goes' technique, sensitivity, composition, and the exquisite observation he lavished on the slightest accent of color or design. The still life, the character study, the virginity of the blessed undertaking of Mary—

all are to be reveled in separately. Then step back and see the whole of it in all its importance.

Before this altarpiece I did indeed feel humbled, because I had never honored it before as it should be honored, and because it allowed me to be a worshiper with the others of the light of the world, the Child of truth.

It was a terrible realization that clutched me those few days in Florence . . . how little I had seen before, on Tour 22. The only consolation was that at that time I didn't know what I know now, so I didn't miss it. But I was determined not to skip a thing this time, if I could help it. I saw the Angelicos in the cells of San Marco, the grand Masaccios, the Uccellos, Ghirlandaios; and on the last day we went to see the Medici tombs by Michelangelo. Florence was swimming with people in the highest Christmas spirits. The streets were too much fun to leave for a museum or a church, so we wandered happily for hours, enjoying the city enjoying itself.

It was during this excursion that we picked up the basket Mary had promised to buy which would shrink the thirty Lucca Christmas figurines into portable size. I have seen pictures of a person being hauled up ancient walls in baskets, but Mary found one that would carry *two*. I timidly said it was a little large for the crèche, but it seemed she had no intention of stopping with thirty figurines—and she didn't. Before we weighed in, en route back to the United States, there were *fifty*. The basket was just the right size for them—and ten or fifteen other little knickknacks we picked up in those last ten days.

I swear I didn't do it on purpose, though Mary accused me of it. We rounded a corner and found ourselves in front of the Accademia where the original of Michelangelo's "David" lives. I told her the story of thinking the one before the Palazzo della Signoria the original, when I was sixteen, and—intent on continuing our street-seeing—she said it was probably a good copy and we'd seen it. I then said I'd always dreamed of seeing the original and that that was the only reason I'd wanted to come to Florence, to which she gave a lengthy recital of the three dozen other "only" reasons I had come to Florence, all of which we'd reasoned out, in her mind, by seeing. I countered with guidebook information: there were other goodies inside . . . to which she gave me the *coup de grâce* by saying that her feet hurt! I suggested I just run in, see it, and run out. Eureka! I'd hit the bull's-eye! She refused to wait outside, so we went in!

Big thrill number two! Everything I have ever said (and I've said everything) about the difference between copies, reproductions, and the original was declared valid, even by Mary and her tired feet. "David" ain't "David" nowhere else but here. Once again, Michelangelo has created the *man* himself. Moses and David—they aren't in the Bible at all. They're in Rome and Florence. "What a piece of work is a man!" . . . Buonarroti! . . . What a statue is "David."

I guess by now I've seen almost everything Michelangelo ever did. I've read his poems, and I even went to Bruges one weekend from England, just to see his Madonna there. I knew him so well I could almost take him for granted, granting him to be a genius. But that he was more than a genius I never knew until I saw, in the same room as the "David," those unutterably divine, humanly godlike, incomparable and colossal "Slaves"!

I've thrown a few adjectives around here and there in this little voyage through my eyes. I remember at least ten thousand greats, five thousand magnificents, and a thousand assorted beautifuls, marvelouses, heavenlys, etc. But I don't know any other language for art. Therefore, I am at a loss (unless I string them all together and then *light* them) as to how to blow up to their proper place in the achievements of all mankind, these unfinished "Slaves" and that one unfinished "Pietà." Genesis! There's the word, the only word to describe them—Genesis!

We had hoped to drive to Venice, but Florence taught us a lesson. Get there as fast as you can if you haven't much time, and hope to come back for the in-between stops another year. Italian trains are furious, frantic, and great fun. They have nothing to do with sightseeing. They just want to get there, and they do. We were in Venice so quickly we could only think how lucky Renaissance man was not to have had any swifter means of locomotion than he did. The whole country, city by city, would have been destroyed if those ambitious and civilized barbarians could have gotten at each other's throats more quickly. I'm convinced the very existence of these cities is largely due to their antique mode of transportation. And let's be thankful for that.

What has kept Venice where it is and how it is for all these centuries is one of the great mysteries and one I don't care to solve, as long as it stays just like it is! The night we arrived it was cold and clear, and to Mary, who had never been there before, the ride from the station to the San Marco stop seemed like one of those "tunnel of love" rides at beach amusement parks. In succession the Rialto, the Cà d'Oro, the Gritti, and, finally, the Palace of the Doges turned up out of the dark like abandoned sets on a movie lot.

I had suspected winter in Venice would not be a post card, so I'd reserved a room in the Royal Danieli, a hotel we probably could never have gotten into in the tourist season. The room I wanted in this old converted palace, next door to the Palace of the Doges, was on the third floor, overlooking the Grand Canal. Years before, when I was a starving student, I met up with a couple of rich American girls who had this room, and the comparison between it and the one I had at the time—a back canal room near the station—gave me the ambition to move upstream the next time I came to Venice.

The room was ours, and whatever misgivings we'd had about Venice in the winter were immediately dispelled. It let in off the marble, balustraded balcony of the five-floor, central court-stairwell of the old palace, through beautiful heavy mahogany doors. The whole room was "papered" with golden brocade; the furniture was copied from the famous eighteenth-century Venetian style, painted gold and green, and in the center of the ceiling hung an intricate and enormous Venetian glass chandelier. Mary was delighted, and so was I. . . . The HEAT was on!

We had shivered in Athens, frozen in Istanbul, mildewed in Rome, actually seen our breath as we went through the Uffizi in Florence, and here we were in Venice—with heat! It was a good thing, too, because from that moment on the rain and fog moved over Venice without surcease or "let." I finally understood that lovely expression in Venice in wintertime. The canals seemed to rise out of their stone-lined routes and cover the entire city, and the palaces and churches dripped, poured, and gurgled on, in, and seemingly under the water. Our beautiful room at the hotel took on the shambles-look of a locker room as everything we owned was piled on the radiator to thaw and dry.

The Venetians, bless them, being half duck by this time, apparently couldn't have minded this weather less. The gaiety of the people was infectious, and we had more fun those few wet days in Venice than anywhere on the trip. I discovered a drink called "China," (pronounced "Keena"), made from the grape stalks. Hot, it warms the soul, and it became our radiator away from the radiator during our entire stay.

I don't honestly think the Venetians are kidding anyone, including themselves. They are naturally delighted to be where they are, and except for one elevator boy who longed to go to America, everyone we met was happily content to be where he was and to be doing what he was doing. Our concierge summed it up by saying that Venice in the winter belonged to the Venetians, and while they missed the sun, you got the feeling that they didn't miss the tourists.

With China to keep us going, we swamped our way from church to church, to museum to antique shops, to restaurants, to more China, to radiator, out again, around again. While Mary was wringing herself out one day, I took off for the Accademia . . . something else I'd missed on Tour 22.

Everything I had studied since about Venetian art seemed always to be labeled "Accademia, Venice." Every public building in Venice seems to be a converted palace or monastery, and so was the Accademia, but the conversion in this case was completely successful. It has been made into one of the most beautiful galleries in the world, and the presence of many of the world's most beautiful paintings doesn't hurt any. There you can see the full glory of Venetian painting from the

298

earliest Gothic religious masters to a tantalizing, huge fragment of a fresco by Tiepolo.

It's hard to say when Venice hit her peak artistically, or in whom, there are so many great talents involved in the artistic generations of that city. Certainly they are all Venetian to the core, and you feel a very different vision here than anywhere else in Italy. They did not take on the current influences of the sixteenth or seventeenth centuries —those of Raphael or Michelangelo—and they were the last to pro- duce a great Italian painter in Tiepolo. This artificial little city has retained its individuality right down to today, though the great painters, unfortunately, are no longer bred there. Venice is a shrine of the past, but a shrine that will forever be worth visiting, even if you have to swim to it and through it, as we did.

There are very few paintings in the world that have real mystery about them . . . where their origin, their subject matter, their painter all have something almost supernatural. It's like the whole mystery of Shakespeare. How could anyone this famous, this great, be so little known? There is much conjecture about Giorgione, about his birth, his death, and especially about which paintings are his and which are not. Most critics agree there are only ten or twelve that can honestly be said to be his, and many of those come up for re-examination from time to time. But that there was a man called Giorgione, there is no doubt, and that certain pictures have a special quality unlike any others, there is also no doubt.

"The Storm," in the Accademia, is almost surely by his hand, ac- cording to the experts, and definitely it has a rare and mysterious beauty that none of the other masters of his time ever achieved. I think one of the overlooked clues to a Giorgione is the quality of youth. We know he died very young, and everything I've ever seen of his has the extraordinary purity of youth. "The Storm" is an unworldly picture and at the same time out of this world. It is Keatsian in its poetic communication, and youthful as Keats is youthful. The melancholy is the disillusion of youth—not that life isn't wonderful, but just that it's not quite as good as it should be. The storm of age approaches, and the lovers can feel it coming between them and their ecstasy, dampening their passion.

There are some of the most famous Bellinis in the same room, and great as the teacher is, the pupil retains a freshness which, while derived from the master, was not to be seen again in the worldly art of Venice—even in the greatness of his supposed pupil, Titian.

There are Lottos, Cimas, Titians, Tintorettos, Veroneses by the dozen, all great, for this is the cream of Venetian art, brought together under one roof. But the hit of the Accademia for me was Carpaccio. "The Legend of St. Ursula" is made up of a half dozen enormous canvases which tell the enchanting tale of St. Ursula and the martyrdom of the eleven thousand virgins. Carpaccio approaches this story with as much skepticism as I do—the idea of eleven thousand virgins! As you look at his delightful narrative, you feel a reverent good humor about the whole thing. Far more than being the story of St. Ursula and her eleven thousand virgins, it is the story of the Venice of Carpaccio's day. There has never been a series of pictures that showed in such detail and with such charm the whole panorama of a period. The dress, the manners, the conceits, the horseplay, the houses, washing, chimney pots, the animals, the interiors and exteriors, and the people—all are there, while in the foreground Ursula and her friends go proudly on their way to martyrdom.

You really owe it to yourself to spend half a day in that small room, which I did, and when I came out I was surprised to find myself in the twentieth century, so thoroughly had I been a part of Carpaccio's fifteenth.

Mary went back with me the second time. Since her profession is costumes and her greatest knowledge the costumes of the past, I was afraid the fifteenth century might claim us both for keeps before I could get her out of the Carpaccio room.

The rain took over completely the second half of our stay, making it impossible to do the "little" kind of sight-seeing that's such fun. You had to run from place to place or else dissolve. But the second evening, we happened on a gallery showing the work of Franco Gentilini, one of the most individual of the younger painters. It was so cozy inside that gallery, with the rain beating down outside, we just couldn't bring ourselves to leave—without a Gentilini. That's the way it is with us. The dealer has a "hard sell" on his hands; in fact, he doesn't even have to be there, as he wasn't the night we bought the Gentilini.

We decided to bring it with us, so the question was not so much how to get it back to the States, but how to get it from the gallery to the hotel without liquidating it in the rain. We finally made it, with some of the showiest open-field running in the history of the sport of collecting.

On our third day Venice disappeared altogether. You could now no longer see the boats on the canal. You could only hear them, moaning and groaning and clanging through the fog. But, fog or no fog, I was going to see Tintoretto's supreme achievement, the Scuola di San Rocco. It involved a great deal of hot China and some mighty strange directions, given by some mighty perplexed Venetians, for us to find the way. Why on earth the only two Americans in Venice were crazy enough to want to see a roomful of paintings, even I didn't have an answer to.

I'll make this short, because if I let myself go all those adjectives will start flying again. I've loved Tintoretto ever since I first made his acquaintance in St. Louis with a not too great one called "The Finding of Moses." I'd seen a lot of them since, even in Venice on Tour 22, but it is in the Scuola di San Rocco where he's completely alive. The entire two floors of this enormous building are Tintoretto from top to bottom . . . ceilings, walls, everything. It is the greatest decoration by one man ever achieved, including the Sistine Chapel, for Tintoretto was a painter and Michelangelo never pretended to be one. He was first, and by his own appellation, a sculptor.

Someday, if you want proof of how lazy you are, go see every Tintoretto in Venice . . . just in Venice. You'll never believe that one man could cover this much canvas with paint, let alone re-create with inexhaustible brilliance heaven and hell, the entire Bible, and the history of every saint who ever lived. As I've said, we had more fun underwater in Venice than anywhere on dry land on our entire trip.

I'm sure Mary would like to see Venice someday, for I had a hard time convincing her that it was *on* the sea, not *in* it. But we felt like Venetians when we left, because in the most popular tourist spot in the world, we were the only ones. Just for those few rainy days it was our city, and that's a feeling you don't often have anywhere, even at home.

We took the train to Rome to make our connection by air to Madrid. Venice had moved to Rome, where it was raining whatever the Italian equivalent of cats and dogs is . . . which reminded Mary that there were some animals in those stalls in the Piazza Navona that would complete her Christmas crèche. The taxi driver took us there without complaint, and the animals were stored in her enormous basket, and we were on our way to the airport.

We only had an hour to wait, and we were on the plane—basket, Gentilini, handbags, coats, and all. As sometimes happens, we were told to get off the plane, since one engine wouldn't start. Then we were told to get on the plane. The engine was fixed. Then we were told it wasn't fixed and we should get off the plane. Five hours later the plane was fixed, and we gaily took off for Madrid. Three hours later we were in Barcelona. As sometimes happens, we were told we would have to stay in Barcelona until noon the next day, but on second thought, the next day was already upon us, so we'd better get some hasty sleep and get back to the airport by noon. As sometimes happens, our four-hour flight from Rome to Madrid took eighteen hours.

In Barcelona, however, I was able to point out to Mary those art nouveau-apartment houses by Gaudi, a phase of art we otherwise would not have seen. In my semi-conscious state I recalled a television debate I had had with Salvador Dali, who predicted that those florid, floral scrolls and furbelows would one day be considered the greatest architecture of the twentieth century. I'm sure it wasn't just my comatose condition after that flight, but, seeing them, somehow I doubted it.

Whence comes the preconceived notion? We have spent endless psychological hours of research, tracking down the source of every other pattern of human behavior. But who or what makes up our minds about who and where, before we meet or see them, to my knowledge has been grossly neglected.

Mary and I, who love Mexico City madly, had dreamed of Madrid for years. Three times we have had tickets to go there, which were canceled because of jobs. I'm glad I took the jobs, because they at least paid off. Madrid didn't.

I thought Madrid was an old city. It isn't. I thought it was cheap to live in. It isn't. I thought it was one of the great shopping centers of the world. It isn't. I even thought it was beautiful. It isn't. It's just a city, with the usual charms of any great metropolis, but very little that's unique or that sets it apart from others, as, say, in the case of San Francisco.

The weather was pretty rotten there, too, but where it made the Venetians feel more at home and in better spirits, it turned the Madrilenes into a surly, complaining mass of sad-looking people who would just as soon as not trample you to death crossing the street.

I read a guidebook which said that it wasn't until the early hours of the morning that Madrid revealed her charms. I'm afraid she never got a chance to reveal them to me at that hour, because by that time the city had so exhausted me, I was asleep.

This may all seem unfair, since we didn't meet the people . . . get to know them. But everywhere else we'd been, we were welcome as strangers. Not here. We arrived strangers and we left strangers.

The only welcome we felt was in the Prado, and in a gallery we chanced into, where there was an exciting exhibition of a young Spanish painter named Lucio Muñoz. We were really "sent" by his work, and it pleased me to find that Tapies, to whom my Carnegie jury had given first prize just before I left, was not a uniquely fine artist in Spain, but one of many.

The pictures were shown us by a very pleasant young man, to whom we tried to impart our enthusiasm in our unenthusiastic French. He spoke no English, and better French than we did. Finally, we decided, after much controversy over two paintings—one Mary liked, one I liked—to blow ourselves to both of them. This was our last stop on the trip, and we'd saved our money to buy in Spain most of our take-home gifts. We couldn't find a thing. Antiques were not only not very good, but very expensive, so these two really fine Spanish contemporary paintings were a bargain and a joy to find.

Our minds were made up, and we told the young man so, but we had to figure out a way to pay for them since our traveler's checks were running short and we still had our hotel bill to pay. We asked him if he could hold them until the next day. He said he would, and then he gave us his card. What a lovely custom that is, one that has almost died out in America, except for businessmen. But it's a custom that can burst your wallet and make for a fine guessing game, once you're home, trying to remember who so-and-so is and where you met him.

I had gotten so used to taking them with thanks, slipping them with a knowing touch into my already bulging wallet, that, had I not dropped this one on the floor, I might never have known that the name on it was that of the artist whose pictures we had just decided to buy.

When I saw Lucio Muñoz, I immediately tried to tell the young man, in my bad French, that we knew the artist's name and what we needed was the gallery's. Much gesticulating and laughing, and then out of the miasma of our French it came to light that the young man was Lucio Muñoz, himself.

Since we'd just bought two of his paintings, we weren't the slightest bit upset, but what if we had hated the pictures! Even my French would have gotten that message across, and I shuddered to think of my possible embarrassment, had that happened.

As it turned out, it was the beginning of a series of events that made Madrid almost a joy. Through Lucio we met other young artists —one in particular, who I think will be great. He's twenty-two and has already had two successful shows: Antonio Lopez Garcia. I think I can best describe his work (in a way I hate to do) by saying he's a Spanish Ben Shahn. I love Ben Shahn, but add the background of Spain and you have something extraordinary.

Hedda Hopper, with whom we had dinner that night in Madrid, where she was doing her annual Christmas tour with Bob Hope, fell in love with a reproduction of one of Garcia's paintings, and we're all at work, at the moment, trying to get it for her to buy. What an amazingly receptive woman Hedda is, and I think, in buying a Garcia, she may be making a prediction of greatness that will outlast her yearly forecasts of who-will-be-who in Hollywood for the following year.

Through Lucio we were able to see some inkling of what is going on in Spain today, a country which many people (I, for one) had thought dormant, artistically. Also, through him, we got an insight into what contemporary Spanish painters think of the great ones of their past.

They certainly aren't the first to say that Velázquez is the greatest painter who ever lived, but they may be the most vehement. I have never met a painter who has not ranked him in the top two or three of all time, and as far as the technique of oil painting goes, number one.

I had always sort of taken this for granted, not being a painter, and I had no argument against it, since I had seen very few of his paintings. In Toledo, Ohio, I had been captivated by the smiling man with a glass of wine. I'd seen a few infantas and several other portraits and the beautiful Venus in the National Gallery in London, but as in the cases of Piero della Francesca in Arezzo and Ghirlandaio in Florence, you must go to Madrid to see Velázquez.

Here is absolute truth in painting. It is unsentimental, unemotional, completely mental—pure, unadulterated truth. Velázquez takes no personal liberties with his subjects. They existed, and he merely allows them to exist forever by his genius. Something I didn't know is that he is credited with being the first artist to use oil as an absolute medium. He painted with oil directly on the canvas, where others prepared their canvases with under-painting, then added oil glazes. Whether he was first or not, he was responsible for the modern use of it as a medium. A detail of a Velázquez will give you more insight into the freedom of modern painting than a Jackson Pollock.

In between Velázquez and Goya is a fascinating school of Spanish still-life painters whose *bodegónes*, or kitchen still lifes, are among the most charming pictures ever done. The Prado is rich in these, especially the ones by Mendenez, though the best, which are by Zurbarán and even Velázquez, are often to be found in the United States. For instance, in Chicago is a still life by Velázquez that is one of the real prizes of that great museum. Behind the still life itself is a Negress, looking out at the viewer with shy pride at the gleam of the copper she has cleaned. And in St. Louis there's a marvelous Zurbarán of fruit and china.

I was a little disappointed with the Zurbaráns in the Prado and unfortunately didn't get to see his best things in Spain, which are in other cities. But we have superb examples in this country—in Cincinnati, Chicago, St. Louis, San Diego, and particularly in the Wadsworth Atheneum in Hartford. Here is the epitome of his art in the pathetic figure of the English St. Serapion. However, the Crucifixion, with a self-portrait, and the "St. Casilda," both in the Prado, are marvelous examples too, and give you a real insight into this aesthetic man who caught, more than any other painter, the simplicity of saints.

The Riberas of the Prado are a revelation. I had not seen too many, and the impact of his tortured saints and gnarled old men is tremendous. The macabre in Spanish painting is one of its arresting qualities, for it never seems to be employed for its own sake, but to make humanity aware of its own inhuman shortcomings.

It's impossible to make an inventory of the Prado's collection or even to attempt to convey the superior quality of the paintings. We visited it five times and didn't begin to digest it. The Titians, Rubenses, the other Spanish painters, the other Italians like Luca Giordano and Tiepolo, the Vandykes . . . all represented by great quality and numbers . . . make it an art experience of overwhelming magnitude. The Roger van der Weyden "Descent from the Cross" and the famous "Garden of Delights" of Hieronymous Bosch would make it a must if they alone were on exhibition. I finally had to slice it up and do one section at a time, and still I came away with a case of art indigestion that could only be cured by constant study and many more visits.

I save Goya for the end, because for modern man he is the most immediate voice to be heard in Spain, especially through the dozens of his finest pieces which make up a whole section of the Prado.

None of these was executed for the rooms in which they hang, but they certainly belong there. The installation is perfect . . . not too crowded . . . and with that rarest of blessings in European galleries, good light. You enter the Goya wing through a small room where the majority of his drawings for the "Caprichos," the "Proverbios," and the "Bullfight" are displayed. Loving drawings, and loving Goya, I was hard put to leave this room, but I realized they were intended for an introduction to the man—the big man who lived just around the corner.

It's not often you get the chance to go hand in hand with an artist through his career, from beginning to end. When you enter the first rooms of his early work, you are seized by a hand that has all the strength and strenuousness of youth, the hand of a man vitally alive to everything around him, the hand of a life-lover, a Casanova of the act of living. Such exuberant well-being glows from these scenes of Spanish life, you are immediately nostalgic for those days which must have existed in Goya's time but don't exist any more—because he painted them, and he was not a liar. All the characters of this frivolous drama are simply people enjoying themselves, the kind of people we had seen in Venice the week before, reveling in innocent merriment. They are so beautiful in their joy, and surely no period ever recorded was more romantically costumed.

The air of romance that bathes all these charming genre paintings as you move through the years with Goya becomes heavy with impending storm until, at the end of his life, the night almost takes over entirely. The same people have lived on, but they are old and embittered, awaiting death in the shadows that will eventually take them in, whether they die or not.

One painting from this last period has some hope, but it, too, is the hope of death . . . this time as a release from loneliness. This canvas, when you first look at it, could be by any one of today's abstract expressionists. It is just color—a whole canvas of subtly applied gradations of the same tones. Near the bottom is a vertical division of a more intense color . . . Spanish colors . . . red-oranges, rusts. In the bottom center a gray-blue-black, head-like shape, intriguingly placed, appears out of this warm nothingness. Slowly it identifies itself to you as the head of a little dog. A little mutt . . . a Goya dog . . . stares up the canvas with a look of such longing you can hardly stand it. Mary said it was Goya's dog, waiting to die to join his master.

After you've seen these end-of-his-life paintings, you think like that!

Elsewhere in the Prado are the great satirical portraits of the royal family, and the luscious Duchess of Alba, clothed and unclothed. And in a little church near the royal palace are the lovely frescoes of angels, and the dome from which the life of Spain looks down on Goya's tomb. But the most moving of his paintings, and one of the few religious ones of his that comes off, is in the cathedral in Toledo.

In a chapel in that cathedral are over a dozen El Grecos, including "The Apostles," and at the end, over the altar, his superior "Betrayal of Jesus." But over a side altar, in the same room, is the same subject by Goya. No one could be expected to portray the betrayers better than Goya, who had recorded the betrayal of human dignity throughout his career. It is the face of his Jesus that, to me, will always be the face of Jesus betrayed.

He had caught in the face an expression of utter incomprehension of the act being perpetrated—of utter "lostness" in and stunned resignation to the cruelty of his fellow man. Someone else's will is being done, and the Man, Jesus, is being torn from His humanhood to become divine on the cross of inhumanity.

Guido Reni to the nineteenth century epitomized in his sentimental heads of Jesus the taste of that period. To me, El Greco's spiritual content is almost as vacuous. Marvelous technically—dramatic almost beyond the boundaries of the theatrical limits the mind can stand—he soars in his vision of what the spiritual should look like, way beyond my conception of it. I can't take a sentimental saviour of the world. I don't understand the saint, portrayed as though his ecstasy is other than successful shuffling off mortality. When they look as they do in Greco—as though they knew all the time they were blessed—they lose me.

He is a great painter, without a doubt, but I think the reason the public holds him in such high esteem at present is because he gives them spirituality, completely achieved—by him, not by the subjects he painted. It is as though he created the standard make-up for a saint: poached eyes, sunken cheeks, and preferably a beard. Then, of course, long fingers and a costume made of sackcloth, soaked in plaster and allowed to dry in big folds over an attenuated skeleton.

Where Greco shines is in his portraits of real people, and he shines like the sun itself in the "Burial of the Count of Orgaz." I hate to keep harping on this, but when you see a painting presented the way this one is, with wonderful lighting, somehow I think the original purpose of the picture is restored. If church pictures were meant to teach and inspire, first you must be able to see them, and for the most part the churches which house some of the most famous treat them as though to be able to see them were an intrusion on their sacred privacy. This Greco, on the other hand, is aglow with a light other than its own. Edison and Greco mutually benefit from this marriage.

In the Frick Collection in New York, in the same room, you can perhaps understand what I am trying to say about the spiritual content of Greco, who is famous for it, and that of a painter who really has it and needs no publicity to put it across—Giovanni Bellini. Greco's beautiful, rich "St. Jerome" is a portrait of an idealized old cardinal, while the "St. Francis" of Bellini is the scene of a miracle. St. Jerome sits for his portrait, but St. Francis is unaware that anyone has witnessed the act of his receiving the stigmata.

Spain is a fascinating country, I'm sure, and I hope to see more of it and like it better on another trip. Unfortunately, what we saw of old Spain, so magnificently reported by Velázquez and Goya, did not help brighten our picture of modern Spain . . . so drab and poor by contrast. But it is unfair to judge a country, either by its former glory or the cursory look we were able to give it in those few short days. I'm sure we will go back and fall in love with it, as so many people have, and perhaps when we do the Spanish people will have regained some of their joy of life.

The morning of our departure we spent roaming around the city, and since it was the Sunday before Christmas, there was a pathetic kind of gaiety in the faces of the children, buying figures for their nativities. We missed the eagerness of the Italians, but some of their spirit was visible in the flea market—at least in the customers in search of bargains. However, if there are bargains there, someone else must be finding them. We're both pretty good at making finds, but these shops were mostly filled with junk, and damned expensive junk at that. And the shopkeepers gave us the impression they knew it was junk but that we were stupid enough to be taken in by it.

On the way to the plane we looked over the catalogue of Lucio Muñoz' work, and both of us felt that meeting him and seeing his exhibition was the high spot of our visit—and, of course, the Prado. We couldn't wait to get home and show our friends this young man's paintings. They reflect modern Spain in their dark and brooding abstraction, for it is difficult to put your finger on what makes this country's mood so disturbingly depressing. Spain seemed to us a land abstracted from the rest of the world . . . a landscape shadowed by those ominous clouds of Greco; a people dark with the despair of Goya's last great frescoes.

Besides the fun and excitement of seeing so much in so little time, we left Europe with feelings of regret but with even greater feelings of joy to be coming back to America. It wasn't just to be home by Christmas—which is the only place to be at that time—but to be home in a country that, all around, holds the greatest promise of greatness to be found on the earth today.

Greece succumbed to greed and idleness; Rome was killed off by its own opulence; Spain died in a massacre of intolerance and inability to progress. They have all been dead, then born anew. They think anew because, as Lincoln said, their case is new. They have had to think and act anew. In each of them you find a profound respect for their past and equally great respect for our present which they see in the documented light of their past, and they cannot help but wonder if we will survive the material success which helped to destroy them. They have learned, through the tortures of defeat, that what survives is the greatness of their thinkers. There is not enough gold in Fort Knox to buy the "Last Supper" of Leonardo or the "Last Judgment" of Michelangelo. During periods of economic distress, they sold much of their artistic treasure to us and to other nations to whom the ball of wealth had been tossed. But now they cherish what is left . . . protect it . . . almost worship it as the symbolic record of their time in history. The museums of Europe are warnings to us to create, in our own time, what will be the lasting symbols of our moment of power . . . our creative contributions.

Our qualifications as a (or *the*) world power for good depend entirely on two elements of our intellectual life: our teachers and the ability of American parents to continue in intellectual growth, to inspire their children to *want* to learn. In other words, as individuals, and as a nation, we must be aware that the only real wealth of any civilization has been, and is, its mental contribution.

Everyone will admit that our teachers are of the utmost importance. Therefore, we must see to it that they are better paid and, further, that those we pay are thoroughly equipped to impart their knowledge so that it will pay off for the students, not only during school and college, but throughout their lives.

Millions of adult Americans have come to the rude conclusion that they learned very little in college, and as leisure time becomes a more and more important factor in their lives, they have a desperate need to know how to utilize it. Extension courses in almost every major American university are jammed with people who want to fill this leisure time with the most rewarding nourishment human beings can assimilate—the arts.

A very great scientist once told me that atomic power, if used for the good of mankind, could create, in a hundred years, an economic situation wherein no one would be allowed to work more than two

311

days a week. Not only the use of that power, but the alarming increase in population would force us into a position where, to avoid catastrophic unemployment, these working days would have to be law. Then, he said, the main problem confronting us would be the education for leisure. Man, without something to do, can go berserk, can become an undisciplined animal; but man, with the time in which to improve his mind, can become greater and more productive of the great things of life than ever before.

And what are the *great* things of life? Somehow or other, most of them involve the creative act, thinking, and hard work.

Hundreds of art students have asked me if it is worth while to try to make a life in music, painting, or the theatre. They cite the apathy of the public in appreciation of the arts. How can you make a life, to say nothing of a living, in work so few people are willing to accept as part of life?

Happily, I've discovered that more people than you realize are interested. There is hardly a town of any size in America that does not contain some dedicated group whose whole endeavor is to supplement the slack in their cultural entertainment. Theatre groups try to make up for the fact that the professional theatre is centered in one or two great cities by bringing often wonderful talent to their local drama; national groups, like the American Federation of Art, make it possible for small museums and art centers to have fine traveling exhibitions at minimum cost. The Archives of American Art in Detroit is making known to the public through the collection and preservation of its history the importance of American art.

There is no reason to fear lack of acceptance or the fact that there are too many artists. There is, because of increased population and increased interest, a much greater audience than ever before, and if the demand is greater, so must the supply be greater.

I heard recently of one co-operative group in El Paso, Texas, who takes on the decoration of churches and public buildings. There are stained-glass workers, mosaicists, muralists, wood carvers, metal workers who submit plans and completely carry out the work. The excellent

312

symphony orchestra in that town, under the direction of a brilliant Italian conductor, Orlando Barera, is comprised of men and women, seventy per cent of whom are under thirty and many of whom are in their teens. They have the admiration and support of the entire city.

The need for the arts is growing every day, therefore the need for the artist. It is not easy . . . it never was . . . but then, it isn't easy to be good at anything. The best demands the greatest effort. The sloppiness many of us have come to accept as a way of life is not tolerated in the arts. Even those seemingly indolent and dissolute fellows like Modigliani turned out a prodigious amount of work, and one who thought himself lazy, Delacroix, produced fourteen thousand works—paintings, murals, drawings, etchings, and lithographs—in his not too long lifetime.

I've cherished my eyes, and I've *seen*, through my own and through the eyes of others. I still have much, much seeing to do, and one thing I know for sure. . . . The world can never grow old for me as long as there are young people, seeing it differently every second of every day, for all my days—and yours.

Through the young artists, I can see the world *young* as long as I live, and if I'm keen enough not to let myself get trapped into thinking any day gone by is better than tomorrow, I have a chance to be my own contemporary. If I can continue to make my judgments on art out of my knowledge of it, and not just my preferences in it, I'll always have the pleasure of being alive in the most living experience . . . art.

Since I started this book, I've seen American art open the world's eyes to our vitality as a cultural entity. I've seen young American artists recognized as leaders in a new movement, a new vision. But most important, I've seen others not recognized, as yet, who will be. Wherever I go—and I'm sure this applies all over the world—I will find talent. It isn't just there for one to *find*—it's *there*—and anyone who wants to see it can.

I know what I like—I like art—and I like what I know.